From Slave
to Statesman
The Legacy of
Joshua Houston,
Servant to
Sam Houston

From Slave

The Legacy of Joshua Houston,

to Statesman

Servant to Sam Houston

Patricia Smith Prather *&* Jane Clements Monday

Introduction by Dan Rather

UNIVERSITY OF NORTH TEXAS PRESS

Requests for permission to reproduce material from this work should be sent to
Permissions
University of North Texas Press
Post Office Box 13856
Denton, Texas 76203-3856

Library of Congress Cataloging-in-Publication Data
Prather, Patricia Smith, 1943–
From slave to statesman : the legacy of Joshua Houston, servant to Sam Houston /
by Patricia Smith Prather and Jane Clements Monday ; introduction by
Dan Rather. — 1st ed.
p.   cm.
Includes bibliographical references and index.
ISBN 0-929398-47-5 (alk. paper) : $32.50
1. Houston, Joshua, 1822–1902.   2. Statesmen—Texas—Biography.   3. Afro-
Americans—Texas—Biography.   4. Houston, Sam, 1793–1863—Friends and
associates.   5. Afro-Americans—Texas—History—19th century.   6. Texas—
History—1846–1950.   I. Monday, Jane Clements, 1941–   .   II. Title.
F391.H79P73   1993
976.4'061'092—dc20
[B]   93-25464
CIP

The paper used in this book meets the minimum requirements of the American
National Standard for Permanence of Paper for Printed Library materials,
Z39.48.1984. Binding materials have been chosen for durability.

Frontispiece and endsheets courtesy Constance Houston Thompson and the
Sam Houston Memorial Museum—Huntsville, Texas.

Contents

Preface

Joshua created a path and left a legacy. We retraced that path searching for clues about his life. What we found was astounding, but we have not stopped our search. This book, therefore, is only a beginning. We hope others, including his descendants, will continue the search for information about Joshua Houston and the other unheralded heroes of the Reconstruction period in Texas and throughout the South.

Researching the life of anyone who lived a century ago is challenging, but researching one who spent half of his life without a last name has been a special challenge. Our good fortune was that Joshua Houston had spent over twenty years with Texas's greatest hero, General Sam Houston. By studying the hundreds of personal letters that Sam and his wife Margaret wrote to each other, as well as reading documented accounts of their lives, we were able to chronicle the life of his servant Joshua, who eventually became a hero in his own right.

Although this book centers on Joshua and how he and other ex-slaves made a difference in Walker County, Texas, we discovered quickly that similar stories were occurring throughout the rest of the state and the South. These men and women formed networks throughout their religious, political, social, and educational organizations that helped them steer through the troubled waters that existed before the Civil War and after Emancipation. We hope that this book will inspire others to study their own communities and counties, discovering men and women, both black and white, who made a positive difference in the lives of all Texans during this turbulent time.

A note on our decision of when to use the terms "Negroes," "Colored," "Blacks," and "African-Americans," might be necessary. Rather than going back and changing all the terms as they were used in our sources to what is considered politically correct *now,* we decided to use the terms that were politically correct *at the time the sources were written.*

Our indebtedness is *first* to General Sam Houston and his wife Margaret, who left a paper trail of letters which allowed us to determine Joshua's role in their lives. We are grateful to the Houston family descendants who preserved and shared these letters. Most of all to Madge Thornall Roberts, great-great-granddaughter of the General and Margaret, we say thank you for her interpretations, research and patience as she gave us insights into Joshua's relationship with the family.

We owe a special debt of gratitude to two of Joshua Houston's granddaughters. Constance Houston Thompson died at the age of 92 during the course of this research, but left us invaluable oral descriptions of her ancestors. Hazel Houston Price has been a constant supporter, contributing both information about and insight into this unique family. One of our most rewarding experiences while writing this book has been discovering so many of Joshua's descendants and sharing with them the results of our research. One of our trails led us to Tony Sherman, an outstanding artist living in Houston, who is Joshua's great-great-grandson and contributed artwork to this volume. To others of Joshua's descendants who have helped us: the Harold Fobbs family, the Georgia Mae Wagner Jolley family, Port Arthur Todd, Eloise Johnson, the Ruby Sims family, and the Helen Demby family, we say thank you for sharing your stories and pictures.

We thank Fran Vick, director of the University of North Texas Press, for her vision and dedication to the idea that stories such as Joshua's must be preserved for the generations yet to come. We thank our editor Charlotte Wright for her patience, insight, and support as she so ably molded our pieces of information into a readable manuscript.

To Dan Rather goes our gratitude for helping us bring Joshua's story to a wider audience.

We want to thank several authors, among them Merline Pitre, Ph.D., whose in-depth research on elected officials during Reconstruction helped us understand the political climate in which Joshua lived. Thanks also go to Dr. Naomi Lede, whose early books about the son and granddaughter of Joshua Houston provided us valuable information. We found that many oral histories had been recorded during the 1930s, providing us with excellent resources. We are very grateful for the WPA's interview project, to Mae Wynne McFarland, and C. W. Wilson (Joshua's nephew) for their work. We appreciate the many people who consented to sharing their knowledge with us through oral interviews, and are glad to aid in the preservation of their knowledge.

To the wonderful historians across this state who reached out to assist us we say thank you: Dr. Mike Campbell of the University of North Texas; Stanford Douglas, director of the Samuel W. Houston Cultural Center; Dr. Louis Marchiafava, Archivist, Houston Public Library; Bernice McBeth, Chairperson, Texas United Methodist Historical Society; James Patton, County Clerk of Walker County and consummate local historian; Dr. Mary Francis Park, Dr. Patrick Nolan, Lois Pierce, Dave Wight, Richard Rice, and Kathy Shute of the Sam Houston Memorial Museum; Dr. Jim Olsen, Dr. Gregg Cantrell, Dr. Donald Coers, Dr. Emmett Jackson, Dr. Paul Culp, Ann Holder, and Linda Fowler of Sam Houston State University; Brice Donely and John Anderson of the Texas State Archives; Robert Schaadt at the Sam Houston Regional Library at Liberty; Revelles Photography; Jena B. Hill at Photographic Images; Chester Hines in Crockett; our superb deed researchers Diane Fuller and D'Anne Crews; and Nancy Tiller for her excellent maps.

To Sam Houston State University—President Martin Anisman, Pam Anisman, and the faculty, administration, and staff—we are grateful for their support and dedication to preserving the legacy of Sam Houston and his times.

Dr. A. I. Thomas, President Emeritus of Prairie View University, lent invaluable, ongoing support. To the county commissioners of Texas who followed in the footsteps of Joshua Houston—especially Cecil Williams, who became the first African-American county commissioner in Walker County since Reconstruction, and El Franco Lee, who led the same battle in Houston—we salute you.

Every team has a coach. Bob Lee, sociologist, deserves that title for all his efforts, beginning with his arranging for the two of us to meet after he learned that we were both in pursuit of information about Joshua Houston and his family. His constant advice throughout the book was invaluable.

Finally and most importantly, we thank our families, especially our children, Robert Prather and Keiba Holt, and Kimberly, Julie and Jennifer Monday for their understanding and support. Thanks also to Pat's sister Brenda and her family and to Jane's brother, Joe Clements and his family, and to her husband, Charles. Charles was our most generous supporter and deserves the patience award for his continuing support, encouragement, and advice. Now we present our readers Joshua's story, *From Slave to Statesman*.

Patricia Smith Prather and Jane Clements Monday

Introduction

For most Americans, slavery is a condition so monstrous that it's unimaginable.

On the one hand, that's good—if we can no longer imagine slavery, we must be far from it.

On the other hand, that's bad—because our understanding of who we are as a nation depends upon our understanding slavery.

We study history to understand how we got from point A to point E, and for most African Americans, slavery is point B. Not the last point, but an important point upon which much is built.

For a long time Americans indulged in fantasies of a benign servitude called slavery. The purpose of these fantasies was to alleviate white guilt and (if black concerns were even considered) to smooth over a troubled past and allow blacks to move onward.

Their achievements, their triumphs and tragedies, their courage and their love have been unknown to too many Americans. We have not known their names, we have not seen their faces.

Because Jane Monday and Patricia Prather sent me a picture, I can see Joshua Houston's face every day now. It hangs in my office.

Here is the proud paterfamilias surrounded by his good-looking, prosperous kinfolk (and underscore that *proud:* Joshua's quiet strength and confidence jump out at you from the picture, and his pleasure in the people around him is visible). Joshua Houston, Jr., is getting married; it's 1898. The Houstons look like any other Texas family grouping of the Victorian Age—except that they're black.

How did they get to this day, this fine family portrait?

For too long, we haven't been told.

Now, thanks to Jane Monday and Patricia Prather, we are finding out.

If you can't imagine what slavery was like, it's in part because we've seen too many romanticized, sanitized, bowdlerized treatments of slavery, on print and on screen.

The book you are holding is not like those other, earlier books. It is a product of diligent research and absolute fact. There is good here, and there is bad. But with it we can understand something more of who we are, whatever our color.

This is the story of a family, in slavery and in freedom. Joshua Houston and his family were a kind of black aristocracy in Texas, but, as you'll see here, they were a hard-working aristocracy never content to rely upon the achievements of the past—or the achievements of their former master.

That's impressive because the legacy of Sam Houston (general, governor of two different states, congressman from one state and senator from another, citizen of the Cherokee nation and Cherokee ambassador to Washington, President of the Republic of Texas and—he didn't make it, but he surely wanted it—President of the United States) still carries a lot of clout in Texas. The college I attended is named for him. So is the city where I grew up, got married, and had children.

As that thumbnail resume suggests (and I'm leaving off a lot—school-teacher, actor, poet), Sam Houston had a remarkable rapport with the Cherokee nation. He lived among the Cherokee for a long time on two separate occasions. The first time, he was a boy, a runaway. He came alone. He did not try to overpower, he did not try to harm. He did not come meekly or weakly. He *did* come *peacefully*. He showed that he cared. He immersed himself in a culture that was alien to him. He learned a language with next to no relation to English. He learned the ways and the culture of those with whom he lived. And he respected them. And he was a lifetime friend, who continued to show his caring long after he'd left the protection of the Cherokee nation.

It's worth asking ourselves how Sam Houston "got it" in his dealings with the Cherokee and didn't "get it" in his dealings with the African Americans around him. In that day, it was unusual for a white man to show any sympathy for another race. Why didn't Sam Houston show as great a sympathy for blacks as he did for Native Americans?

How the Houstons white and black got along, and didn't get along, is a tale full of lessons for all of us.

The greater part of this country's existence is given over to the seemingly simple business of getting along. We came here freely or not, from all over the map, no two alike. Americans don't worship alike, don't look alike, don't think alike. Some visionaries suggested, in a Declaration and a Constitution two centuries ago, that we might have better luck getting along if we accepted each other *as equals*—at least in God's eyes and under the law. And ever since, we've tried to do just that.

We have very seldom if ever succeeded on anything like the grand scale our ancestors envisioned. But sometimes we have come just close enough to taste, to know how wonderful equality must be.

We have always been equal; we must study the times we didn't know it.

Dan Rather
New York
Spring, 1993

Joshua Houston Chronology

1819
Margaret Lea born in Alabama.

1822
Joshua born a slave, apparently in the Temple Lea household
in Marion, Perry County, Alabama.

1834
Temple Lea dies and leaves Joshua to his daughter Margaret.

1836
*Joshua's son Joe born (to Anneliza).

1837
Margaret graduated from Judson Institute.

1839
Joshua meets General Houston when he visits the Lea family in Alabama.

1840
Joshua comes to Texas after General Sam Houston marries Margaret Lea.
*Joshua's daughter Lucy born (to Anneliza).

1841
Houston elected President of the Republic of Texas for the second time.

1845
Joshua drives the family to see Andrew Jackson and attend funeral.
Joshua documented making improvements on home at Raven Hill,
eleven miles from Huntsville.
Texas joins the United States.

*According to family oral tradition.

1846
Sam Houston elected as one of the first two Senators from Texas
to the U.S. Congress.

1848
Joshua's daughter Julie born to Ann (Anneliza).

1853
Joshua working for a Huntsville stage line, most likely Colonel Grant's.

1856
Joshua's daughter Ellen born (to Mary Green).

1859
Sam Houston elected Governor of Texas.

1861
Joshua, Jr., born (to Mary Green).

1862
Houston frees his slaves. Joshua and others elect to
stay with the Houston family.

1863
Joshua listed as property in Last Will and Testament
of General Sam Houston.

1864
February— **Joshua's son Samuel Walker born (to Sylvester).

1865
June 19th—Slaves in Texas learn of their freedom.

1866
January 15th—Joshua buys property for homestead
on 10th Street in Huntsville.
Joshua is trustee to the Union Church and school in Huntsville in
cooperation with the Freedmen's Bureau.

1867
Joshua appointed city alderman in Huntsville, Texas, under Governor Pease.

**For alternate dates, see text.

1869
Joshua trustee for Union Church.
November 9th—New Texas Constitution ratified.

1870
Joshua appointed city alderman in Huntsville, Texas, under Governor Davis.

1875
Joshua's daughter Minnie born (to Sylvester).

1878 (–1880)
Joshua is elected and serves as county commissioner of Walker County.

1882 (–1884)
Joshua is elected and serves as county commissioner of Walker County.

1883
Joshua is a supporter of Bishop Ward College in Huntsville.

1888
Joshua elected as a delegate to the National Republican
Convention from Texas.

1898
October 11th—Joshua, Jr., marries Georgia Carolina Orviss in Huntsville.
November 21st—Joshua's wife Sylvester dies.

1899
Joshua writes out his last will and testament, leaving land
to his sons and daughters.

1902
Joshua dies January 8th and is buried in Huntsville's
Oakwood Cemetery next to his wife Sylvester.

Prologue

Joshua was born a slave. After his mistress Margaret Lea married General Sam Houston, he served the couple for over twenty years before slaves were freed in Texas. With Houston's death in 1863, Margaret was left a widow with eight children. Almost all of the family wealth was tied up in land, and Margaret had a hard time making ends meet. Ironically, Joshua had saved the wages he had earned when he hired out as a blacksmith. When he learned of the plight of his former mistress, Joshua paid her a visit. The story of that visit is documented by another former Houston slave, Jeff, in his book, *My Master:*

> Uncle Joshua waited until Mrs. Houston finished her dinner, and then . . . asked her if he could talk to her alone. . . .[He] laid an old leather bag on the table . . . [and] told [Mrs. Houston] there was over $2,000 in gold and United States currency in the bag and that he wanted her to use every cent of it. . . .[She] was so overcome with the unselfish devotion which one of her slaves had shown, that she could not speak for a minute. But she handed the bag of money back to Uncle Joshua and said: "It is noble of you to want to help us. You have no idea how I appreciate your kindness, and I shall never forget it, but I cannot accept your savings. . . . I want you to take your money and do just what I know General Houston would want you to do with it, if he were here, and that is give your own boys and girls a good education."

CHAPTER ONE

1822–1845

"Sometimes I Feel Like a Motherless Child"

Joshua was only twelve years old but already valuable property when his master, Temple Lea, died in 1834 and willed the boy to his daughter, Margaret.[1]

Joshua and Margaret grew up on the same soil in Marion, Alabama, but their worlds were oceans apart. She was just a few years older than her slave, Joshua. Her days were spent learning the art of being a lady and preparing to be wife and mother in another well-to-do family. Joshua's days were spent working from sunup to sundown like a grown man.

In all likelihood, Joshua's day consisted of rising every morning before daybreak, rolling up the floor pallet on which he slept, and breakfasting on something like corn pone and cow milk before he left his slave cabin to feed the animals.[2] Joshua especially liked the horses,[3] and he may have dared to dream that one day he would have one of his own. During those early morning hours, Joshua may have even pretended that the horses he fed and groomed were his. But his early morning daydreams would have given way to the harsh reality of slavery as the sun rose higher in the sky and Joshua's work load became heavier.

Thus was Joshua's monotonous life of labor as chattel. His days were spent carrying his share of the load of the many chores necessary to make Margaret Lea and her family comfortable on their plantation. There were fruits and vegetables to be cultivated and harvested, meats to be cured, fences to be mended, buildings to be repaired, shrubs to be trimmed, animals to be cared for and wagons to be mended. By summer's end, all the slaves were involved in producing the main crops. The hot sun and rich Alabama soil were perfect incubators for the lush green plants whose fruits burst to yield white cotton, a crop which turned to gold in the pockets of plantation owners but signaled back-breaking woe to the black hands that reached down to wrestle the fibers from their stubborn seed pods. After cotton picking came the sugar cane harvest. The work of boiling the cane to make sugar seemed endless. Joshua and the others often worked eighteen-hour days during the harvest season. Some sugar factories operated all day and night, seven days a week.[4]

When the long, exhausting days ended, Joshua probably collapsed on his floor pallet of dirty rags. If he did not fall asleep immediately, he may have spent a few moments wondering what kind of world created so much hardship for a man simply because his color was not white. He had learned at a very early age that skin color made a difference. People with black skin were subservient to those with white skin, and people with red skin were to be feared by both. It was a lot for a twelve-year-old to comprehend, even one with Joshua's intelligence.

It is almost certain that he did not have a father around to help him understand. His parents' names are lost to history since slaves had no last names and few records were kept on parentage. Sometimes late at night, Joshua may have wondered about his ancestors. Where in Africa had they come from? How had they felt as they crossed the Atlantic in the hold of a ship? How could they have understood the orders given by men speaking foreign tongues? He no doubt listened to the stories and songs repeated by the older slaves around him and may have felt an inner kinship with distant relatives and traditions dating back hundreds of years. He was probably fascinated by the sound of African dialect, but he also knew that speaking it was strictly forbidden.[5] Joshua had so many questions, but there was neither the time nor the opportunity to pursue answers.

Whatever his heritage was, Joshua had special qualities, and the Lea family noticed his intelligence when he was very young. This insured that he was apprenticed to learn several trades, which in turn made him quite valuable to the plantation. His other good fortune was belonging to a family that did not allow overseers to render harsh treatment to their slaves.[6]

Joshua was probably born about 1822,[7] not long after Alabama became a state. Broken treaties with the Creek Indians kept tensions between the Anglos and Native Americans a constant threat. But Joshua was largely oblivious to those circumstances as a young slave. He likely spent his first few years in a plantation nursery being cared for by women too old to work in the fields. He and the other slave children may have shared meals from one large bowl that was passed around to each child until the mush or bread with milk was all gone. Evening meals likely consisted of greens and finely chopped pieces of meat mixed with cornmeal and sometimes dumplings.[8]

By the time Joshua was five, his daily duties probably included gathering firewood, tending animals, milking cows, toting water, sweeping the yard and helping out with babies in the nursery. He, like other slaves of the time, probably wore cotton shirts with slits on the side, allowing him easy movement to do chores and a free-flow of air to keep him cool in summer.[9]

By age ten, he would have been given pants to wear and considered a plantation laborer.[10] He probably began his apprenticeship as a blacksmith about this time, taking on chores like heaping wood into the furnace, pumping the bellows and fetching tools.[11] Because he liked horses, he probably looked forward to his days in the blacksmith shop filled with the familiar smell of horses, sweat, and fire. He began to learn toolmaking and horseshoeing. Early each morning he would probably have gone out and caught the horses in the pasture while they were frisky and hungry. He would have groomed them and occasionally even gotten to ride them. Thus he began his second apprenticeship, as rider, trainer and caretaker.[12] His blacksmith training had taught him how to shoe the horses and to make and repair their harnesses. He had also learned the importance of keeping the equipment in top condition. Part of his days were likely spent oiling the harnesses, cleaning the buggies and repairing the wheels and axles. Everything had to be in tiptop shape and ready for use when the Lea family needed it. Because Joshua was skilled at working with his hands, he also began learning carpentry skills and apprenticed in woodmaking.[13] He was intelligent enough to be aware that on large plantations like the Leas', the slaves with the most skills became the most valuable, and so were treated the best.

Another good thing about working in the blacksmith shop was the chance to hear the latest news. Joshua gradually began to participate in the chatter among the adult slaves, who repeated every word they heard in the main house about visitors, nearby plantation slaves, masters, elected officials, Indians and other topical issues of the day. Around 1832, there would have been whispers about the Nat Turner revolt which had taken place in Virginia in 1831, and how Turner and the others had been publicly hanged to discourage other rebellions. But in reality it did not matter that such things were happening in faraway places or that the President of the United States was Andrew Jackson. Joshua and the other slaves knew that their fate was not much better than that of the farm animals they cared for.

So instead of looking toward the Nat Turners and the Andrew Jacksons, slaves created their own heroes from people who were around them. For instance, they looked up to the slaves who could do some good by preaching whenever they could slip away from their cabins into the nearby woods. Their heroes also included the occasional slave who escaped plantation life and fled to freedom in Mexico, Canada, or nearby Indian villages which would sometimes shelter runaway slaves. And everyone looked up to the blacksmith and other skilled slaves, along with the ones who worked in the main house, since these were the ones who had a better chance of being accepted by the whites as nearly human.[14]

There can be little doubt that Joshua looked forward to late evenings and Sundays when he and the rest of the slaves had a few hours to themselves. The Leas always observed the Sabbath and required that only necessary chores be done on that day.[15] They were one of the leading Baptist families in the community and fervently believed in sharing the word of the Lord. Temple Lea had been a lay minister before his death and his widow, Nancy, often insisted that the slaves be included in morning and evening Bible readings.[16] It was during these readings that Joshua may have begun to decipher words from the Bible in the process of learning to read.[17] He would have to have been discreet, however, because it was against the law for slaves to read.

Joshua probably used his free time fishing at the creek or hunting and trapping with the older boys, which were the only leisure-time activities available to young male slaves. Adult slaves often used their free time tending their small gardens. Other times they used the time to bathe, although scrubbing the skin and hair with homemade lye soap to get rid of dirt and even lice cannot have been altogether pleasant in spite of the soothing hot water in the wooden tubs. But the favorite leisure activities for young and old were the times everyone gathered around the old slaves who repeated stories told by their forefathers.[18] They were probably unaware that thousands of miles away African griots were engaging in the same ritual, preserving ancient history through oral teachings.[19]

But most of Joshua's life was filled with long work days followed by nights spent recuperating and resting his weary body for the next day's work. His cabin in the slave quarters would likely have been one room, with a big fireplace, dirt floors and no windows.[20] Slave quarters were ordinarily located away from the main house, with a long, worn path leading to them.[21] In winter, Joshua probably helped put mud in the cracks between the logs to keep the wind and cold out, then in summer knocked it out again to encourage the breezes.[22]

Plantation owners as fastidious as the Leas would insist that the cabins be kept clean and the yards swept. As a young boy, Joshua would probably have slept on a pallet, but some of the older slave men with families attached wooden logs to the walls to make beds. Mattresses were supported by rope woven as lattice. They were stuffed with straw, moss or leaves. Every season the mattress stuffings would be changed to eliminate the bugs. Joshua and the other children were probably in charge of gathering moss from the trees or straw from the barn. The men who were good with their hands made tables and chairs out of wood, using corn shucks to stuff the seats. At night, fireplaces would provide light, but some enterprising slaves fashioned lamps out of lightwood torches.[23] Joshua was undoubtedly watching and learning everything he could.

Life for Joshua would have continued until his death in much the same way as this, had fate not intervened. In 1839, General Sam Houston visited Mobile, Alabama.[24] Everyone was talking about the hero of the Battle of San Jacinto, especially how General Houston led the Texas army to victory over Mexico's Santa Anna, thus securing Texas land from Mexico. The General was forty-six years old and had recently ended his term as President of the Republic of Texas. But his legendary status dated back to his days as Governor of Tennessee when he enjoyed a close friendship with General Andrew Jackson, who later served as President of the United States.

In fact, General Sam Houston was on his way from Mobile to visit Jackson and his wife in Tennessee when he stopped to visit the Lea family in Alabama, and met Margaret, Joshua's mistress. Sam and Margaret met at a Strawberry Festival at Spring Hill given by her sister, Antoinette Bledsoe. The General was smitten with violet-eyed Margaret. He soon proposed marriage, but Margaret's family was uncomfortable with his intentions toward her. They had heard about his legendary drinking and his scandalous divorce. In addition, the General was twenty-six years older than twenty-year-old Margaret, and worst of all, had not been baptized. Nancy Lea had a chance to express her views to the General when he returned to Marion in August. He was ill in bed, and she took advantage of the opportunity to read the scriptures aloud at his bedside for two days.[25] Joshua may have heard about the incident from the two slaves who helped keep the restless Houston in bed.[26]

As for Joshua, he was no doubt impressed with the General. He could see that they shared a common love for the fine blooded horses that Master Bledsoe owned. Still, he and the other slaves probably enjoyed speculating on

Sam Houston in 1840. This photo was taken around 1840, when Joshua first saw him. Joshua loved to tell the story of how the gallant hero of the Battle of San Jacinto came courting his mistress Margaret Lea of Marion, Alabama.
Courtesy Sam Houston Memorial Museum—Huntsville, Texas.

Margaret Lea in 1840. At the death of Margaret's father, Temple Lea, Joshua was willed to Margaret. His life changed drastically when Margaret married General Sam Houston on May 9, 1840.

Courtesy Sam Houston Memorial Museum—Huntsville, Texas.

what would happen when the strong will of Nancy Lea clashed with that of General Houston.

Margaret was undaunted by her family's warnings, telling them, "He has won my heart." She wrote letters and poems to the General after he went back to Texas, and he reciprocated. Meanwhile, her mother and the Bledsoes accepted the General's invitation to visit Texas and consider land investments.[27] Joshua and the other slaves lit up the grapevine telegraph with the news about the gallant General and their fair mistress. Joshua knew things were moving fast when Eliza told him that Margaret had already started sewing a white satin dress, a purple silk one and a blue muslin. Less than a year after their first meeting, Sam Houston and Margaret Lea became man and wife on 9 May 1840, in Marion, Alabama.[28]

Thus began Joshua's rise out of obscurity as a slave in Alabama. At eighteen years old, he was on his way to Texas to live with the Republic's most famous hero. Fate had altered Joshua's life forever. As he boarded the steamer at Mobile, Alabama,[29] and journeyed west in the Gulf of Mexico, he was no doubt full of curiosity about what would be the most exciting segment of his life as servant to Sam and Margaret Houston.

Joshua's excitement may have waned a bit during the boat trip. There is no reason to believe he had ever been on a boat before. It helped that some of the other servants were with him, huddled together in the hold of the ship as it rode the waves. Joshua and the others may have even compared this experience to the stories the old men told about the first slaves crossing the ocean. But Joshua's experience was luxurious compared to the stench of the holds of the slave ships. Joshua, like those before him, was headed for a new life, but he was not being compelled by brute force.

It was summer when he got his first view of Texas, at Galveston's port, which looked like a picture out of one of Margaret's books. The harbor was filled with ships from all over the world, places that Joshua had never heard of like Vera Cruz, Tampico and Havana. The city itself was big, with two hotels, six taverns and several hundred homes.[30] Once off the steamer, Joshua and the others gathered their baggage, loaded it in a wagon and headed to the home of Nancy Lea, who had already moved to Galveston.[31]

Joshua was probably greeted by Dinan, Polly, Jet and Bingley, servants who had come to Texas with Nancy Lea.[32] They would no doubt have cautioned Joshua that Galveston had one of the largest slave markets west of New Orleans. And Joshua learned that the city had an ordinance requiring all free blacks and mulattos to register at the office of Mayor Syndor, who was also the slave auctioneer. He also learned that free slaves were frequently arrested and sold at auction in the market at a place known as the Strand.[33] So he knew to be careful. Even though he belonged to General Sam Houston, Joshua was a stranger in town, so at first he would be seen as just another slave.

It would not have been long, however, before people in Galveston started to recognize him. As buying fresh water was a daily task for those who lived there, it may have been one of Joshua's jobs to go to the dock and buy fresh water every day from one of the steamers off the San Jacinto River.[34] Joshua would likely have passed by one of the many slave markets on his daily trip, in full view of the men, women, and children lined up in the hot sun waiting to be called on the block for auction. Some of them were fresh off the boats, and new to both Texas and the Americas. Most of these spoke no English and were nearly starved from their journey. Others came from plantations in other parts of Texas. Crowds of people were always milling around.[35] Joshua would undoubtedly have hurried through this area, trying hard not to attract any attention.

But even the strict laws about blacks and the general hostility toward men of color probably did little to squelch Joshua's excitement about being in Texas. It is hard to imagine that he could have been homesick for Alabama. Not only was he still with Margaret, whom he had served practically all his life, but now his duties extended to the famous General. And he still enjoyed the company of several other Lea family servants who had moved to Texas to serve Sam and Margaret.

Eliza, the cook, had been with them almost as long as Joshua had. Margaret had fallen in love with little Eliza when her father brought her home from the auction block where he had purchased her. Eliza told the family she had been living on a plantation in the tidewater area of Virginia when a friendly white man came up in a carriage and asked her and her little friends if they wanted a buggy ride. When they climbed in, the man whisked them off to be sold.[36] Another household servant, Charlotte, about the same age as Joshua, had been with the Lea family as long as Joshua could remember. Vianna was the oldest of the four slaves who had been left to Margaret in her father's will. Vianna had probably looked out for Joshua, Eliza and Charlotte much as a mother would.[37] So Joshua was still surrounded by the only family he could remember, and he was ready to take on whatever duties were assigned to him on this new soil.

After a short time in Galveston, Joshua was told that he was going to travel with the General to Houston, the town that had been named for his new master. They boarded a steamer and began the slow journey up Buffalo Bayou.[38] The land was flat and treeless and the banks of Houston's bayou were lined with tall grasses, a haven for mosquitos. The city had been carved out of the marshy land only a few years earlier by the Allen brothers, two enterprising northerners. They distributed handbills depicting the land as a paradise, rather than the mosquito-infested mudhole that Joshua saw when he arrived with the General.[39] One thing that the Allen brothers did right was predict that Sam Houston would be the President of the Texas Republic, which is why they named the new town for him and gave the General a block of land downtown. When Houston was elected President, the Congress designated this city as capital of Texas.

Joshua's first sight of Houston was a bit different from what he had seen in Galveston. He was probably surprised at the large number of Indians there who were trading their wares of skins, wild game and ornaments in exchange for cloth for their clothing and lead for their rifles. Most of these Indians were descendants of those who had hunted buffalo on the bayou named in memory of the magnificent animal.[40] Seeing so many Indians in such a peaceful setting may have helped allay some of his fear of them. Nancy Lea had been badly scared by Indians in Alabama and had instilled this fear in all her slaves.[41]

While the General was making speeches and campaigning, Joshua got to observe other aspects of Houston. One of the most curious things he may have seen was the city of Houston's effort to clean up the streets and rid them of rats. Young boys were paid "a bit a head," one eighth of a dollar, for each rat they killed and turned in. The town was concerned about epidemics like yellow fever, so residents who did not clean up their lots or use carts to haul off their trash were fined. The spring rains had been so heavy that year that the teamsters were having trouble getting their wagons into town, so fresh fruits, vegetables and other supplies were coming in on boats and barges. Rumors were rampant about more trouble with Mexico, and men were signing up for the Texas army.[42]

It is likely that Joshua had to sleep on the porch of the hotel while the General wrestled with indoor quarters that were in all likelihood hotter than the porch.[43] The General missed his new bride even though their letters kept them in touch. He assured Margaret in a letter on June 30th that he would "take care of Joshua."[44] In another letter on July 1st he told her, "I left Joshua well."[45]

After spending time in Houston, Joshua was sent to help the other slaves working on the home and property owned by the General at Cedar Point, located near Galveston Bay on Cedar Bayou, a two-hour ride from Galveston.

There was no bridge between Galveston Island and the mainland, so all travel was by boat. Joshua found there a roughly-hewn cabin with two rooms, one on each side of a hall, with doors that could be opened to catch the breeze of the bay and the distant Gulf of Mexico.[46]

Although it had been exciting to see Galveston and Houston, Joshua was probably glad to be back in his favorite environment: on the farm, in the outdoors, and among his animals. He found, however, that another set of problems faced him at Cedar Point. He had to learn to work with Tom Blue and Esaw, slaves who had belonged to the General before his marriage.[47] It took a team effort to transform the casual bachelor's cabin into a comfortable first home for their master and mistress. Joshua no doubt adjusted gradually to the personalities of other slaves, as well as to working in the hot, humid Texas weather.

He probably received plenty of coaching from Margaret, who traveled back and forth from Galveston to oversee the work. Before long the cabin had her special touch. Transportation between the two places was difficult so two of the men slaves would have to stop work to accompany Margaret between Galveston and Cedar Point. She always brought Eliza, to the great joy of Joshua and the others, who looked forward to her good cooking. Eliza assumed responsibility for all of the domestic chores when she was at Cedar Point.[48] She coordinated the work of Charlotte and Vianna, and made sure that Charlotte's ill temper fits did not get out of hand.[49]

Eliza could bake a wonderful apple crisp and bread pudding, and the smell of her cooking may have stirred special memories in Joshua's mind. He had been eating Eliza's good cooking since she was a teenager working in the Lea kitchen in Alabama. She quickly adjusted her recipes to vegetables and fruits that were available in Texas. When the Cedar Point garden began producing fresh vegetables, she prepared them to go with her scrumptious cornbread. Blackberries grew everywhere and could be made into tasty desserts. Okra grew well in Texas and was a good gumbo thickener. Often when the General was at Cedar Point she would fix her specialty, which she named Cedar Point Gumbo.[50] Most of its ingredients could be caught in the bay. Joshua and the others probably used the old method of tying bacon or chicken necks on a string to attract and then scoop up the big Blue Claw crabs in nets they made.

Once the vegetable garden was taken care of, Margaret had Joshua plant a flower garden and help the rest of the male slaves plant a grove of oak trees that extended to the bayou. By the time the furniture arrived from Alabama in July of 1840, the cabin was almost like Margaret wanted it. Some of the furniture arrived broken at the landing on Cedar Bayou but Joshua got right to work putting it back in good shape.[51] He was probably glad to see Margaret happy and adjusting so well to Texas and married life.

But just about the time the home was ready for the newlyweds, Margaret's happiness was marred when she saw a copy of the newspaper speculating that the General would enter the race for President of the Texas Republic. She responded by going off by herself, staring toward the Gulf, and gently strumming her guitar and singing softly. She had so hoped that her husband would retire from public life and settle into their newly decorated home.[52] Joshua and the other slaves were no doubt aware of Margaret's disappointment.

But the General had plans to combine both a happy marriage and a productive public life. He was eager for the people of Texas to meet his new bride, so he took her to Houston in July to meet both his public and his closest friend, Ashbel Smith, Surgeon General of the Texas Army. The visit went well and everyone agreed that the marriage appeared sound.[53] During their boat trip up Buffalo Bayou toward Houston they had passed the San Jacinto battleground where, four years previously, the General had defeated Santa Anna. The battlefield full of bones, and the tree where the wounded Houston had rested while Santa Anna surrendered, were both visible from the boat.[54]

Joshua may have been glad to return to the excitement of Houston, and he probably enjoyed preparing Eliza, who had spent her time at Cedar Point and Galveston, for her big-city experience by telling her about the city. He might have shared what he had learned about the Indians so she would be less fearful. He would almost certainly have warned her about the slave laws preventing them from gathering in groups of more than four without the presence of their owners and forbidding them to gamble, carry weapons, buy liquor or sell anything without their masters' permission.[55] Of course, it is doubtful that these matters would be a problem for Eliza, whose biggest fear was the possibility of being kidnapped and sold.

Within less than three months after coming to Texas, Joshua had already traveled more than he probably ever dreamed possible. He had become familiar with both the perils of pioneering in Texas and the well-known orations of General Sam Houston, who by this time had recognized what a valuable addition Joshua was to his family.

The General had Joshua begin preparing for a trip to the Redlands in northeast Texas, where the General still maintained his law practice.[56] The 150-mile trip to the Redlands would take at least six days on roads barely passable. Joshua's blacksmithing and wheelwrighting skills were about to be tested.

A coach was borrowed to help Margaret withstand the weather and bumpy roads.[57] The lowlands along the Trinity River bed would be wet and the roads muddy. It would have been Joshua's job to check the equipment and horses carefully and take along tools for necessary repairs. A successful journey depended on the animals remaining strong or, if they became sick, on the woods yielding plants and other natural medicines that Joshua could utilize to heal them. Joshua probably drove the hardspring wagon while the General helped maneuver the coach. At night the three would camp under the trees, Joshua likely the one to build a fire for preparing supper and keeping curious animals away. After supper he would secure the horses and finally fall asleep under the bright Texas stars. The aroma of his hot chickory coffee would signal breakfast the next day, and well before daybreak they would be on the road again.[58]

Both the General and Joshua carried rifles to ensure their safety and to hunt game as needed.[59] Joshua had probably learned to shoot and hunt in Alabama, since he was entrusted with a gun at this point. It may have been during the several days remaining on this trip that the General began to tell Joshua stories about his life. Joshua may have begun to understand why the General had such knowledge of and respect for the Indians when he told Joshua about living among the Cherokee as a young boy and then again after he resigned as Governor of Tennessee. Joshua also eventually learned about the General's dislike of slavery, his dedication to Texas, and his burning need to serve the Republic.[60]

Joshua continued to hone his skills at navigating the treacherous Texas roads, river beds and trails. He would have immediately recognized the Redlands by the distinctive crimson color of the soil. The forest was dense and the pine trees abundant. The area was still considered home by the General, who was campaigning to represent the district in the Texas Congress. Because he had friends throughout the area, accommodations were never a problem. Many nights they visited Houston's friends and enjoyed hot meals and warm hospitality, although some nights they slept out in the forest.[61] The General spoke at many barbecues and dinners and his friends were delighted to note he did not touch any of the liquor that was so prevalent at these affairs.[62] Joshua began to meet the most important citizens of Texas. At night he would spend time with their slaves and quickly learn the latest news. His social sphere was increasing, and he likely began getting special attention from many of the female slaves.

Joshua may have had a chance to work on his reading skills during this trip. His informal education had begun by association with Margaret and other members of the Lea family. When they learned that Joshua could decipher small words from the Bible, they encouraged him and allowed Margaret to share some of her books.[63] Whenever Joshua had a few moments, he would thumb through the General's books to increase his understanding. Houston did not discourage Joshua's learning although it was illegal to teach slaves to read. In fact, the General probably appreciated being able to talk to someone about important subjects during their long rides over Texas's crude roads.[64] Besides, it was an extra bonus for him that Joshua could help keep records of expenditures and other transactions while he was traveling.[65]

Upon returning from the trip to the Redlands, Margaret became ill and Houston took her to Grand Cane, the sugar cane plantation of Margaret's sister Antoinette and her husband William Bledsoe, located on the Trinity River just up from Liberty. The General was frantic over Margaret's illness. He sent Joshua to get Dr. Ashbel Smith, who was on holiday in the city of Houston. Joshua would have had to ride all night to make the thirty-five mile trip, a dangerous journey for someone who could be mistaken for a runaway slave. Smith left with Joshua soon after the message was delivered, giving the latter little time to rest and certainly no time to sleep. When he arrived at Grand Cane, Smith found that Margaret was merely suffering from exhaustion, much to the General's relief. As for Joshua, he no doubt fell asleep immediately after taking care of the overworked horses.[66]

Joshua was excited but tired after returning to Cedar Point. He probably shared stories of what he had experienced and the people he had met with the other slaves, then slept like a log, savoring the nightly bay breeze. But all was still not well between the two "families" of slaves, so the General decided to ease the friction by hiring out some of his own slaves for wages.[67] Those with skills such as carpentry or blacksmithing could earn up to $150 per year.[68] The General was generous in frequently allowing his servants to keep small portions of their earnings, while most other masters kept all of their slaves' earnings to tide them over during lean times.[69] But his plan didn't work well in this instance, for two of the servants escaped. The General was furious and wrote one of his friends that he would be late paying back a loan because he lost two of his slaves valued at about $2,200.[70]

Joshua probably heard that the runaways made it to Mexico.[71] Speculations as to how they escaped might have included the old trick of putting pepper in their shoes to throw off the dogs and then walking through fresh cow manure to further confuse them.[72]

When the General learned in September of 1840 that he had been elected to the Texas Congress, he decided to move his family to Houston. So Joshua helped load their belongings onto a steamer and the family made their way up Buffalo Bayou. He remembered landmarks he had seen in June, but the trip was much more pleasant with the cooler fall weather. The comings and going of the General always attracted considerable attention, but this time he was accompanied by his wife, and among their belongings was a beautiful rosewood piano. The Houstons and their piano became the talk of the town.[73]

As soon as Margaret and her servants were settled in Houston, Joshua accompanied the General to Austin to be sworn in to the Texas Congress. Margaret didn't go, and a week after he left she went to Galveston to stay with her mother.[74]

While Congress was in session, the General traveled between the cities of Houston and Austin, and Margaret went to Cedar Point to check the progress of construction on the homesite. Joshua was also busy traveling.[75] Sometimes he was in Austin with the General and other times he was at Cedar Point helping with construction. He became quite good at navigating Texas terrain in all kinds of weather. And everywhere he went there was talk of the General's campaign for President of the Texas Republic. Houston was formally nominated in the spring.

Houston resumed his travels and campaigning in late summer and Margaret went with him. He also took Dr. Fosgate from Houston City to care for Margaret's recurring bouts of illness. Joshua had his hands full with the three of them. Every time they reached a town there were celebrations, camp meetings, weddings, dances and barbecues to attend. Between towns, Joshua would maneuver the springless coach along the weedy roads and through walls of pine and oak. At night he would unhitch the horses, set up the tent and gather a bed of leaves for the General and Margaret. He would build a big fire between the tent and the coach. For six days they traveled.[76] Shortly after they arrived in Nacogdoches, it was announced that Houston had been elected President of Texas.

Joshua prepared the coach and animals for the next trip, one hundred miles southwest from Nacogdoches to Washington-on-the-Brazos. They were treated to a great feast of "barbecued hogs and two thundering big steer, well roasted with lots of honey, taters, chickens and goodies in general," according to one guest.[77]

Then back on the road, in a drizzling mist, Joshua drove the coach again through the Redlands eastward to San Augustine. General Sam Houston rode the Tennessee mare he had purchased three years earlier during the summer he met Margaret in Alabama.[78] San Augustine's whitewashed cottages behind picket-fenced yards bordering red dirt streets were a welcome sight for the Houston family, accustomed to other towns in Texas which were mere dots in the wilderness.[79] The Houstons were guests of a well-to-do merchant whose tall, galleried house was built on a corner of the town square. Joshua, Eliza and the other servants probably shared news of their travels with the slaves of the Thomas family, and all watched in awe the next morning when so many callers came to meet President Sam Houston and his lady Margaret.[80]

During their month-long stay in San Augustine, Joshua and the other servants were kept busy readying the Houston family for a dizzying social agenda. It would have been Eliza's job to help Margaret with her clothes and hair. When Joshua was not seeing to the General's other needs, his job was to keep the horses and other animals in fine shape for their travels.

Their next visit, with Nacogdoches society, was drab in contrast to San Augustine. Nevertheless, with no less fanfare, city society lavished Texas's first family with a public barbecue.[81] There Joshua became acquainted with the slaves of their host, Adolphus Sterne, who had been one of the General's first friends in Texas. When Houston had set up his law practice in Nacogdoches in 1833, Sterne's wife had sponsored his membership in the Catholic Church, a requirement for obtaining a Spanish Land Grant. The General thought so much of the couple that he deeded his lot in the city to the Sterne's new baby, Eugenia.[82]

A highlight of the Nacogdoches trip for Joshua was the chance to visit William Goyens, a free black who was one of the leading citizens of the city. Goyens owned an inn for travelers, was a blacksmith, and manufactured wagons. In addition he owned thousands of acres of land. He rendered invaluable assistance to the General in negotiating treaties with the Indians, as he spoke their language and was their friend. Goyens had accompanied the General on one of his trips to Washington-on-the-Brazos.[83]

Joshua also had quite a scare in Nacogdoches when the horses ran off one night. It took him several days to find them and get them ready to resume their trip.[84]

From Nacogdoches, the Houstons visited the log farmhouse of Dr. and Mrs. Robert Irions, located on the Angelina River. Joshua may have sensed that the visit was difficult for Margaret. The General had once courted Anna Raguet, who became Mrs. Robert Irions. It had been Anna to whom the General wrote from the battlefield of San Jacinto right after defeating General Santa Anna and to whom he had sent a wreath from the battlefield. Later the General had encouraged his good friend, Robert Irions, to marry Anna. This was the first meeting between the two women, and Joshua was probably relieved when all went well.[85]

After two months of travel, the Houstons returned to the city of Houston on 9 November. The entire town turned out for their arrival. The revelry included a presidential parade accompanied by booming cannons throughout the day. Joshua was the elegant driver of Margaret's carriage, but it took all his strength and skill to keep the horses under control with all the noise. The parade was quite a spectacle, with the marching of the Houston Dragoons, the Fannin Artillery and the Milam Guards. Joshua undoubtedly beamed with pride as he drove the Republic's First Lady. When he stopped the carriage for Margaret to visit the Main Street Presbyterian Church, she and the President were greeted by a roomful of well-wishers. The President made a rousing speech before Joshua took Margaret home so Eliza could help her get ready for the big ball that was planned in their honor that evening by Mayor J. D. Andrews and his wife.[86]

Later in the month, on 25 November 1841, the new President gave another rousing speech in Houston and then began preparing to leave for Austin, now the capital, to be sworn in. It was December and the roads were drier and less cluttered with brush, but the weather was cold. Margaret stayed in Houston, with Mayor and Mrs. Andrews, under the care of Eliza and her herb medicines to restore her health. She did not want to slow the trip down or spend too much money by going along.[87]

When the General got to Austin he refused to stay in the extravagant house that President Lamar had built. Instead, he stayed at the Eberly House, an inn. Joshua stayed in the lean-to out back. Letters from the General to his wife at this time were filled with discussions of the difficulty he was experiencing in trying to maneuver the Republic through bad times. One letter explained that because of the severe financial crisis the new Republic was having, he had decided to cut his own $10,000 salary in half. He suggested that Margaret hire out the servants to help with their own personal finances.[88] Joshua was particularly valuable because of his blacksmith skills. On 30 December 1841, President Houston wrote and told Margaret he would "write to Captain Black to go down and arrange matters at our place! Major Western will hire Joshua, if it should be proper to hire him out, and of this you must be the sole judge! In all matters referred to you, do as you deem best, and it will meet my hearty concurrence!"[89]

Early in 1842 Margaret was still concerned with keeping Joshua hired for extra money and in a letter to her husband dated 7 February 1842, she told him, ". . . Joshua is here, but I have not been able to hire him, so Col. Andrews keeps him employed."[90] Colonel (Mayor J. D.) Andrews had a great use for Joshua because he operated an overnight inn for stagecoach passengers and Joshua's skills came in quite handy.[91]

Toward the end of February, Houston headed home from Austin. Although he usually rode his favorite horse Saxe, for this trip he chose to ride a chestnut-haired mule named Bruin. He had decided that mules had more sense than horses and that they could make their own way, leaving him more time to think. Houston and Bruin set a record, making the trip in just two hours less than four days. As Joshua was in charge of the animals, he would have cared for Bruin once Houston got back home.[92]

Shortly after Independence Day, on 2 March 1842, the General got the news that San Antonio had again fallen to the Mexican Army. Many of the citizens of Houston and the Republic wanted to immediately declare war and march toward Mexico to fight the enemy. President Houston knew that the young Republic was in no position financially or militarily to defeat Mexico again. When Congress declared war on Mexico, Houston vetoed it. The citizens were very angry with him and threats were made on his life.[93] Joshua and the other servants were undoubtedly afraid, not only for their own lives, but also for those of the Houston family. Joshua knew that his master had defeated the Mexicans once before, and he had every confidence in the General, but it is also likely that he had heard stories about war from some of the General's friends who had lived through that spring of 1836.

The threats on his life only made President Houston mad. In late June, when he saw figures moving around the house at night, he ordered the servants to light the candles and open the windows and doors. He then asked Margaret to play her piano so that all the people of Houston could see that President Houston was not afraid.[94] As the familiar sounds of the piano went out the windows of the house, Joshua may have thought back to the days in Alabama when he had first heard his mistress play on the Lea plantation and how the sounds had soothed his fears then too.

President Houston remained calm that night, and made plans to organize the militia and move the Republic's archives to Houston for safekeeping. However, he had underestimated his old friend Angelina Eberly, who ran the inn where he stayed in Austin. She did not want the capital or the archives

moved from Austin, as she felt it would be bad for business. So she fired a
cannon waking up the town to alert them that Houston's men were moving
the archives and thereby preventing the move from Austin to Houston.[95]

In the meantime, Margaret was suffering from malaria and had an asthma
attack. So for her health and safety, Houston decided to send her back to Alabama for a while, accompanied by Eliza.[96] While she was gone, the General
hired out Vincy (Vianna?) for $15 a month. In a letter dated 21 May 1842,
the General wrote Margaret that he might ". . . hire out Joshua and board
[him]self. . . ."[97]

By the fall of 1842, Margaret was back in Texas and Joshua was making
preparations for the family to move again, this time to Washington-on-the-
Brazos, which had been made the new capital city of the Republic because
it was farther from the Mexican Army than Austin was, and considered a
little safer. Joshua once again helped load most of the furniture and other
belongings in wagons and they started their trek. The wagons' progress was
slow. One good thing about the frequent stops was a chance to pick up native
pecans just fallen from the trees. Joshua set up the tent at dusk, folded it
at dawn and left the natural leaf mattresses to their role of replenishing the
forest. For part of the trip the family was lost among the perilous forks and
turns in the road before finally reaching its destination on the East bank of
the Brazos River.[98]

The twenty to thirty-five buildings making up Washington-on-the-Brazos
were unpainted, wooden and shabby. The Houstons had to share a house with
another family, and the slaves made accommodations as though they were
still traveling.[99] However, thanks to some help from a wagonmaster named
Rohrer, the famous Houston piano was safely installed for the use of the President and the First Lady.[100] Once again, Joshua would be able to hear the soft
music, and diplomats from other countries would dine in the wild frontier
with beautiful rugs on the floor and light by silver candelabras. Margaret once
again was making a lovely home for her husband on the rugged Texas frontier.

The good news was the fall weather, which brought relief from the muggy
summer days. But the best news of all was that Margaret was going to have
a baby. The General was overjoyed and Eliza could hardly contain herself.
Joshua had other priorities but was no doubt also pleased that the household
had cause to celebrate and turn their attention, if only momentarily, from its
other problems.

Margaret spent a lot of time resting under the care of her mother Nancy.
Her only outings were the occasional buggy rides she and Eliza enjoyed over

the rolling hills of the Brazos River countryside under the watchful care of Joshua, who drove them.[101] He was cautious on the rough roads. By spring, an abundance of bluebonnets and other wildflowers turned the hills into natural gardens.

Sam Houston, Jr., was born in May of 1843 and several Lea family members visited Washington-on-the-Brazos to welcome him.[102] Eliza was kept busy cooking for the guests and caring for the baby, who was put in her care right after his birth.[103] Although Eliza had helped with other Lea family babies, she was probably especially excited that Margaret and the General had their own child. Joshua had his hands full caring for the extra horses and wagons belonging to all the company. He may have also been responsible for transporting the necessary extra fresh water from the town well. Presents for the newborn, from local townspeople and Indian friends of the General, ranged from a silver cup to beaded moccasins.[104]

Margaret's other precious gift came from her husband. The carriage he ordered for her arrived in Galveston about this time. Although not the fine vehicle Margaret longed for, she accepted the carriage with no complaint.[105] At least her travels would be more comfortable, especially with the baby. And Joshua was probably proud that he finally had a proper carriage in which to drive Texas's First Family.

President Houston had need to travel also, and while Margaret spent most of the summer with Mrs. Lea and the Bledsoes at Grand Cane, Houston was traveling in East Texas. July 4th found him at Cedar Bayou near Cedar Point, at one of the oldest churches in Texas, for a special celebration. Sam Houston and his guest Andrew Jackson Donelson were there to debate Texas's annexation into the union. Houston, Mirabeau Lamar and Donelson debated annexation and notables from all around were invited. Joshua and the other servants looked forward to these occasions so that they had a chance to visit, catch up on the news and enjoy the festivities. There was a large barbecue of deer, beef, hogs and wild turkeys, and other good foods were available from the kitchens of the landowners all around the Bayou.[106]

But there was ordinarily little time for frivolity in their lives, as President Houston wrestled with many important issues, including his attempts to get the Texas Republic annexed to the United States. The issue was not resolved before the General's term as president ended. Because he could not succeed himself, Anson Jones, known to oppose Texas entering the Union, was elected President in 1844.

After the election, Joshua accompanied General Houston to Grand Cane to spend Christmas with Margaret and Sam, Jr. Amidst the celebration, Houston's interest turned to moving again. He wanted to spend life as a civilian, away from the politics of city life, so decided to move his family to land he owned near Huntsville. He sent Joshua to the area with house plans and orders to begin construction. Houston named the new home Raven Hill after the name the Indians gave him, "The Raven." In a letter to Margaret on 27 January 1845, he described the progress that Joshua and the other slaves were making: "I have bargained to have a good lot and some fence enclosed around a neat garden inside. It will be 220 ft. one way and 200 the other . . . so that rabbits cannot get into it." Houston described the house he planned for Joshua to build as "two story . . . [with] each room to be 20 by 24 feet. Galleries the whole length of the building 12 feet wide. The length of the house will be 62 feet." Houston estimated a cost of $1,200 to include the house, a separate kitchen and 60 acres of land, but vowed to acquire it for less money.[107]

A year later, in November of 1845, Joshua, with the guidance of the General, had produced a house that suited the Houstons. A wagon train, complete with the rosewood piano and the yellow coach, pulled up to the pine-covered highlands of East Texas to a raw trail encircling a hill covered with trees. Raven Hill beckoned its new inhabitants. The house was similar to the one at Cedar Point, only bigger. It was constructed from axe-squared logs and the windows were mere openings protected by slab shutters. Two large square rooms under a board roof flanked an open hallway. The chimneys were wide and built of native rock. The kitchen was a separate building in the yard among other buildings still being constructed by Joshua and the other slaves. By early spring, Raven Hill was alive with new leaves on grapevines, rose bushes and bois d'arc and ash trees.[108]

Not long after the Houstons settled into this domestic tranquility far from the public life they were accustomed to, Donelson came to visit to try to convince his old friend that his support was needed to bring Texas into the Union, and of course, he was successful.[109] Joshua would have surmised that the General and Donelson were discussing some issue of utmost importance when they stayed up late at night talking. Eliza would have kept the pots bubbling with good things to eat during Donelson's visit, and Joshua would have been responsible for taking good care of his horses. It may have been during this visit that Donelson told Houston of Andrew Jackson's grave illness, since it was right afterward that Houston decided to go to Tennessee to visit his old friend.

Joshua had never been to Tennessee, but experience had taught him how to prepare the family for travel. Joshua drove the family to Galveston. Then they traveled east by steamer on the Gulf of Mexico. Joshua no doubt slept in the ship's hold with the rest of the slave passengers. By day he might have enjoyed the fresh winds when he was not tending to the General's needs. Joshua would have gotten a look at the Mississippi River when they boarded a riverboat on the mighty waterway headed to Nashville. From there they rented a carriage and Joshua no doubt took the reins, steering the horses on the Lebanon Pike and other roads leading to Jackson's plantation, the Hermitage. Less than an hour from the bedside of the former President, Joshua saw a carriage coming from the plantation. One of the passengers was Jackson's doctor, who informed the Houstons of his death. Joshua pushed on toward the Hermitage while the General and Margaret tried to deal with the shock. As Joshua pulled the carriage up to the steps, they were met by house servants. The General jumped out and ran into the house. Joshua helped Margaret and gently handed her Sam, Jr., who had fallen asleep during the trip. As they stood over Jackson's deathbed, the General told his sleepy young offspring, "My son, try to remember that you have looked upon the face of Andrew Jackson." The General then gently closed the eyes of his dead mentor.[110]

They were all exhausted from the long trip, so Joshua drove them to the Donelson's homestead across the road, known as Tulip Grove. But Joshua had to tend the horses before he could bed down. As he worked, he might have been able to see the General through a window, writing at the desk. The letter he wrote that night was addressed to President James K. Polk, informing him of Jackson's death.[111]

NOTES

1. Will of Temple Lea, Perry County (Alabama) Will Book A, p. 57–58.

2. This and other assumptions about how Joshua spent his days as a slave are based in large part on Thomas L. Webber, *Deep Like the Rivers* (New York: W. W. Norton, 1978); James Benson Sellers, *Slavery in Alabama* (Birmingham: University of Alabama Press, 1950); John W. Blassingame, *The Slave Community* (New York: Oxford University Press, 1972); Paul D. Escott, *Slavery Remembered* (Chapel Hill: University of North Carolina Press, 1979); Leslie Howard Owens, *This Species of Property* (New York: Oxford University Press, 1976).

3. The assumption that Josh liked horses is based on the fact that Houston nearly always left him in charge of them. That he learned to care for them in Alabama is

based on the fact that he was placed in charge of them immediately upon coming to
Texas, rather than going through a training period.

4. Sellers, p. 69–71, 79; Blassingame, p. 153.

5. Webber, p. 35.

6. Jeff Hamilton (as told to Lenoir Hunt), *My Master: The Inside Story of Sam Houston and His Times* (Dallas: Manfred Van Nort & Co., 1940), p. 38. This memoir by an
ex-slave of the Houston family was told to Lenoir Hunt, who did the actual writing
and copyrighted the book. In it, Hamilton states that he was the only Houston slave
ever to be whipped by the General. Also, interviews with Houston family descendants Madge Roberts and Peggy Everitt confirm that the Leas and Houstons prided
themselves in humane treatment of their slaves.

7. Will of Temple Lea listing slaves and their ages.

8. Webber, p. 10.

9. Webber, p. 16.

10. Escott, p. 16; Owens, p. 205–07.

11. Joshua reached Texas in 1840 (at around age 18), and was shortly thereafter
hired out as blacksmith to a stagecoach owner, so it can be assumed that he had
already developed his smithing skills in Alabama.

12. This assumption, too, is based on the skills he already had upon reaching
Texas. He was put in charge of the General's horses shortly after his arrival.

13. Because of evidence that Joshua built Raven Hill and helped with the building
of the Cedar Point home, it is assumed his carpentry skills were the result of many
years of apprenticeship, begun in Alabama.

14. Escott, p. 60; Sellers, p. 74.

15. Temple Houston Morrow, "Intimate Stories of My Grandfather, General
Houston, and His Family," typescript in letter to Grace Longino, 1957, at Sam Houston Memorial Museum, Huntsville, Texas. This documents the Houston family's
attitude toward Sundays. Much of this was due to Margaret's influence, since she
maintained a strict attitude toward religious matters all her life. It is assumed that
Margaret probably followed the pattern set by her own parents for acceptable behavior on the Sabbath. There is also a general reference to Sunday being a day of relative
rest for the slaves in Sellers' *Slavery in Alabama*, p. 188.

16. Meredith Morrow Madison, "Margaret Lea Houston," Master's thesis, University of Texas at El Paso, 1960, p. 5.

17. Peggy Everitt, Meredith (Madison) Spangler, Mrs. A. R. Teasdale, and Madge
Roberts, all descendants of Sam and Margaret, agree that slaves were included in
Bible readings and were taught to read from the Bible; also Hamilton/Hunt, p. 20
records that General Houston told Jeff he would teach him to read.

18. Webber, p. 17.

19. A griot is a figure out of West African culture who is the keeper of the tribal

history, and thus the tribe storyteller. Helen Dudar, " 'Griot New York' Sets the City's Rhythm Dance," *Smithsonian Magazine* (September 1922): 102–09.

20. Sellers, p. 86.

21. Blassingame, p. 159, 188; Owens, p. 136.

22. Sellers, p. 86.

23. Webber, p. 7–9.

24. Marquis James, *The Raven,* (Indianapolis: Bobbs-Merrill Company, 1929), p. 308. Madge Thornall Roberts, *Star of Destiny: The Private Life of Sam and Margaret Houston* (Denton: University of North Texas Press, 1992), p. 18.

25. Donald Braider, *Solitary Star* (New York: Putnam, 1974), p. 191.

26. Roberts, p. 12.

27. Roberts, p. 25–26.

28. Madison, p. 23.

29. Braider, p. 197, states that Joshua accompanied Sam and Margaret Houston on this journey.

30. Gary Cartwright, *Galveston* (New York: Atheneum/MacMillan, 1991), p. 77.

31. William Seale, *Sam Houston's Wife* (Norman: University of Oklahoma Press, 1970), p. 35.

32. These were the slaves given to Nancy Lea in her husband's will. Bingley and Polly are mentioned in various family letters as being in Texas with her, and it is assumed the others came too.

33. Cartwright, p. 79.

34. Cartwright, p. 77, says that fresh water was brought to the island on a regular basis; we have assumed that Joshua would have gone to get the Houston family's share at least part of the time.

35. Cartwright, p. 79.

36. Hamilton/Hunt, p. 102.

37. Temple Lea's will lists these slaves and their ages. It is evident from the many books on slavery that an older female slave often "mothered" the younger ones, and we have assumed so here.

38. Braider, p. 199; George Fuermann, *Houston, The Feast Years* (Houston: Premiere Printing Co., 1962), p. 42.

39. David G. McComb, *Houston, the Bayou City* (Austin: University of Texas Press, 1969), p. 15, 43.

40. McComb, p. 26.

41. Seale, p. 48, 88.

42. McComb, p. 31; Gustav Dresel, *Gustav Dresel's Houston Journal,* trans. Max Freund (Austin: University of Texas Press, 1954), p. 103.

43. Fuermann, p. 42; Hamilton/Hunt, p. 47, notes that this is how he slept when he traveled with the General.

44. Sam Houston, letter to Margaret Lea Houston, 30 June 1840, Franklin Williams Collection, Huntsville, Texas.

45. Sam Houston, letter to Margaret Houston, 1 July 1840, Franklin Williams Collection, Huntsville, Texas.

46. Seale, p. 38.

47. Braider, p. 200.

48. Hunt, p. 98; Seale, p. 38–40.

49. Hamilton/Hunt, p. 98.

50. Family recipes in possession of Madge Roberts; also, Study Club of Huntsville, *Taste and Traditions* (Kearney: Morris Press, 1992), n.p. Interviews with Peggy Everitt and Madge Roberts reveal that Margaret did not cook at all, so Eliza did all the cooking for the Houston family.

51. Braider, p. 200.

52. Ibid.

53. Ibid.

54. Roberts, p. 39.

55. Fred R. Vonder Mehden, *Ethnic Groups of Houston* (Houston: Rice University, 1984), p. 13, 15.

56. Braider, p. 205.

57. Seale, p. 41–42.

58. Braider, p. 205.

59. Madison, p. 30.

60. The assumption that Sam and Joshua conversed on a personal level during these trips is based on the information in Hamilton/Hunt's *My Master*. Hamilton discusses his trips with the General and some of the stories Houston told him. As Joshua was older and had been with the Houstons longer than Jeff, it is assumed that he would have been even a more trusted servant, and taken into greater confidence.

61. Roberts, p. 63.

62. Clifford Hopewell, *Sam Houston: Man of Destiny* (Austin: Eakin Press, 1987), p. 256.

63. Hamilton/Hunt, p. 20. Interviews and writings by Houston descendants all indicate that the Leas and the Houstons taught their slaves to read. It is assumed that Joshua began to learn in Alabama when still a young boy.

64. This assumption is based on the General's behavior towards Jeff Hamilton, as recorded in *My Master*.

65. Assumption that Joshua could understand the money system and read well enough to handle the shopping errands is based on a letter from Sam Houston to Margaret Houston, 21 July 1848, that states Joshua did the errands at the Gibbs store, the Tanners store, and other places in town.

66. Seale, p. 42.

67. Seale, p. 44.

68. Sellers, p. 197–99.

69. Hamilton/Hunt, p. 123; Sellers, p. 312.

70. Sam Houston, letter to Margaret Lea Houston, 4 September 1840. Franklin Williams Collection, Huntsville, Texas.

71. Seale, p. 44 states that they made it to Mexico.

72. Elizabeth Silverthorne, *Plantation Life in Texas* (College Station: Texas A&M Press, 1986), p. 45.

73. Seale, p. 44–49.

74. Braider, p. 201.

75. Seale, p. 47.

76. Seale, p. 59.

77. Seale, p. 60.

78. Ibid.

79. Llerena Friend, *Sam Houston: The Great Designer* (Austin: University of Texas Press, 1954), p. 100.

80. Seale, p. 60–61.

81. Seale, p. 63.

82. Archie P. McDonald, editor, *Adolphus Sterne, Hurrah for Texas* (Waco: Texian Press, 1969), p. 68.

83. Archie P. McDonald, compiler, *Nacogdoches Past and Present: A Legacy of Texas Pride* (Odessa: B&C Publishing, 1986), p. 81.

84. McDonald, *Adolphus Sterne,* p. 68.

85. Seale, p. 64.

86. Roberts, p. 64; Seale, p. 64.

87. Braider, p. 206; Seale, p. 65.

88. Braider, p. 209.

89. Sam Houston to Margaret Lea Houston, 30 November 1841, Franklin Williams Collection, Huntsville, Texas. Captain Black and his two sons had fought at San Jacinto with General Houston and he helped to oversee the work at Cedar Point. He had an ox-wagon freight business called "Black's Run" which hauled goods between the Trinity and Brazos Rivers (Ruth Davis, "Stage Routes of Huntsville," typescript copy in Thomason Room, Sam Houston State University Library, Huntsville, Texas).

90. Margaret Houston, letter to Sam Houston, 7 February 1842, Franklin Williams Collection, Huntsville, Texas.

91. S. O. Young, *Thumb Nail History of the City of Houston, Texas,* (Houston: Rein and Sons, 1912), p. 42, lists J. D. Andrews as the mayor of Houston. Madge Thornall Roberts, interview with Jane Monday in Huntsville, 1992, revealed that Andrews ran a stagecoach stop in Houston.

92. James, p 326

93. Ibid.

94. Ibid.

95. James, p. 329.

96. Braider, p. 215; Seale, p. 69.

97. Sam Houston, letter to Margaret Lea Houston, 21 May 1842, Franklin Williams Collection, Huntsville, Texas.

98. Braider, p. 219; Seale, p. 76.

99. Seale, p. 74–75.

100. James, p. 330.

101. Seale, p. 76–77.

102. Madison, p. 42.

103. Madge Roberts, Peggy Everitt, and Mrs. A. R. Teasdale, Houston descendants, state that Eliza took care of the babies from the minute they were born.

104. Seale, p. 88.

105. Seale, p. 90.

106. Amelia Williams, *Following General Sam Houston, 1793–1863* (Austin: The Steck Co., 1935), p. 163.

107. Seale, p. 74.

108. Ibid.

109. Braider, p. 242.

110. Braider, p. 242; Seale, p. 98.

111. Braider, p. 242–43; James, p. 357; Roberts, p. 114.

CHAPTER TWO

1845–1859

"Nobody Knows the Trouble I've Seen"

Joshua would have seen the who's who of the nation at the funeral of former President Andrew Jackson. General Sam Houston was happy to see old friends even though it was during one of the saddest times of his life. The Houston family stayed in Tennessee for most of the summer and accepted many social invitations from friends he had not visited in six years. Joshua likely drove the General from house to house and from one barbecue feast to another. Occasionally Margaret got dressed up and accompanied the General, leaving Sam, Jr., in the able hands of Eliza. But for the most part, Margaret spent her time at the Donelsons' home.[1]

As the weather started turning cooler, the General sent Margaret, Eliza and Sam, Jr., to Marion, Alabama to visit her relatives. He and Joshua returned to Texas and Raven Hill to continue work on the new homestead.[2] The General supervised whenever he was there, but he kept busy traveling and listening to discussions about annexation. There was much speculation about the General being a candidate for the United States Senate if annexation passed, and he was interested. He felt the political fever rising in his blood again. By fall he had announced intentions to run for the Senate, and in a letter dated 9 December 1845, he shared his political philosophy with his friend, Andrew Jackson Donelson.[3] Joshua may have wondered how Margaret felt when the General conveyed his plans to her, knowing her aversion to the enormous amount of time he would spend away from home in the pursuit of a political career.

When Margaret, Eliza and Sam, Jr., returned from Alabama just after the New Year, they traveled by steamer up the Trinity River to Grand Cane. Margaret was grieving about the deaths of her brother-in-law, William Bledsoe, and her sister-in-law, Mary Lea, but was glad to be back near her family. By the time the General and Joshua arrived at Grand Cane in late January, 1846, there was a joyous reunion.[4]

Margaret was overjoyed not only at being reunited with her family, but also because her husband agreed to attend church with her at the Concord Baptist Church, not far from Grand Cane, which Joshua and other area servants had built.[5] On the Sunday the General had chosen to attend, excitement was in the air and everyone was up at the crack of dawn. Eliza prepared a sumptuous breakfast and dressed Sam, Jr., and when the General stepped out of his room, Margaret was radiant and holding on to his arm.[6] Joshua may have wondered if the General's agreement to attend church was a subtle way to appease Margaret for his decision to reactivate his political life. Joshua drove them to church in the buggy, but he probably waited under a tree for the service to end.[7] To pass the time, he may have gone over the events of the past year, including General Jackson's death, talk of Texas joining the union, and now the General's candidacy for the Senate. Joshua's small world was rapidly enlarging.

Within a month, they were back in Raven Hill. On a clear, crisp, winter morning, 25 February 1846, a rider appeared in the clearing bearing news. General Sam Houston was going to Washington as Senator from Texas. As much as the General loved his family, the lure of being on the national scene beckoned. They made plans to pack up and leave for Washington in three weeks, but when Margaret learned that she was again with child, she decided not to accompany him to Washington.[8]

On 8 March 1846, Joshua loaded the wagon with Houston's trunk and traveling case and started down the steep road to the Trinity River, where the General would take the steamer to Galveston. From there, on 12 March, he would set sail to New Orleans and on to Washington as Texas's first Senator.[9]

This was a particularly bad time to leave his family alone. The entire countryside was caught up in the news of possible war with Mexico, which of course directly affected those living in Texas. Zachary Taylor came through the state on his way to the Mexican border, and he stayed at the Fanthrop Inn in Anderson, Texas, a place both Joshua and the General were familiar with. Interestingly, three other Army officers also stayed there during this time— Robert E. Lee, Ulysses S. Grant, and Jefferson Davis.[10]

Once again, Margaret stayed home and took care of the family while her husband was gone. Joshua helped by managing the farm chores and Eliza took charge of the household. Margaret had to depend more and more on Joshua with the General so far away. Travel time to Washington was six weeks, so their letters often took that long, and many were even lost.[11] Joshua may have sensed Margaret's loneliness and tried to do things to cheer her up. He worked especially hard to make her flower beds pretty by planting grapevines, rose bushes, and bois d'arcs.[12] At night, Joshua would hear the sounds he had heard since childhood, Margaret playing the piano and guitar. During the day Margaret would sit on the porch doing needlework.[13]

Once a month, Joshua hitched up the coach and drove his mistress the fourteen miles to Huntsville to visit friends for the weekend and attend church all day Sunday. Margaret would stay with either the Josiah Merritts or Reverend and Frances Creath.[14] Reverend Creath was pastor of the Huntsville Baptist Church, which held services in the Brick Academy erected in the early 1840s to educate the young boys of Huntsville.[15]

Huntsville was chosen as the county seat when Walker County was created in 1846. The town square was surrounded by several buildings, including three stores—Smithers, Gibbs and McDonald; a well known hostlery and stagecoach stop known as the Globe Tavern; and a mercantile store run by Pleasant Gray, who founded the town in 1835. Goods were in very limited supply since most were brought by wagon from Houston or by steamboat from Cincinnati, Texas. Pleasant Gray would not sell more than three yards of cloth to any one customer because of the short supply.[16] Besides tending to the horses and wagons while he was there, Joshua bought supplies for the Houston family and exchanged crops for supplies. He would also go by the stagecoach office to mail letters that Margaret wrote to the General and other family members, and pick up any letters that arrived.[17] He knew how precious mail was, especially from the General. He probably looked forward to seeing Margaret's face light up when letters came from her husband and other family members.

Joshua was quite busy when they went to Huntsville, but he may have been glad for the chance to break the monotony of the farm work and catch up on the local news, politics or talk of war. On Mondays after the Huntsville weekends, Joshua would re-hitch the horses to the coach and prepare for the trip back to Raven Hill over rough roads and through tall pines and thick underbrush, returning to the day-to-day routine.[18] The most welcome breaks from farm life were the letters brought back from the trips to Huntsville. The General and Margaret had established the tradition of letter writing from the very beginning of their courtship, and due to Houston's frequent absences, they still corresponded with one another several times a week. Margaret would share the news sent by the General to the servants.[19]

Sometimes Margaret would invite friends and relatives to Raven Hill for several days for picnics and visiting to help fill her lonely days. The General's sister Eliza Moore and her family lived right down the road and Sam, Jr., was always glad to have the company of his cousins. Margaret would often spend time teaching the young girls to play the piano. Eliza was kept busy cooking for all the extra guests, while Joshua ever had a watchful eye out for young Sam, Jr., since the General had left Joshua in charge.[20] Joshua was never far away when the family picnicked by the lake or when Sam, Jr., was climbing trees or fishing.[21]

In the quiet hours after sunset, Joshua would often sit with the Houston family, listening to the frogs croak, watching the children chase fireflies, and whittling or rock carving. He may have learned the art of whittling from the General, who in turn had learned it while living among the Cherokees in Tennessee.[22] Margaret was particularly proud of a box and pipe that Joshua made out of prairie rock and on 20 June 1846 wrote her husband, "I send you a box and a pipe out of prairie rock. It is some of Joshua's work, and rather rough but I suppose it will be a curiosity in Washington, and that it will give you some pleasure to present to particular friends."[23]

The other breaks in the routine of plantation life came with each changing season. Spring was the time for tending to new young animals and planting new crops. Corn, planted in early spring, was sustenance for both man and animal—roasting ears, bread, grits, succotash, chowder, pudding, and popcorn, as well as food for the animals. The corn shucks were used for mattresses, chair bottoms and toilet tissue, while the cobs were used for fuel, fertilizer and smoking pipes. Peas were another staple crop planted early, as were beans, cabbage and grains. Trees were cut and rails were split during spring in preparation for making fences in the fall.[24]

In late spring, second crops of corn and peas were planted. By summer, days were spent chopping cotton, harvesting grain, making flour, fighting weeds, preparing and repairing machinery, and making baskets for fall harvests.[25]

Regular work nearly ceased around the Fourth of July, a time of celebrations and political gatherings where memorable speeches were made by General Sam Houston and other prominent men of the day. Servants began preparing meals days in advance. Joshua would have helped dig pits in which to barbecue deer, hog, wild turkey and other meats. Eliza would have been busy with pound cakes, and pies made from wild dewberries, grapes and plums. The feasts were complete with roasting ears, watermelons, cantaloupes, potatoes and whatever other fresh vegetables and fruits were ripe.[26]

In the fall, although the work pace was just as hectic, the cooler days and nights brought relief from the hot, muggy Texas summers. The season was spent planting fall vegetables and storing food for the winter. Vegetables such as sweet potatoes, white potatoes, white turnips and beets were buried in deep holes on mounds of dry sand, dry cornstalks, straw and grass. Cornstalks were then piled on them "tepee style" and covered with dirt to keep the vegetables from rotting. Fall was also the time for soap- and candle-making, for the sugar cane harvest and for building and mending fences. The children helped with some of the easier chores such as pecan picking. They were allowed to keep a few to play a game similar to what later became marbles. The adult slaves would hunt wild game and fish to supplement their diet and give them a diversion from the daily routine.[27]

Although the work of slaves was never done, winter was a slower time, consisting of chores like making preparations for the spring plantings and doing hand work, such as weaving baskets, sewing clothes, and making and repairing shoes. Joshua and the other servants also had more time to whittle in the winter. Like other slaves during this time, they might have made wooden dishes, bowls, spoons and churn paddles. Cotton production, a year-around chore, started with the preparation of the ground in January. But during the early days at Raven Hill cotton production suffered from the cotton worm, wet weather and low prices.[28]

Joshua, often left in charge while the General was away, knew how to plan for chores that were necessary to maintain the farm year around. But his major responsibility as blacksmith and driver was the daily care of the animals. Joshua was also the farm veterinarian and had to treat as well as try to prevent illnesses among the animals.[29] Many of his remedies were the same ones used by Eliza and the other female servants who treated people. Spiderwebs stopped bleeding; poultices made of clay mixed with garden herbs were made for treating snake bites; jimsonweed was used for making salves to treat cuts, and turpentine mixtures soothed rheumatism and other ailments.[30]

Christmas at the Houstons' provided a major break from farm life. If the Houston household was like the majority of plantation homes in Texas during this time, its preparations for the holiday season would begin weeks in advance. The smell of pine would fill the house. Joshua may have been the one in charge of gathering pine branches, holly, and other evergreens from the thick woods surrounding Raven Hill. He may also have scouted the woods for the perfect tree so that it could be cut just before Christmas to surprise the children. The servants, including Eliza, Vianna and Charlotte, would probably have been the ones to decorate the tree with strings of popcorn, cotton balls and other homemade ornaments, making the whole house looked festive.[31]

Joshua's extra duties during the holiday season included caring for the extra horses brought by visitors to the Houston family. He also would have helped the other servants haul huge logs into the house for the yule celebrations. Vianna and Charlotte may have made fireworks for the children by filling dried hog bladders with air and tying them to long sticks. When the children held these near the fire, they exploded. Eliza, as cook, no doubt outdid herself making sure Christmas dinner was perfect, with stuffed turkey, wild duck, turnip and other greens, sweet potatoes and all sorts of pies and cakes.[32]

But the General knew all of this activity was not keeping his wife from being lonely while he was over a thousand miles away in Washington, D. C. A letter of his in the spring of 1846 suggested a companion for Margaret.[33] Anna, he said, was the sister of a man the General had helped in Washington and she was looking for employment. Margaret's answer to the General was, "My love, I would be glad indeed to have Anna's services, if you think she would be satisfied with our rude fare."[34] But Anna did not prove the companion Margaret needed and she left within a short time of her arrival.[35] Not long afterward, Houston came home. The couple's second child, a girl, was born on 6 September 1846, and named Nancy Elizabeth after both grandmothers.

Soon Joshua was hitching up the buggy to drive the General to speaking engagements around Texas. Houston did not have much time before he had to return to Washington, but he had to keep in touch with his voting public and at the same time make sure his personal business was in order. Often when the General was home Joshua would accompany him to Vernon Lea's (his brother-in-law's) home at Council Hill, because Sam met his Indian friends there. It was about fourteen miles from Raven Hill, and the two men would either go on horseback or in a carriage. Houston planned his trips to spend every few days at home with his family, except when he had to go north to the Redlands or San Augustine. The roads were improving but travel was still slow and the General spent a lot of this time instructing Joshua about his duties to the family and farm chores. Joshua was probably pleased when the General took time to explain issues of great importance in Washington as well as Texas. The General was especially concerned about Mexico's growing interest in recapturing Texas.[36]

Before the General prepared for his fifteen-hundred mile trip back to Washington in late fall, he made detailed preparations for his family's welfare during his absence. He hired out eight of his twelve servants to Captain Frank Hatch, editor of the town newspaper, in exchange for Mr. Hatch agreeing to help as overseer at Raven Hill.[37] Joshua's instructions were to begin construction on a new building, a law office for the General's books and papers.[38] Raven Hill was expanding. The sound of the axe was common around the place. Joshua's split rail fences extended deep into a partially cleared forest south of the house.[39]

His work ceased when Margaret became ill in February, 1847. Margaret's breast had been bothering her for quite a while and the pain became unbearable. She thought she might die and decided she didn't want to do it at Raven Hill. Joshua hitched up the horses and yellow coach and drove his mistress to her sister Antoinette's home near the Trinity River. Joshua was sent to get a doctor in Liberty but had to travel again to get Ashbel Smith because Margaret would not let the first doctor examine her breast. Joshua knew it was serious and was probably able to give Smith, the trusted family friend and physician, some information about the situation. It was hard to keep secrets from the servants, so Joshua was likely to have overheard the news that the breast had burst open and was bleeding.[40]

Dr. Smith decided to operate immediately. Joshua surmised that the operation would be painful but knew that there was no way Margaret was going to use whiskey, the only painkiller they had. Her brother-in-law Charles Power offered a silver dollar, probably one of the few in Texas, for her to bite on to help withstand the pain. Eliza probably assisted Dr. Smith by providing clean linens and boiling water for sterilization.[41]

The General was so worried when he got word about the operation that he hurried home from Washington. By the time he arrived in April, however, Margaret was already taking short walks and under the able care of her mother.[42] Seeing that Margaret was better and getting proper care, the General had Joshua drive him to Huntsville so he could deliver the San Jacinto Day speech commemorating April 21, that fateful day more than a decade earlier when Houston and his army had defeated Santa Anna, and transferred the vast lands known as "Tejas" from Mexico to the Texas Republic.[43]

By June, the General, Margaret and the family had returned to Raven Hill.[44] Houston won re-election to the Senate, but Margaret still did not want to move to Washington. So the General began plans to move his family closer to Huntsville where Margaret could get better health care and not be so isolated from friends. She had recovered from the cancer and was looking forward to

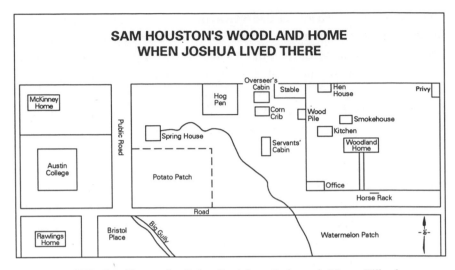

Layout of Woodland home when Joshua lived there. Redrawn by Nancy Tiller from an
original diagram by Mrs. W. A. Leigh in 1935.
Courtesy Sam Houston State University—Huntsville, Texas.

moving to their new home, which was just two miles from the city and nearer
to church. The General acquired the land with a small house on it by trading
some of the land from Raven Hill with Frank Hatch.[45]

The Hatch house was a small log cabin with a chimney of mud and sticks.
It was situated on a hillside that sloped down to a creek and on one side of the
house the land spread rather flat to a natural pond. A short distance from the
house was a public road leading to the Huntsville town square. The Houstons
were satisfied—they had the privacy of the country within an hour's walk to
the center of Huntsville. Joshua and the other servants worked all summer
expanding the log house to accommodate the sizeable household. The General's design included an open hallway which joined the old house to a new
addition with a porch across the front.[46]

On 7 September 1847, Houston wrote Margaret from Montgomery, Texas
saying, ". . . if the hands are not engaged in getting in the corn I wish them
to be getting 3 or 4 boards and making rails until I get home. The boards will
be important to my cribs and stables. Let the sheep be kept up in the loft, or
if they are let out at all do not permit them to be alone for one moment or
they will run off and mix with the flock from which they came."[47] The new

homestead became known as the Woodland home, and by October Joshua was sent to bring the furniture from Raven Hill. Margaret wrote Houston on October 3 and told him, "Smith met Joshua and took his wagon from him, so that Mr. Moore was under the necessity of borrowing William Palmer's to bring up his things."[48]

The General remained with his family during the Christmas of 1847, but he left in January for Washington. Margaret, expecting another baby, was sick again. In February, she wrote her husband with bad news: "Mother's Negro woman Vianna . . . survived a short time and I can say with safety that her death was one of the greatest trials I ever endured first on account of the state of mind in which she died and secondly because I knew she had died from the want of medicine, for mother was so alarmed about me at the time that she neglected her on my account."[49]

According to this letter Vianna, who had been with the Lea family for nearly twenty years, had died of pneumonia. She had been like a mother to Joshua, who had known her all his life. Eliza and Charlotte would probably have prepared her body for burial. The ritual involved washing her with soap and hot water, then wrapping her in a long sheet. The body was then placed on a "cooling board"—similar to an ironing board but with sturdier legs— and covered with another sheet. Joshua and Prince probably made this board, as well as the wooden coffin in which they buried Vianna in the slave section of the cemetery.[50]

Two weeks later, on February 28, Margaret wrote to her husband reporting that everyone was well except Mary, who she feared was consumptive. Joshua would have observed that Margaret turned to Dr. Rawlings for treatment this time, perhaps in an effort to avoid repeating Vianna's fate. Margaret wrote Houston on March 21 that he should not "expect too much from the farm as we have only three hands, Prince, Joshua and Bingley."[51] In the same letter she also recorded that the sheep had been scattered and presumed drowned at Calhoun's Mill. All but thirteen sheep and three goats were lost.

Life at Woodlands settled into a routine, the only interruption taking place on a spring morning, April 13, when the newest Houston family member was born. She was named for her mother, but came to be called Maggie, the nickname the General had for his wife.[52]

About the same time, Joshua and the others were beginning to harvest early spring vegetables. In addition, they were still making improvements to the 173 acres of hilly woodlands. Joshua helped to clear pasture for the General's horses and continued to keep the animals in tip-top shape as he had done for over eight years. He and the other servants followed Houston's instructions and kept planting until July 4, even though they were still busy tending and harvesting what had already been planted. Joshua was also assigned duties back at the part of Raven Hill that the Houstons retained, as well as at Cedar Point, the Houston's summer home near Galveston on Trinity Bay.[53]

At age twenty-six, Joshua had a lot going for him. He was a trusted servant who could travel alone on behalf of General Sam Houston, much like a free man. He was also allowed to carry firearms and to keep a portion of any wages he earned as a blacksmith and wheelwright. Living closer to town meant he had more opportunity to earn extra money than he had living in the country, especially with the stagecoach line being there. And, to boot, he could read and write and handle the buying for the Houston family whenever there was not an overseer to do the job.

Even though Joshua was kept very busy, he also had time for a personal life, including the formation of his own family. Sometime before 1848, he began a relationship with a slave woman named Ann (also known as Anneliza),[54] although the first documentation of it is in a letter Margaret wrote to Houston in 1848: "Joshua and Ann have a daughter [this is almost certainly Julie Houston], and I believe that is all the news I have of them, but you will have perceived that they are prospering, and I am sure you can not rejoice more at it than I do."[55] Even though it was against the law for slaves to legally marry,[56] Joshua and Ann had started and maintained a family. Ann may well have lived on a nearby plantation where Joshua could have visited her.[57] Two other children had earlier been born to Joshua and Ann—a son, Joe, and a daughter, Lucy.[58] The couple probably did not see one another very often, but as was the common practice of the day, slaves were allowed to have mates on nearby farms and plantations and to visit one another when it was feasible for their owners. Any children born to them were considered the property of the family that owned the mother.[59] It is not known what family Ann belonged to, but she and her children later lived in a community known as Hall's Bluff, not far from Crockett, Texas.[60]

During this time, in the absence of an overseer, Margaret began to have trouble managing the slaves, even though her mother Nancy Lea was there to help her. In a letter written on 30 May 1848, Margaret complained to her husband that "the servants are tolerably lazy and stubborn . . . they will not be governed by mother."[61] She wrote another letter in June telling a strange tale about a specific slave named Albert. She said that he "was so cunning that he was very near getting into the church but fortunately his hypocrisy was discovered and I fear he is planning some great act of villainy."[62] Apparently the Houstons tried to deal with Albert by hiring him out as much as possible. By February of 1849, the General was explaining to Margaret that Albert "had been guilty of bad conduct and had been sent home. I regret this. Hire him to anyone that you can."[63]

In addition to expressing disappointment in her servants' behavior, Margaret also shared her concerns for their welfare. On June 28, she wrote to her husband about Eliza, who had been ill. She described her as a "pitiable object indeed. She is so disfigured with the scrofula, that you would not recognize her. I have sent her to Dr. Evans, and he seems to have hopes of curing her."[64] The General wrote back on July 16: "I am truly distressed at the situation of poor Eliza. I hope that she can be cured and if not otherwise, I have no doubt but the sour lake would cure her and if needful, or you think well of it, contrive to get some of the oil from the lake and give it to her."[65] Another servant, Mary, became consumptive in February, and a doctor was sent for in that case also.[66] Joshua was undoubtedly pleased to belong to the kind family who would provide medical help for their servants. He knew from his travels that this was not the norm, and that he and the other servants were lucky to belong to the Houstons if they had to belong to anyone at all.

Evidence that Joshua was relied on to fetch doctors or run errands in town is evident in the many letters from the General which contain specific messages of work for Joshua to do. For instance, on 21 July 1848 the General wrote Margaret from the Senate Chamber to "give Joshua money to go to the Tanners and . . . tell him to attend to the Buggy and not let it be injured."[67] Joshua knew exactly what to do when he got the message from Margaret. He was used to carrying out the General's orders and looked forward to his returning home so he could show him all he had done and talk over his work with him. Joshua had become comfortable running errands for the Houstons, and the Huntsville community appeared comfortable with Joshua.

In mid-July, Margaret hired a new overseer, a young man named Thomas Gott. He was put in charge of everything around the farm except the horses.[68] On 16 November 1848, Margaret wrote that "Mr. Gott is even tempered and positive with the servants."[69] Problems soon began to arise, however, for by January Margaret was asking her husband to "write to Mr. Gott about your regulations for the servants and their going to town at night, entertaining their visitors, gambling, drinking and things of that kind." She also asked him to discuss with Gott the "meat to be weighed for them [the slaves] and how much." She wrote that "Gott is a good man but . . . Prince and Joshua

I fear will soon have him blinded."[70] Then on January 30, Margaret wrote that, "Mr. Gott stands much in awe of Prince and Joshua. He had tried to whip Joshua once, but did not succeed and I presume he will not attempt such a thing with any of the grown ones again."[71] Joshua was obviously having trouble with the new overseer, and part of the reason may have been that Gott was having an affair with Virginia Thorn, Margaret's ward. Within just a few months, Gott and Virginia ran off together.[72]

Further evidence that the Houstons were both kind and concerned in their treatment of their slaves can be found in a letter the General wrote Margaret in November of 1848, giving his permission for a patch of land they could use to grow their own vegetables. He thought they "would probably like to have the land between mother's [Nancy Lea's] land and town. So they may have a patch of equal size in any part of the field Mr. Gott may think appropriate."[73] Joshua and the other slaves would have been glad of the chance to supplement their rations with vegetables of their own. They apparently had trouble with thefts from their garden, as Houston instructed Margaret later on: "They may put it in the middle of the field so it will be secure from Rogers."[74] The same letter mentions that Houston had sent to Cuba for tobacco seed, which meant that Joshua and the others would be planting it in the spring.

Meanwhile, expansions continued on the house in order to accommodate the growing family. The Houston household, including the servants, had grown to nineteen people. In 1849, two second floor bedrooms were added, each with a fireplace, and Joshua built a staircase leading upstairs from the porch.[75] The General was well pleased with the progress when he returned from the Senate in mid-September, welcoming the sight of his new family farm. He felt it bore some resemblance to his birthplace in Virginia.[76] William Seale's biography of Margaret Houston incorporates a description of the Houstons' homelife here:

> Eliza operated the kitchen and cooked the cakes that brought compliments to Margaret. Houston's friends never hesitated to stop by for a meal, according to the custom of a day when there were insufficient means of preserving food and quantities of it had to be cooked and eaten or thrown to the hogs. Henderson Yoakum . . . [often] met with Houston, spending entire days talking business in the office [which was separate from the house]. At mealtime, Houston and his guests walked to the house, where in the summertime they were served at the cherry banquet table Margaret placed

in the loggia. She set her table with monogrammed silver and surrounded it with homely mule-ear chairs whose cowhide seats, the general liked to note, retained their animal hair.[77]

Houston's private office, built of squared logs, was in the side yard. There he could whittle and scatter papers and pipe ashes to his heart's content. The General kept his books here, including his journals, a law library, and his favorites from classical literature. What tidying he permitted was entrusted only to Joshua.[78]

Local talk in Huntsville at this time concerned plans for a college to be built on ten acres of land known as "gin hill," donated by a Mr. Hatchet. Everyone in the community was hopeful about the city becoming a center of learning. For the moment though, Huntsville citizens were busy watching the building of the county courthouse and the state penitentiary.[79]

Joshua was probably glad to see how happy Margaret was in Huntsville. He often drove her to church activities or to visit friends.[80] And, whenever the General was home, the house maintained an air of carnival. There were always visitors, including traveling ministers, political friends and others, who were spellbound hearing the General's stories. There can be little doubt that Joshua looked forward to these visits, too, as a chance to catch up on the latest news. Whenever the General would return to Washington, the carnival atmosphere would end, and it was back to running the farm.

By the time the General returned home in May of 1849, things were running smoothly again after the fiasco with Mr. Gott. Dinners were served by Eliza and the other servants on china, accompanied by silver and other cutlery and placed on damask tablecloths brought from Alabama. The monogrammed punch bowl they used for parties had been a gift from the Sultan of Morocco. Sometimes as many as twenty people ate dinner together, and when there were not enough chairs, supplemental seats such as the prized mahogany medicine chest of Santa Anna (a trophy from the Battle of San Jacinto), were used. Prayer services always followed meals and were held on the front porch. It may have been Joshua's duty to line the chairs in rows. Margaret and the guests and children would sit on the front row with the servants seated behind them. When the General was home, he stood before the assembly, read the Bible and delivered a short explanation of what he had read. A hymn and prayer ended the service.[81]

Joshua knew how strict Margaret was about the observance of the Sabbath and that she maintained the same routine even when the General was home. Under her orders, Eliza and the other servants cooked on Saturdays the food they would need on Sunday. All toys and playthings for the children were put away on Saturday evening, including the dolls. The Houston family spent Sundays reading religious books and meditating, and they also allowed their servants the day off.[82] Although they were expected to keep their minds on spiritual matters, the servants were also allowed to catch up on their personal chores, such as gardening, mending, housekeeping, laundry, or even bathing. Sundays could also be spent visiting friends or family on a nearby farm.[83] This would probably have been the time Joshua, Ann, and their children would get to spend time together, assuming all of his duties to the Houstons were fulfilled. He may also have used the time to hunt or fish with his son Joe, who was getting old enough to accompany him on such ventures.[84]

Often when the General was home, his Indian friends would visit the Woodlands. The Cherokees, in particular, liked to camp on the grounds of the Houston farm when they were traveling.[85] Sometimes before leaving Washington, Houston would send word to the Indians giving them his arrival date and inviting them for a visit. At the same time, he would write and tell Margaret to expect them, and she would send Joshua to town to get extra supplies. Joshua was never surprised by the Indians' arrival if the wind was blowing from the north, because the old gray mule in the corral would snort and jump and nearly tear up the place about an hour before they arrived. When that happened, Joshua would tell Margaret so she could have Eliza and the other servants already cooking by the time the Indians would ride up. Then everyone would be seated on the back lawn, with the General and the Chief in the center of the circle. Eliza and the others would serve the feast, with baked beef ribs often being the main dish. The stripped bones were placed in a dishpan in the center of the circle after each person finished eating.[86]

In late 1849, Joshua said his goodbyes to another servant who had been with him since childhood. Charlotte had long been testing the Houston family's patience with her insolent behavior.[87] Joshua knew that it was not uncommon for servants to rebel against their masters by being slow to accomplish their work or by doing it wrong. Other than whippings as punishment for bad behavior or rewards for good, there was not much the owners could do. Neither the General nor Margaret believed in whippings, so someone like Charlotte who maintained a continual bad attitude created difficulties for all concerned. Rather than hiring her out like they had done Albert, by December Margaret decided to sell her. She explained to her husband:

I am sorry to tell you that Charlotte's conduct was such that I was compelled to sell her. I fear you will not be pleased at the price I received for her, but I assure you, I was compelled to dispose of her. I sold her to Col. Gillespie for five hundred dollars. I bore with every kind of insolence until a mixture of some kind was discovered in one of our dishes, and circumstances fixed it on her as the guilty one.[88]

It is hard to know how Joshua felt about Charlotte's leaving. She had been with the family for a long time, but she had also helped to create a mood of conflict in the family. In addition, the fact that she was so easily sold probably reminded him that no matter what kind of work he did, he was still property which could be disposed of at will.

In spite of sporadic problems like these, for the most part life on the farm was predictable and constant for Joshua. There were always horses and other animals to care for, crops to plant or harvest, and the needs of his own small family to see to. He had to be ready at any time to drive the Houston family to church, to Margaret's mother's home in Independence, to the family summer home at Cedar Point on Trinity Bay or to the in-laws' house at Grand Cane. During the eight months that the General spent in his Senate duties in 1850, Joshua continued his role of blacksmith, keeping the iron hardware for the wagons and carriages in mint condition and making whatever new kitchen utensils that Eliza needed. And, as always, he kept his own tools sharp and in top shape. He had to administer any medicine the animals needed and was constantly learning new things about local plants and other homemade remedies for them.

It is likely that when Joshua went to town to pick up supplies and mail, he would bring home a copy of the *Huntsville Item* newspaper.[89] Joshua would not have had much time for reading, but when he did, newspapers would have been a good source of keeping up with the news when the General was not in town. The Houstons taught all their young slave children to read along with their own children,[90] and Joshua was grateful to the Houstons for encouraging him. He knew they were breaking the law in his behalf, so he would have guarded his knowledge for their protection.

Early in 1850, Joshua was hired out again. The General wrote to Margaret on 12 January: "As to the hire of the servants, I can say nothing. If you hired out Joshua for the year, it is done and it must remain so. I mentioned to Col. Yoakum that Mr. Smith of the steam mill would hire Joshua for a few months."[91] Joshua probably preferred to stay at the Houstons because he could be sure of the treatment he would receive, but being hired out also gave him the chance to make some extra money. A contract between the Houstons and Daniel B. Guerrant and John McAdams in 1851, which states the terms for Prince and Mary to be hired out for a year, indicates that the Houstons tried to see to it that their slaves were well cared for even when working for other people. The contract stated that Margaret would receive $200 for Prince and Mary's work, and that Guerrant and McAdams would "furnish each Negro with two summer suits, one winter suit of clothing, shoes, a wool hat for the boy, and take care of Mary's children and furnish them with suitable clothing and return them if alive at the end of the term."[92]

Working elsewhere also gave Joshua the opportunity to get to know more people in the community, and for them to become familiar with his skills. One of the people for whom Joshua worked was Colonel Grant, who owned a stagecoach line.[93] Huntsville was a major stagecoach stop on the route from Nacogdoches to Houston, so working for Grant would have given Joshua the opportunity to see many of the travelers who stopped to spend the night at one of three inns in town.

The oldest of these inns was the Globe Hotel, built by Pleasant Gray, founder of Huntsville, and later bought by the Woodalls, publishers of the *Huntsville Item*. It had a large artesian spring behind it that furnished water for the travelers. The Keenan House and the Eutaw House, owned by Benjamin Wilson, were the other two inns.[94] All three of these establishments would have been glad to have access to such a skilled animal handler and blacksmith as Joshua.

The big news in Huntsville during the summer of 1851 was the excitement about building Austin College. The dedication of the cornerstone for the first college building attracted a large crowd from out of town.[95] During this same summer, many of Houston's friends were also in town for a meeting of the Grand Chapter of Masonic Lodge. Among them was Adolphus Sterne of Nacogdoches, who had served in both the Texas House and the Senate. He attended both ceremonies with the Houstons. It was so hot that the General held an umbrella over the head of the college president Samuel McKinney as he delivered the dedicatory address.[96] It may have been at this ceremony that Joshua began to realize the importance of a formal education in addition to merely being able to read, an idea that would remain central to his own life and also be passed down through several generations of his progeny. Certainly he would have heard a lot of people talking about how a college would improve the town by offering additional schooling to children who had previously had the chance to study only in the lower grades.

On his way back to Washington in the fall of 1851, Sam Houston continued to keep in close touch with family matters through correspondence with his wife. He frequently gave her instructions to pass along to Joshua, as well as the other servants. On 15 November, he wrote from Nacogdoches saying, "I hope the servants are well and Joshua takes care of the horses."[97] Then again, from the mouth of the Red River on November 28, he wrote, "I have not my dear, mentioned to you for Joshua, if there is any rye left after sowing the patches, to have it sowed in the stable lot where I had peas sown last December. Let it be done!"[98] Margaret, eight months pregnant at the time, described her daily routine in one of her letters to her husband:

> My household matters move on more smoothly and harmoniously than they ever have done since I was a housekeeper. I am astonished at my own success, and wish you were here to admire it. But will give you a small insight in my arrangements. . . . We do not confine [the children] long to their books but allow them an abundance of time for exercise. Thus one duty after another is taken in regular succession and all confusion is avoided. We have supper before dark that the children may be present at worship.[99]

The young slave children were also included in the lessons and all the servants were included each evening in the worship service.[100]

As the birth of her next child and the anticipation of another holiday season without her husband drew near, Margaret struggled with loneliness. One Saturday, which was her regular day to write the General, she was told that the mail would not go out until Thursday owing to an accident involving the stagecoach on the way to Huntsville. Margaret waited until 23 December to write Houston, explaining: "Instead of writing I borrowed Col. Yoakum's horse and buggy and attended our church meeting. Do not look so frightened my love, for I assure you I felt very well, and although it was a cold day, I wrapped myself in my cloak, and had mother to drive me and Joshua to walk before the horse."[101] As it was the usual custom, Joshua probably heated some bricks and wrapped them in cloth to put in the buggy to keep Margaret's and her mother's feet warm. He would have been extra careful with the buggy due to Margaret's condition.

On 20 January 1852, Antoinette Power Houston was born and named for Margaret's sister.[102] She joined Mary William Houston, who had been born two years earlier, on 9 April 1850.[103] Joshua would have been glad that the baby and Margaret were well. Eliza already had her hands full with the two toddlers and two older Houston children, but she was no doubt also pleased. The General had been hoping that the child would be another boy, but was pleased with his four daughters and one son, the latter of whom was approaching his tenth year.[104]

But 1852 was also a year for bad news. Joshua had to drive Margaret to Independence to comfort her mother, Nancy Lea, when they received word that her son Henry Lea had died in Alabama.[105] Minor problems continued as well. On 28 May, Margaret wrote her husband concerning their problem servant Albert:

I suppose Col. Yoakum has told you that Albert is at home. They could get no lumber in Independence and therefore there was no work for him to do. Bro. Baines thought it best to send him home. I do hope my love you will not blame Bro. B. for it, as I do not see what else he could do. No one here wants Albert, except Dr. Kittrell, and as he is not willing to give more than 20 dollars per month. I told Col. Yoakum, I would keep him at home for the present as I did not think you would be satisfied with that.[106]

Houston answered her on 28 June, saying that she should go ahead and let Kittrell have Albert for $20, as he would be "of no use at home until fodder time." He continued:

Indeed, I suppose, Joshua or Bingley could be spared as the crop is laid by, or soon will be. The fodder and peas are all the crop we have together this year with the pumpkins. If they are hired out or any one of them, I do not wish them to be out of reach of Doc. Evans practice. I have written to Col. Yoakum to direct the fixing of the spring in a handsome manner. King and Green may wish to hire Albert. He may go to them but not about the machinery.[107]

Joshua was used to being hired out by this time and probably took it in stride. He continued to do work for the Houstons during this year, too. On 28 June, the General sent a letter to Margaret reminding her that "Joshua told me he would fix the hand mill and sharpen it. Let it be done right off, and Cousin Martin give Nash his orders about its preservation. It is a great saving of corn." The General also mentioned in this letter that if there was more corn wanting, it could be got at the Hoague's plantation.[108] Joshua would likely have been sent there for the corn, just as he often went to the Hodge plantation to exchange equipment or supplies. His good friend Memphis Allen, who was a servant at the Hodge's, also visited the Woodlands occasionally.[109] At the time, the two servants had no idea of the important roles they were destined to play in Huntsville after the Civil War and the end of slavery.

Late in the fall of 1852 the Lea family suffered another misfortune. A major hurricane on the Gulf Coast destroyed the sugar cane plantation belonging to Antoinette and her husband, leaving them penniless. Joshua and Antoinette were about the same age and he had witnessed many of her trials—including the death of her first husband William Bledsoe in 1846—and triumphs, including her second marriage, to Charles Power, in 1847. Now Joshua was witness to yet another trial, as she and her husband arrived in Independence, their oxen dragging cypress trees so they could begin to build another home for themselves.[110]

The General's political disappointment that year was his failure to get the Democratic presidential nomination. But he was consoled when he returned home to Huntsville in January 1853 and learned that he had been re-elected to a second full term as Senator. Margaret wanted to be nearer her mother and sister now that the General was leaving again, so the General agreed that his family should move to Independence. Besides, Sam, Jr., was old enough to enroll in Baylor College there.[111] Joshua did not have to be told what to do for this move. He was by now an expert at moving the Houston family.

Before they left, however, the General acquired another servant. He was in Huntsville one day when he noticed a young boy being auctioned on the slave block in front of Gibbs general store. He could see the child was scared out of his wits and noted he might be a good companion for Sam, Jr. Houston purchased Jeff for $450, then took him into Gibbs store to feed him. The General had Tom Gibbs draw up a bill of sale to pay McKell, the seller, for the boy. He told Gibbs he would send Joshua for the boy later, and then bought Jeff his first store-bought hat. This settled the child, who instinctively knew that his new owner was different from most white men he had ever come in contact with. And when Joshua came to pick him up, Jeff noticed the quiet mannerisms of the older servant, whom he came to call "Uncle Joshua," and felt he would like his new family.[112]

Jeff's first view of his new home was at night. Joshua took him to the kitchen where Eliza fed him food left from dinner. All the servants crowded into the kitchen to inspect the newest member of their family. Joshua took Jeff to his cabin and bedded him down on a pallet next to his own bed. Jeff could see candles burning in the windows of the Houston family home and felt comforted by the presence of Joshua. He drifted off to sleep that first night to the sounds of a banjo and a clear singing voice.[113] As Joshua watched the sleeping boy his thoughts must have drifted back to his own boyhood days on the Lea plantation. He knew Jeff's fate, just as he knew his own and the fate of his own son, Joe. No matter how smart or educated, he thought, they would always be someone else's property.

The next morning, Jeff stood in front of the cabins where the servants lived and saw the blacksmith shop, barns, horse and cow lots and the deep well where Joshua and the other slaves drew water. Slave work started with feeding and watering about a dozen horses and mules. Jeff's job was to climb the ladder to the stable loft and throw Joshua bundles of fodder to feed the animals. From there, they went to the cow lot where another barn was used for cows and calves. The cows were fed fodder and cottonseed mixed with corn meal. A large pigpen adjoined the cow lot. There Jeff met Prince, who was General Houston's foreman and had almost as much authority as Joshua. Prince was feeding the hogs purslane, a local wild vine which the hogs were fond of and which everyone believed was a natural medicine.[114]

On his way to breakfast with the field hands, Jeff noticed a large garden with radishes, onions and other herbs and a nearby turnip patch. The smokehouse was near the kitchen and inside it were barrels of sausage and salted pork, along with slabs of bacon and hams strung from the rafters for "home-curing" over a slow hickory fire. Joshua pointed out the small building that was the General's office. Then he took Jeff to the ash hopper to show him one of the jobs he would have. Joshua explained that when ashes were removed from the fireplaces they were thrown in the hopper. When the rains came and wet the ashes, a lye was formed which dripped into a bucket at the bottom of the hopper. The lye was then mixed with fats from the hogs to make lye soap, which was used for all sorts of things, especially for washing clothes.[115]

Jeff's first real dinner at the Houstons' was cooked by the woman he was told to call "Aunt Liza." It was a feast compared to what he was used to: corn bread or hoe cakes and molasses and buttermilk. He ate Eliza's dinner of pork, tripe, fried sweet potatoes and cracklin' bread like he had never eaten before. Decades later in his memoirs, Jeff said that although he was only a small boy at the time, he realized that this was no normal household where treatment of slaves was concerned.[116] Some servants even had store-bought shoes rather than home-made ones.[117]

In fact, Jeff learned a lot about General Sam Houston during this first day. It just so happened that the General was in the house when the servants were eating and when he saw them reaching into the platters and eating with their hands, he got very upset with Joshua and Eliza for letting the servants eat like hogs. He ordered Joshua to hitch up the buggy and drive him to Gibbs store so he could buy tin plates, knives, forks, spoons and cups. At the store, while Joshua and Jeff loaded the buggy with the new utensils, Houston struck up a conversation with Mr. Gibbs about teaching slaves to eat in a civilized fashion. Gibbs told the General a story he had just heard from a churchman that "the Negro was not a human being but an animal without a soul." But Gibbs was also quick to point out that he did not believe the theory.[118]

On 25 October 1853, not long after Jeff settled into life on the farm in Huntsville, Joshua packed up the family belongings to move to Independence, Texas. Joshua knew the fifty-mile trip to Independence well. On moving day the entire Houston family helped with final details until they were ready to take off. The General led the entourage in his black buggy, followed by Joshua driving the big yellow coach and the wagons filled with the other servants, luggage and furniture.[119]

The General purchased a home with 365 acres of timber and cultivated land and made arrangements to rent out the Huntsville home. The new home was located on the longest avenue in Independence, not far from the hill where the college stood. It was set back from the road, and had an orchard and a spring. The house was small and made of logs, with an open hallway and a wing of rooms at the rear.[120]

The family, especially Margaret, liked Independence. The two oldest children, Sam and Nannie, were enrolled at the school and walked there. At noon, Joshua or Eliza climbed the hill to take lunch to them.[121] In addition to the tuition he paid for his own children, the General made a gift of $330 to Baylor to be spent on the education of young ministers.[122] He probably did not realize that his doing so was sending a direct message to Joshua about helping the underprivileged to receive an education.

Meanwhile, Margaret was becoming close friends with the wife of the college president, Georgia Burleson. Joshua would often drive the two women to visit friends in nearby Anderson, Texas. The General and Rufus Burleson were often at loggerheads but restrained themselves from open warfare.[123]

Once the family was settled in, the General resumed his speechmaking throughout Texas. Portions of his speeches contained harsh words for those who were anti-Union.[124] By December he was headed back to Washington. Shortly after his arrival, a letter from Margaret reconfirmed the news that she was pregnant with their sixth child.[125] In another letter, dated 3 January 1854, she assured the General that the family would do well and that she "was able to hire Prince to Mr. Madden for $175 and his clothing." [126] In a letter on January 24, she wrote "Mother has put Martha at Mr. Wilson's and that is another piece of good news. She is also to let him have Bingley at a dollar and a half per day, while at the same time he will be learning the carpenter's trade." [127] Jeff was hired out as a houseboy.[128] Joshua took charge of farming duties and frequently consulted with Charles Power, Margaret's brother-in-law who had a farm nearby.[129]

In June of 1854, the General's wish to name a child for Andrew Jackson came true when Margaret gave birth to their second son.[130] In October, when Houston came home from Washington, Margaret thought it an opportune time to approach her husband about being baptized. At first the General resisted, but with his family's continued efforts he finally gave in. The news of the General's baptism aroused the public's excitement and anticipation. On a bright sunny November, with a crowd of onlookers including the entire Houston family lining the edge of Rocky Creek, the sixty-one-year-old General was baptized at high noon.[131]

Margaret's influence on the General went deep. He had long ago ceased his heavy drinking and become a model family man, and now he was a confirmed Christian. The one thing she probably knew she could never influence was his thirst for public life or his lust for travel. The Houston family was as "mobile as the cavalry." A notion to trek would strike the General and within the hour, the children would be readied for travel by Margaret and the maids. One observer described it this way: "With trunks lashed to [the sides] and a flourish to Tom Blue's long whip the great yellow coach and four horses would be off in a cloud of rolling dust. General Houston led the way in a single-seated top buggy beside the gigantic Joshua, his driver." [132] In spite of all the turmoil, the servants may have relished these great adventures as breaks from their daily routines. Along the way, they would have the opportunity to listen to the General's stories and visit his many friends throughout the area. This would have given them the opportunity to swap stories with the other slaves about their families or other topics of the day.

During the summer of 1855, Joshua drove the General throughout the state to make speeches. "No matter how hot it was," according to one eyewitness, "the General wore a large, soft-brimmed fur hat. His speech-making attire was usually the same, a vest made out of leopard skin, no necktie and his shirt unbuttoned at the collar." His six-foot-plus frame, sparkling blue eyes and deep "carrying" voice always impressed the crowds.[133] But there was growing hostility toward Houston, due partly to his anti-slavery sentiments and his unrelenting support of the Union. He knew his days in the Senate were numbered, and by November he moved his family back to their Huntsville home, the Woodlands.[134]

There, Margaret resumed her routine, with Joshua driving her to church or to visit her good friend Frances Creath. The garden of flowers and the ivy her husband had brought back from George Washington's tomb brought her some comfort. And the pecan trees that the General had previously planted were old enough to yield nuts. The enduring friendship of Huntsville citizens, including retired military officers, clergymen, farmers, storekeepers and lawyers, provided a support system for the Houston family. Tom Gibbs carried the Houstons' credit at his store and Henderson Yoakum made weekly visits to Houston's law office to examine business papers and pertinent mail.[135]

The Houstons transferred their church memberships from Independence to Huntsville. Margaret was overjoyed when several of the family servants, including Mary and Eliza, joined the Baptist Church. They attended services with the Houston family and sat upstairs. On the day that they were to be baptized, the minister, church members and other servants met at the pool, which had been dug by Bingley, near the Houstons' Woodland home.[136] Joshua observed this baptism as he had many before this, and it is possible that he was baptized himself at some point because after slavery he became quite active in the First Baptist Church. However, no official record of his baptism has been found.

The General returned to Washington in December. By Christmas day, the weather there was bitter cold. It was also an unusually cold winter back in Texas, and Joshua would have had to work hard to keep an adequate supply of wood in the fireplaces, and to see to it that the animals were kept warm. Every available quilt was gathered to keep family members warm, especially during the bitter nights.[137]

Margaret was particularly affected by this winter, and Joshua may have had to take extra care with her. She was so lonely that even on the coldest days she would wrap up in her cloak and wander in the field along the rail fences. Other times, she would play the piano, and Joshua may have been perceptive enough to hear the melancholy in the notes she played. To make matters worse, she received word that her friend Frances Creath was dying, so she went to her side and stayed until she drew her last breath.[138] As Joshua drove her home that night, he might have attempted to console her with words, but she was probably barely listening.

Spring was especially welcome in 1856 even though the General did not come home until summer. He brought gifts of silver for Margaret from Gault Jewelers in Washington, D. C., as well as silver cups for each of his four daughters. The General received the silver they were made from as a pension payment for his service in the War of 1812.[139]

The following spring life changed again for the Houstons. The General had announced his candidacy for Governor of Texas, so he had speaking engagements almost daily. Because he accepted an offer from Ed Sharp, a plow salesman who volunteered to drive him to over sixty-seven speaking engagements, Joshua did not travel with his master that summer.[140] But the General's popularity was waning and during his travels he received several threats. When he got word in August that he lost by 4000 votes, he was whittling an Indian head out of a piece of soft pine and told Margaret, "Wait until 1859."[141] It was the only defeat of his political career. At first he sulked but soon wrote a letter to his long-time friend Ashbel Smith, inviting him to visit so they could have some good laughs together.[142]

While the General was in Washington finishing his last term in the Senate, his third son, William Rogers, was born on 25 May 1858.[143] Soon after, Joshua packed up the family once again and moved them back to Independence. Campaigning and traveling had taken a toll on the monetary situation of the Houston family and the General had to sell his home in Huntsville to pay off campaign debts.[144]

During the summer the General began plans to move his family again, this time back to the original home they stayed in when the newlyweds came to Texas in 1840. Cedar Point had 4000 acres and could sustain cash crops to support the family.[145] Houston hired an architect to draw plans to enlarge the house to accommodate his family and the servants. The house was to have one room large enough to hold two pianos. Houston probably counted on Joshua being able to help make the farm livable again.

On 3 March 1859, the General left Washington for the last time.[146] Three months later, back in Texas, he announced his candidacy for Governor, but he did not hit the campaign trail. Instead he opted to make one public address at Nacogdoches and to publish a letter announcing his intentions.[147] After he and Joshua returned from Nacogdoches, Houston spent six months with his family, the longest uninterrupted time since his marriage to Margaret almost twenty years earlier.

Joshua was probably glad, along with Margaret and the children, to have the General home. No doubt the house was filled once more with Houston's stories about Texas, beginning with the decisive winning of Texas lands from Mexico in the Battle of San Jacinto and ending with the current battle over the question of slavery and a unified Union. The General may have talked to Joshua about the growing friction between the Northern and Southern states and his own allegiance to the Union.

There was a growing fear throughout the country concerning slave rebellions, which came to a peak in October when John Brown seized the federal arsenal at Harper's Ferry, Virginia. His plan was to get enough ammunition to carry on a large-scale operation against Virginia slaveholders. The effect of this raid on the South was electrifying. The John Brown uprising became the major topic of the day. Slave owners became fearful and distrusting of even their most loyal servants. Rumors of local poisonings, killings and runaways were rampant. Several slave owners in counties surrounding Huntsville hired patrols to hunt runaways. Slaves who made it to Mexico were brought back.[148] The General probably cautioned Joshua and the other slaves to be extra careful, especially when traveling.

Amidst all of this, Houston won the gubernatorial election. John Brown was hanged just before the General moved his family to Austin, where he would serve the people of Texas one more time. Rumors of secessions from the Union by the southern states was intensifying. In Austin, the General and his family would face hostilities from those who disagreed with him.

Joshua arrived ahead of the family with two wagons filled with the family belongings, including Margaret's legendary piano. The General led the entourage in the top buggy with Jeff driving, followed by Tom Blue driving the yellow coach with Margaret, the children, Eliza and another maid.[149] During one rest stop, the General asked his young slave Jeff to recite his ABCs, to spell some words, to read a newspaper and then said to him, "Jeff, you will be a learned man yet."[150] By the time they reached Austin, Margaret had a bad attack of asthma and everyone stayed awake during the night administering her illness.[151]

The Governor's mansion was lovely, but it was not large enough to accommodate the entire Houston family. There were twelve servants with Sam and Margaret Houston, in addition to their own seven children and assorted animals, including dogs. A partition had to be erected for an extra room, and more beds had to be brought in. Eliza and the nurses lived on the second floor, but Joshua and the other male slaves occupied quarters in the stable.[152]

While the family and servants adjusted their living quarters and set up housekeeping, the Governor agonized over the disturbing state of affairs in

Texas Governor's Mansion. This is one of the first known photographs of the Texas Governor's
Mansion in Austin, Texas. Joshua lived here while Sam and Margaret Houston served as
Governor and First Lady of Texas.
Courtesy Archives Division—Texas State Library.

the capitol, located one block from the mansion. Less than one month after
Houston became Governor, South Carolina's legislature proclaimed the right
of a state to secede from the Union. The fear of war between the states was
growing.[153]

Joshua was thirty-eight years old now and his duties had once again
changed. He was no longer helping to manage a whole farm, but he was still
in charge of all the governor's horses, buggies, and carriages. What would
not have changed is that he could, from his vantage point in the stables, still
hear Margaret playing the piano. Margaret's music had had a quieting effect
on him since both of them had been children on her family's plantation in
Alabama.[154]

The other constant in Joshua's life was Eliza. A couple of years older than
he, she had always looked after the family, the General, Margaret, the other

servants and now seven children, soon to be eight. Other than being fearful about all of the unrest in the state and the nation, Eliza's main concern was likely how she would feed the family adequately without fresh vegetables from the garden. Nancy Lea calmed her fears a little when she sent them a milk cow and vegetables from Independence.[155] When she was not cooking or taking care of the children, Eliza helped Margaret scour through pattern books looking for dresses that would suit the First Lady of Texas.[156]

All was not smooth at the Governor's mansion. One night a thief broke into the stable at the mansion and stole the General's horses. This was probably as devastating to Joshua as it was to Houston, who told Sam, Jr., about the incident in a letter on 4 June 1860. He assured his oldest son that his gray stallion was not among the horses stolen and would be at the stable when he got there for him to ride.[157]

The Governor also had problems within his own family. His son Andrew Jackson Houston was known for getting into trouble. Once back at the Woodlands he had been out in the yard chasing a rooster. When he caught it, he threw it in a large flour barrel. Joshua heard the rooster crowing and went to his rescue. He pulled the "white" rooster out with one hand, and with the other took Andrew by the ear and led him to the General. When father asked son why he had done it, Andrew just said, "Pa, that old rooster sure is mad." The General broke into laughter and Andrew escaped punishment once again.[158] Andrew's behavior did not change just because he was in the governor's mansion. One day while Joshua was working in the stables he saw Andrew running toward the mansion from the capitol. He soon learned, along with the rest of Austin's residents, that Andrew had locked the Senators in their chamber and run away with the key. After the Senators began to call out the window to people on the ground, the Governor was called upon to convince his son to give up the key. Houston later remarked that his "six-year-old son had shown more generalship in handling the members of the Legislature than he himself had shown with all his power as Governor." [159]

In general, though, the entire Houston family, including the slaves, had more to worry about than a youngster's pranks. With all the rumors and bad news in the air, everyone feared that war was coming. For Joshua, this may have increased his determination to improve his reading and writing skills and to learn as much as he could about taking care of a house, farm and business, just in case the time came when he would be free. Although the thought of providing for Ann, the mother of his son Joe and daughters Lucy and Julie, was probably uppermost in his mind, he was also aware that the Houston family would suffer too. Texas was on the brink of facing the most turbulent times Joshua had seen in his nineteen years on its soil.

NOTES

1. Seale, p. 102–03.

2. Roberts, p. 111–12.

3. Sam Houston, *The Writings of Sam Houston,* ed. Amelia Williams and Eugene Barker (Austin: University of Texas Press, 1938–43), vol. 7, p. 15–16.

4. Seale, p. 105.

5. Roberts, p. 113 states that Sam Houston "joined with the others in erecting a large log house in which to hold services [for the Concord Baptist Church]." Since Joshua was Houston's carpenter, we have assumed that he contributed his labor to the building of the church.

6. Seale, p. 106.

7. In *My Master* Jeff Hamilton states that he would wait outside the church while the Houston family attended services, so we have assumed Joshua did the same thing.

8. Braider, p. 244; Seale, p. 108.

9. Roberts, p. 119.

10. Kathryn Turner, *Stagecoach Inns of Texas* (Waco: Texian Press, 1972) p. 32.

11. Seale, p. 114.

12. Margaret Lea Houston, letter to Sam Houston, 19 March, 1846, Franklin Williams Collection, Huntsville, Texas.

13. Seale, p. 110.

14. Seale, p. 110.

15. D'Anne McAdams Crews, ed., *Huntsville and Walker County, Texas: A Bicentennial History* (Huntsville: Sam Houston State University, 1976), p. 60.

16. Crews, p. 23.

17. Hamilton/Hunt, p. 9.

18. Seale, p. 110.

19. In many of the letters in the Franklin Williams collection in Huntsville, Houston writes to tell one or more of the slaves "howdy" and gives them a particular message of what work to do.

20. Several Houston family stories state that Joshua was "the man of the house" when the General was away, and that responsibility included being in charge of Sam, Jr. Peggy Everitt, Madge Roberts, and Meredith Spangler interviews.

21. Margaret Lea Houston, letter to Sam Houston, 20 June 1846, Franklin Williams Collection, Huntsville, Texas.

22. Marshall De Bruhl, *Sword of San Jacinto: A Life of Sam Houston* (New York: Random House, 1993), p. 33.

23. Margaret Houston, letter to Sam Houston, 20 June 1846, Franklin Williams collection, Huntsville, Texas.

24. Silverthorne, p. 106.

25. Silverthorne, p. 107, 111.

26. Silverthorne, p. 111.

27. Silverthorne, p. 114.

28. Silverthorne, p. 127–141.

29. Thomas Jewett Goree, *The Thomas Jewett Goree Letters* (Bryan, Texas: Family History Foundation, 1981), p. 279.

30. As one of Joshua's major responsibilities was the animals, we have assumed he would have known doctoring techniques. The information concerning the spider-webs is from Goree Hightower. The rest of the folk remedy information is from Silverthorne, p. 149–154.

31. Based on information on traditional Christmases on Texas plantations in Silverthorne, p. 154.

32. Silverthorne, p. 135–40.

33. Sam Houston, letter to Margaret Houston, 16 May 1846, Franklin Williams Collection, Huntsville, Texas.

34. Margaret Houston, letter to Sam Houston, 28 May 1846, Franklin Williams Collection, Huntsville, Texas.

35. Margaret Houston, letter to Sam Houston, 12 June 1846.

36. Friend, p. 182.

37. Seale, p. 121.

38. Roberts, p. 141.

39. Seale, p. 122.

40. Roberts, p. 149–50.

41. Roberts, p. 151.

42. Braider, p. 250.

43. Madison, p. 64.

44. Madison, p. 65.

45. Roberts, p. 152.

46. Seale, p. 128.

47. Madison, p. 66.

48. Margaret Houston, letter to Sam Houston, 3 October 1847, Franklin Williams Collection, Huntsville, Texas.

49. Margaret Houston, letter to Sam Houston, 14 February 1848, Franklin Williams Collection, Huntsville, Texas.

50. James F. Mellon, *Bullwhip Days: The Slaves Remember* (New York: Weidenfeld and Nicolson, 1988), p. 194.

51. Margaret Houston, letter to Sam Houston, 21 March 1848. (Hereafter, all letters are from the Franklin Williams Collection in Huntsville, Texas, unless otherwise stated.)

52. Braider, p. 254.

53. Seale, p. 132.

54. There is no record of an official marriage, and Joshua and Ann may have merely followed the slave custom (based on African tradition) of "jumping the broom" to declare that they were wed. Ordinarily, the woman would wear her best dress and perhaps a flower or ribbon in her hair. Everyone would gather in the yard and someone would hold one end of the broom up in the air with the brush part remaining on the ground. The bride would jump over first, then the groom, then both would jump back over it together.

55. Margaret Houston, letter to Sam Houston, 24 May 1848.

56. Silverthorne, p. 166.

57. We have assumed Ann did not belong to the Houstons, since she is not mentioned in other Houston letters.

58. Based on information on gravestones in the Campbell's Cemetery in Hall's Bluff, Texas.

59. Silverthorne, p. 166.

60. She is buried in this community. The name on the gravestone is Anneliza Halyard, and she is buried near her husband Wharton Halyard and her son Joe Houston. A note in Mae Wynne McFarland's notebook says that Joshua's first wife was a Wynne. We have no other documentation on this, but a Wynne family had a plantation (Wynnewood) in Alabama near the Lea plantation, and this family later moved to Huntsville, Texas. So it is possible that Joshua and Ann were both from Alabama, and that their relationship began there.

61. Margaret Houston, letter to Sam Houston, 30 May 1848.

62. Margaret Houston, letter to Sam Houston, 2 June 1848.

63. Sam Houston, letter to Margaret Houston, 11 February 1849.

64. Margaret Houston, letter to Sam Houston, 28 June 1848.

65. Sam Houston, letter to Margaret Houston, 16 July 1848.

66. Margaret Houston, letter to Sam Houston, 28 February 1849.

67. Sam Houston, letter to Margaret Houston, 21 July 1848.

68. Seale, p. 133.

69. Margaret Houston, letter to Sam Houston, 16 November 1848.

70. Margaret Houston, letter to Sam Houston 3 January 1849.

71. Margaret Houston, letter to Sam Houston, 30 January 1849.

72. Braider, p. 261; Madison, p. 72.

73. Sam Houston, letter to Margaret Houston, 23 November 1848.

74. Sam Houston, letter to Margaret Houston, 13 January 1849.

75. Seale, p. 144.

76. James, p. 375.

77. Seale, p. 138.

78. Roberts, p. 175.

79. Crews, p. 38.

80. Seale, p. 110.

81. Seale, p. 145.

82. Madge Thornall Roberts, interview with authors on the subject of the Houston family's observation of the Sabbath.

83. Silverthorne, p. 186–87; Webber, p. 18.

84. Webber, p. 17.

85. Seale, p. 145.

86. Temple Houston Morrow, "Intimate Stories." Also Morrow's letter to Grace Longino Cox, 17 January 1957, Temple Houston Morrow Collection, Sam Houston Memorial Museum, Huntsville, Texas.

87. Margaret Houston, letter to Sam Houston, 28 January 1850, Temple Houston Morrow Collection, Huntsville, Texas.

88. Margaret Houston, letter to Sam Houston, 17 December 1849.

89. Crews, p. 48.

90. Interviews with descendants Madge Roberts, Mrs. A. R. Teasdale and Peggy Everitt.

91. Sam Houston, letter to Margaret Houston, 12 January 1850.

92. Walker County Tax District Court Records, No. 528, p. 365–66, recorded 24 March 1851.

93. Hamilton/Hunt, p. 10.

94. Crews, p. 133.

95. Crews, p. 39.

96. McDonald, *Adolphus Sterne,* p. 225–26.

97. Sam Houston, letter to Margaret Houston, 15 November 1851.

98. Sam Houston, letter to Margaret Houston, 28 November 1851.

99. Margaret Houston, letter to Sam Houston, 28 November 1851.

100. Temple Houston Morrow, letter to Grace Longino Cox, 17 January 1957, Temple Houston Morrow Collection, Huntsville, Texas.

101. Roberts, p. 226.

102. Madison, p. 83.

103. Seale, p. 150.

104. Roberts, p. 226.

105. Margaret Houston, letter to Sam Houston, 28 May 1852.

106. Ibid.

107. Sam Houston, letter to Margaret Houston, 15 June 1852.

108. Sam Houston, letter to Margaret Houston, 28 June 1852.

109. C. W. Wilson, *The Negro in Walker County* (Huntsville: Sam Houston State University, 1934), n.p.

110. Seale, p. 163.

111. Roberts, p. 235.

112. Hamilton/Hunt, p. 13.

113. Hamilton/Hunt, p. 14.

114. Hamilton/Hunt, p. 15.

115. Hamilton/Hunt, p. 16.

116. Hamilton/Hunt, p. 16–17.

117. T & S Gibbs Ledger, 1858, Franklin Westin Collection, Rice University, Houston, Texas.

118. Hamilton/Hunt, p. 17.

119. James, p. 385.

120. Roberts, p. 235.

121. Seale, p. 163.

122. Roberts, p. 236.

123. Seale, p. 164.

124. Braider, p. 276.

125. Seale, p. 164.

126. Margaret Houston, letter to Sam Houston, 3 January 1854.

127. Margaret Houston, letter to Sam Houston, 24 January 1854.

128. Hamilton/Hunt, p. 27.

129. Seale, p. 167.

130. Roberts, p. 241.

131. James, p. 385.

132. Ibid.

133. Hamilton/Hunt, p. 31.

134. Braider, p. 283.

135. Seale, p. 173–74.

136. Minutes of the First Baptist Church, Huntsville, Texas, 18 November 1855, 16 December 1855, and 21 June 1863.

137. Seale, p. 172.

138. Seale, p. 176–77.

139. Roberts, p. 251.

140. Braider, p. 286.

141. Roberts, p. 264.

142. James, p. 390.

143. Roberts, p. 273.

144. Braider, p. 287.

145. Madge Roberts interview with Jane Monday; also Seale, p. 191.

146. James, p. 390.

147. Braider, p. 292.

148. Braider, p. 295.

149. Roberts, p. 280; Hamilton/Hunt, p. 44.

150. Hamilton/Hunt, p. 44.

151. Hamilton/Hunt, p. 44.

152. Seale, p. 193.

153. Seale, p. 195.

154. Seale, p. 197.

155. Seale, p. 194.

156. Ibid.

157. Seale, p. 200.

158. Madge Roberts and Peggy Everitt interview with authors.

159. Hamilton/Hunt, p. 53–55; Roberts, p. 291.

CHAPTER THREE

1859–1864

"Let My People Go"

Joshua never had much time for personal pursuits, but in the quiet of the night, he may have pondered the complicated problems faced by the General. No doubt the two often talked about the events of the day, especially to while away the time when they traveled over the roads of Texas. If their discussions came around to subjects like the Underground Railroad, abolitionists or slave uprisings, it is likely they were both guarded in their responses. Joshua heard a lot of rumors from fellow slaves via the grapevine telegraph, especially while traveling, but when he listened to the General, he heard firsthand news. Joshua's position gave him opportunities few other slaves could boast of. He would have been especially interested in news about Frederick Douglass, a former slave just a few years older than he was, and one of the most eloquent spokesmen for the anti-slavery movement.

Joshua was present when supporters of Sam Houston nominated him for President of the United States on 21 April 1860, the twenty-fourth anniversary of the Battle of San Jacinto.[1] As Joshua stood on the very grounds where the battle had been fought, his imagination probably turned to images of Houston facing Santa Anna and the noble speech he had made as he spared the life of the Mexican leader.

Joshua was no doubt aware that the General's position against slavery, his legislative proposals, and his strong pro-Union stance were unpopular with many Texans, including the legislature in Austin. Both men had cause for concern on 8 July 1860, when news spread about fires burning in eleven Texas towns.[2] The paranoia created with the John Brown incident was still having its effect and tensions over slavery were in high gear. The fires were viewed with suspicion. Many believed they were part of an organized slave insurrection. It was an anxious and fearful time for both slaves and slave owners, and Joshua and his master would have been no exception. Even living with an enlightened man like Houston, Joshua was probably anxious about his own fate—wondering whether he would die a slave, and if his own children would ever be free.

Not long after his nomination, the General learned there were three other Democratic nominees for President, and that the newly-formed Republican Party had nominated Abraham Lincoln. His quest for the presidency would be a difficult one. In addition, he could not ignore the family problems which kept cropping up. Margaret had a very difficult delivery with their fourth son, Temple Lea, and Houston had to remain by her side for more than a week while she recovered her health. The General decided to withdraw his name from the Presidential race, stating that the Democrats did not have a chance of winning if their vote were to be split four ways. In November 1860, Lincoln was elected President, but before he could take office, South Carolina seceded from the Union. Houston, fearing that Texas was heading in the same direction, stepped up his efforts at promoting the Union. He had Joshua drive him to the larger cities in the state so he could make speeches to try to stop the secessionists. His pleas fell on deaf ears. Southern states began "toppling like a row of dominoes" and soon elected Jefferson Davis as president of the Confederate states. Texans voted to join the Confederacy in February, 1861.[3]

By the time Lincoln was inaugurated, the country was clearly divided, and secession sentiments in Texas were running high. Because of his proximity to General Houston, Joshua was probably not surprised that things had gotten so bad. He had been present just a year earlier when Robert E. Lee (a distant relative of Margaret's), had visited the Governor's mansion on his way to the Texas border.[4] Houston had discussed his presidential aspirations with Lee and his hopes that someday Mexico would be a protectorate. It is possible that the General shared parts of his and Lee's conversation with Joshua at some time during their Texas travels. Joshua was probably not aware, however, that Governor Houston had received secret communications from President Abraham Lincoln offering army protection to keep Texas in the Union.[5] Joshua must have watched carefully as his master handled the daily difficulties which developed during this crucial time in history.

The night of 15 March 1861, was perhaps the worst one ever for the Houston family. During dinner, about 8:00 on a Friday evening, George W. Chilton, a member of the state's Secession Convention, visited the Governor's man-

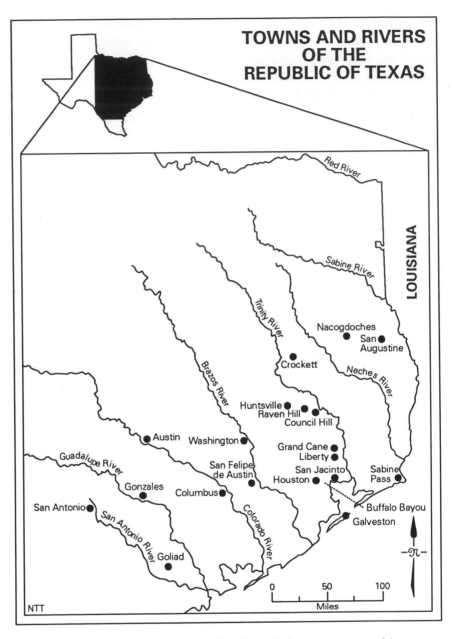

Map of towns and rivers of the Republic of Texas. Joshua went to many of these towns with General Houston.

Courtesy Nancy Tiller.

sion with an announcement. He stated that the next day at noon all officials would be required to meet at the Capitol and take an oath of loyalty to the Confederacy or be removed from office. After dinner, Margaret had Joshua and the other servants place their chairs around the wall of the dining room. She brought the two-volume Bible and placed it in front of Governor Houston. They had prayers, then afterward she took the lamp and led the children upstairs to bed. The servants retired to their quarters. Joshua was told not to allow any more visitors in the mansion.[6] He probably watched lights burn all night in the General's bedroom, and wondered whether his master would take the oath or give up the Governorship.

The next morning, everyone waited for the General's decision. When he appeared he told Margaret, "I will never do it." He refused to take the oath, so the lieutenant governor was sworn in as Governor of Texas. Sam Houston's beloved Texas had deposed him. The state he had seen grow from just 20,000 settlers when he first moved there, to 431,000 people in 1861, had turned its back on him. Slave owners had made their position perfectly clear. They were more concerned about their investment in 182,000 slaves than in following Houston's lead to join the union and end slavery.[7]

Even after Houston made the difficult choice to step down as Governor, he had one more chance to stay in power. On the night of March 19, as the family was packing, there was a loud knock at the door of the mansion. A group of Houston supporters came to tell him that an army was in the hills outside Austin ready to come to his defense and put him back in office as Governor, restore the Republic, and take over Mexico. Joshua no doubt heard about the General's answer to these men; that he appreciated their friendship and loyalty, but for the sake of humanity and justice, he wanted them to disperse.[8]

Instead, Houston accepted defeat and continued with his plans to move his family out of Austin. On moving day, Joshua took the lead wagon loaded with household goods, glassware and several boxes of books and papers which the General always carried with him. Tom Blue drove the yellow coach in which Margaret and her children rode. All of the other servants followed in a wagon, except Jeff. He stayed behind for a few hours with the General, who had to finish some business in town before he could leave.[9]

As he drove, Joshua probably glanced back at Austin, grieved for his master's fate, and pondered the irony in the political defeat of the man whose name had become synonymous with the state of Texas. Houston's many years of dedication and service were being ignored. Knowing the General's fall from power was due, in large part, to his stand on slavery, Joshua probably reflected again about the effects of that institution on his own life and what it might be like without it. He no doubt resented having to hide his intelligence as he traveled, even though he could be open with the General. He had firsthand experience with what slavery did to the body and soul—how it reduced men to the state of animals and how children had no hope but to repeat the same hideous cycle.

Slavery had deprived Joshua of the right to be married and raise his own family. He could not acquire property or educate his children. He could not hold public office or even vote. He had no judicial rights and could not testify in a court of law. The humane treatment Joshua and the other slaves received from the Houston family gave them their only chance at dignity, and it could only be felt within the confines of that environment. Once off the farm or out of the governor's mansion, they faced the constant potential for abuse by any stranger unfamiliar with their connections to General Sam Houston. Joshua or any of the others could be stolen in a moment and sold to some cruel master. The roads were filled with vigilante committees looking for runaway slaves who would often capture any slave who was momentarily without the protection of his master.

Jeff, who had stayed behind in Austin so he could drive the General back home after he finished his business, was also grieved by the family's disgrace. He had grown to manhood with the Houston family, and never expected to see such hatred aimed at his master. At just under twenty-one years old, Jeff was old enough to sense the terrible suffering that would come if the General's predictions came true about a war between the states. Jeff saw that the General, as always, bore the events with great dignity. Everyone knew he was suffering, but his lack of outward grief inspired the entire Houston family to follow his lead and to hold their heads high.[10]

As the General prepared to leave Austin in his top buggy, he said to Jeff, "We have plenty of time now, since we are both out of office, so turn back and we'll drive over to see the Treaty Oak." This tree, not far from the Colorado River, stood over sixty feet high, shading nearly an acre of land. After the General took some time to meditate, he told Jeff the oak's story. Houston said the Indians had been coming to the tree for hundreds of years to have their war dances and other ceremonies under its shade. Also, he said that the first treaty between the Indians and the pioneers (led by Stephen F. Austin) was signed under the tree, defining boundary lines between the two races. Houston told Jeff about an Indian legend that young girls would make love-tea out of the oak's leaves in order to woo their lovers and to keep them safe during wars. Jeff also heard that the famous naturalist James Audubon had estimated the tree's age at five hundred years old.[11]

During this trip, the General apparently did not discuss with Jeff his thoughts about Texas's secession or his fear of war. Once they arrived in Independence, he set about taking measures to protect and to feed his family.[12]

The General's dire predictions about war came true less than a month after he left Austin. On 12 April 1861, the South Carolina Government seized Fort Sumter from the federal government. Although no one was killed, the altercation led by the newly formed Confederate government signaled the beginning of the war between the states. Houston and Joshua were headed toward Galveston when news of Fort Sumter reached them. By the time they returned to Independence in May, everyone was making plans for the war. Houston found himself the object of numerous hostilities. On more than one occasion he had guns pointed at him, and he received many verbal threats.[13]

The Houstons visited briefly with Margaret's relatives in Independence, but because of his shortage of money, Houston wanted his family back at Cedar Point where they could live off their 4000 acres of timberland and rich farming soil. Their credit was also good here, since the Cedar Point land was valued at $150,000 on the tax roles.[14]

Joshua had been sent ahead to help Sam, Jr., get the house ready for the family's arrival. On 31 June 1861, Margaret, Eliza, baby Temple, and the other small children finally got there. The older girls—Nannie, Maggie and Mary Willie—stayed behind in Independence with the Leas in order to attend Baylor's Female Department.[15]

Cedar Point became their sanctuary, shielding them from the public's anger over the General's stance on secession. Houston was slowing down considerably and was even walking with a cane. Often, Joshua or Margaret would walk with him, surveying the property or walking along the Trinity Bay. If he mentioned a taste for oysters, Joshua would gather some and Eliza would have them on the table for dinner. If he wanted gumbo, Eliza would mix up her Cedar Point Gumbo recipe. After eating dinner and reading the Bible to the children and servants, the General would often relate stories about his colorful life. Sometimes during the day he would write letters to old friends, which he and Joshua would mail on their visits to the city of Houston or Galveston.[16]

Although the General was more settled than ever and had no official duties, he was not content to stay on the farm all day. He and Joshua would travel to Houston or Galveston for a day or so where he would visit old friends and learn of the news, especially concerning the war. His close friend and neighbor Ashbel Smith told him that all slave gatherings, even church meetings, were suspected as places where escapes could be planned.[17]

During restless nights at Cedar Point, Margaret tried to comfort him, sitting and reading to him by candlelight from the Bible or other books, or from newspapers. At first, many of the newspapers published editorials criticizing Houston, but soon his name was not even being mentioned. As he walked around the city named in his honor, the General was scarcely noticed.[18]

Still at Cedar Point, Sam, Jr., was growing restless listening to his father's old war stories. He complained to Joshua, not daring to approach his father. The eighteen-year-old youth had spent more of his time with Joshua than with his father, so the relationship between father and son was somewhat formal.[19] Sam, Jr., felt closed in at Cedar Point and wanted more contact with others. To ease his boredom he accepted an invitation to go to Ashbel Smith's nearby Evergreen Farm.[20]

From there he wrote to his parents in the spring of 1861, mentioning that he was drilling with Dr. Smith's volunteer company, the Bayland Guards. Margaret became very upset that her son was considering joining the Confederate forces. The General was more concerned that the boy might not gain acceptance by those who knew what his father stood for. Nevertheless, Sam, Jr., decided to join the Bayland Guards. When he returned home to tell his family, his mother was in shock. When things quieted down a bit, the General presented his son with a Confederate uniform and Margaret presented him with a Bible for his vest pocket.[21] Joshua probably had some words of encouragement for Sam, Jr., which no doubt included pointers about taking good care of himself.

Joshua would have spent at least part of this summer like every other, trying to make Margaret's surroundings as pleasant as possible. This would include planting flowers when he wasn't tending gardens or caring for the animals or traveling with the General. By fall, Houston had figured out several ways to make ends meet. One of the things he decided was that the servants should cut down certain trees on the property so they could be sold in Galveston for firewood. The axe took more and more of the oaks that they had planted many years before, and by Christmas only a few trees were left.[22]

Joshua's biggest problem that winter was how to keep the animals warm and healthy. The cabins and barn that winter were colder than usual, without the trees to help shield them from the elements.[23] Eliza, in one way, had it easier in winter. The fires in the kitchen made her more comfortable then, rather than making her more miserable like they did in the summer. On the other hand, the children probably got more colds in the winter, and she would have been responsible for treating them. Eliza's presence, her cheerful attitude and her hot meals, would have contributed to the family's welfare.

Although spring chased the fierce winds away, Margaret was as sad as she had ever been in her life. Her beloved Sam, Jr., left with the Bayland Guards on 12 March 1862, headed toward Missouri, and she feared she would never see him again.[24] There is little doubt that the whole family, including all the slaves, turned out to say their goodbyes, all of them giving their own parting words of advice.

The General soon resumed his travels to the cities of Houston and Galveston, and it is likely that Joshua went with him at least part of the time, as he had done before.[25] It would have been a break from the monotony of home life for both men, especially for Joshua, since it gave him the opportunity to catch up on news of the war and of the people he had gotten to know during his many trips with his master.

On a family outing in the spring of 1862, to take their minds off the war and Sam, Jr., the Houston family stopped to pick flowers. Little Temple saved some of his pickings for Eliza and when he got back to the cabin he proudly presented them to her. Margaret was so pleased with her son's gesture of affection toward his nurse and friend that she pressed the flowers for safe keeping.[26]

On 28 May 1862, Thomas J. Goree wrote his mother that Sam's cousin Martin Royster had seen Sam, Jr., at the battle of Shiloh, "on the ground with a bullet in his thigh firing at the enemy."[27] When they got the news, the Houstons feared Sam's death or capture by Union soldiers. They began asking for news of Sam whenever they shared their food and water with the many soldiers who stopped at their home on their way upcountry.[28]

One afternoon in late September, a thin, crippled soldier came up to Margaret. She did not recognize him as her son until he spoke and said, "Ma, I don't believe you know me."[29] Margaret praised God that her prayers had been answered. By the time the General and Joshua returned from a trip to Galveston, there was a big celebration going on in the Houston household. Sam, Jr., told his mother that the bullet passed through the Bible she had given him and absorbed the impact. The General and the family, including Joshua and the other servants, got a blow-by-blow accounting of the battle at Shiloh where Sam, Jr., had been wounded.[30]

Word came in December 1862 that federal troops had captured Galveston and erected a blockade. Prices of all goods skyrocketed three hundred to four hundred percent.[31] Fearful for the safety of his family, the General made plans for them to return to Huntsville. He tried to buy back his Woodland home but it was unavailable, so he decided to rent. The house he found was a peculiar two-story wooden structure which local people called the Steamboat House because of its resemblance to the vessel. Joshua made minor changes to accommodate the family and they settled down once again.[32]

The General always welcomed guests and so was glad when his old friend Billie Blount, chief of the Alabama Indians, came to visit. The Alabama tribe had combined with the tribe of the Coushattas, one of the oldest tribes in the Southwest, and the General had been instrumental in getting the state of Texas to deed them 4000 acres of land not far from Huntsville. Blount bore gifts of blankets, beads and toys for the Houston children when he met the General at the big spring near where the Houston family once lived. He had come to seek Houston's help in preventing Indians from being drafted to fight for the Confederate army. By writing a letter to the Confederate War De-partment, Houston was successful in securing the release of the Texas Indians from the army.[33]

The General was now becoming noticeably feeble. His hair was very white and he bent over the hickory walking stick that Joshua had carved.[34] The monotony of home life was almost too much for a man so used to being at the center of things in state and national politics. His prolific letter writ-ing became the main focus of his quest to stay in touch with the public. Joshua almost always had letters to mail when he went to town to take care of the family business or to work for the stagecoach company to earn extra money. Many of these letters were addressed to Houston's long time friend, Ashbel Smith.

By the fall of 1862, the problem of slave runaways had a direct effect on the Houstons. Tom Blue, the coachman who had been with the General since be-fore his marriage to Margaret, made a dramatic escape to Mexico. Blue was a fine-looking mulatto with the manners and speech of a high class gentleman. He persuaded another servant, Walter Hume, to make the escape with him and to pose as his servant. They had no trouble crossing the Mexican border since Blue resembled a Spaniard, but once across the border, Blue carried the scheme a bit further. He sold Hume as a slave for $800, a bargain price, so he could live like the gentleman he portrayed himself.[35]

The General was not too upset about the escape, and in fact made a joke about how the two slaves had left too soon. A little more than a week after they escaped, the General got word that Abraham Lincoln had issued a proc-

lamation on 23 September 1862, that all slaves would be declared free on
1 January 1863. The General decided not to wait that long. Dressed in his best
Sunday suit, the General called all of his servants to the front of the house
and read them a newspaper account of the proclamation. When he told them
that they were free, his voice filled with emotion. But he also told them they
could stay and work for him, and that he would pay them as long as he could.
There was not a dry eye among owners or servants, and for a long while there
was just silence.[36]

It was Joshua who broke the silence by telling the General he would go
right on working for him like he had always done. Joshua had always been
a leader among the servants, so many of them agreed with him. Besides his
loyalty to the Houston family, Joshua was smart enough to know that the war
was still going on and that there were deep hostilities among whites toward
the slaves. He undoubtedly figured that the safest place for himself and the
others was with the Houstons, where they could look out for one another
as they had always done. Besides, the General's health was failing and Joshua
knew he needed help now more than ever before. Eliza got the notion that
the law or government was going to send soldiers to take them away from the
Houston family and began to moan and sway from side to side. Then she took
two-year-old Temple Lea into her arms and hugged him and cried "I don't
want no 'mancipation."[37]

Actually, because of the state constitution adopted by the Confederate government in 1861, it was illegal in Texas for Houston to free his slaves.[38] Still,
he had done everything in his power to make them free.

On 2 March 1863, the General celebrated his seventieth birthday. It was also
the anniversary date of the signing of the Texas Declaration of Independence
in 1836. He had begun to look frail and Margaret suggested he go to Sour
Lake. The hot mineral water from the springs there had been very helpful
to Eliza when she suffered with consumption, and Margaret had found the
waters helpful when she needed relief from her ailments. The General agreed
that he would make the trip during the summer.[39]

Just before he left, a delegation of his Indian friends came with a message
of good wishes from Chief Blount, who had heard of the General's failing
health. The General did not meet them by the spring as he had always done,
but visited with them on his front porch. The eight young squaws and four
young braves formed a circle around the General and talked for a long time in
their language. Just before their departure, the General asked them to sing a
song. The Indians were so pleased with his request that they sang several.[40]

Earlier in the year, the General had written a letter to General McGruder praising his victory at Galveston, which removed the Union blockade and re-opened the port. Huntsville's prison had become important to the state of Texas and the Confederacy because it was furnishing cotton and wool for uniforms. However, when the General found out that captured union officers had been forced to work in the prison, he became angry. One of his last public acts was to convince the superintendent of the prison to release the soldiers and allow them to stay in the home of the Houstons and other Huntsville residents until arrangements could be made to exchange them as prisoners of war with some captured southern soldiers.[41] The General may have been thinking of the experiences of his own son, Sam Jr., while he was a prisoner of war.

The General finally left for Sour Lake in early June of 1863. The fifty-mile drive with Joshua at the reins gave the two time, once again, to reminisce about their travels, trials and tribulations during the years they had spent together in Texas. They may have laughed, for instance, about the time the General's horse kicked Nannie into the baptizing pool on their Huntsville property. Jeff was supposed to be watching out for Nannie and he had the horse "Old Pete" by the pond getting a drink of water. Nannie had a switch in her hand and he told her to hit the horse even though he knew the horse was so vicious that only the General could ride him. The horse reared at her and she fell into the pond. Even though Jeff jumped in to save her, the General gave him a good whipping for causing the accident in the first place. This became a family joke about the only servant to ever get a whipping from the General.[42]

The General and Joshua may have also reminisced about how relieved the whole family had been when they learned that Sam, Jr., had survived the battle of Shiloh. And the General no doubt managed to recall a story or two about his thirteen years in Washington as a United States Senator. Whatever stories they relived this time, they were ones familiar to them from their many long journeys together over Texas roads.

Joshua was savvy enough to know what everyone else around could see, that the old war horse was slowing down. He hoped the Sour Lake waters would help the General. Many people swore that their ailments had been cured by the springs. However, after spending more than a month at Sour Lake, the General seemed in worse shape. To make matters worse, while he was there word came that General Grant had captured Vicksburg.[43]

The General was in low spirits and looked like a corpse by the time he and

*Sam Houston's grave in Huntsville, Texas. Joshua continued to care for the General
even after his death, offering money to his widow and building a fence
around his former master's grave.*
Courtesy Sam Houston Memorial Museum—Huntsville, Texas.

Joshua returned to Huntsville. He was put to bed and family members and
servants took turns giving him medicines, fanning the air to give him relief
from the hot, muggy weather, and trying to keep the flies from bothering
him. Margaret faced the fact that her husband would not live much longer and
sent for Drs. P. W. Kittrell and T. H. Markham, requesting that they make
the General as comfortable as possible. She then sent for a minister and a few
close friends. They kept vigil all day on 26 July 1863. The General was in a
stupor but tried to talk, telling the minister, "all is well." Just before sundown,
the General whispered, "Texas, Texas, Margaret," and those where his last
words.[44]

The General's body was prepared for burial, and final tributes were paid
by the Masons, Odd Fellows and other friends and family members. The next
day, he was buried in the cemetery across the road from the steamboat house
where he had spent his final days.

Joshua was not in Huntsville when the General drew his last breath because
he was working on a stagecoach job. By the time he returned and heard about
the death, the General's family had moved back to Independence.[45] Margaret
had honored her husband's wish to free his slaves and only a few had elected

to go to Independence with her. The only two mentioned by name are Eliza and Bingley.[46]

Joshua was deeply saddened by the death of the General and prepared to visit his old master's widow to offer condolence. Joshua started on his journey long before the sun came up. He had traveled the road to Independence countless times but never without the Houston entourage.

He knew how deeply grieved Margaret was. She now had seven children to raise without their father, and Sam, Jr., was back fighting in the war. Nothing that Joshua had ever seen in the past could prepare him for seeing Margaret's desolation in the face of her husband's death. Knowing of Margaret's love for flowers and how they had always helped lift her spirits, Joshua may have stopped to pick some for her.

He arrived just before supper and waited until Margaret finished her meal. Joshua then asked if he could talk to her alone. He told her how sorry he was about the General and how much he too would miss him. After asking about all of the children, Joshua laid an old leather bag on the table. He told his former mistress that there was over $2000 in gold and United States currency in the bag and he wanted her to have every cent of it.

Margaret Houston was so overcome with the generosity of her former servant that she couldn't speak for a moment, but she then thanked him and politely refused the offer, saying, "I want you to take your money and do just what General Houston would want you to do with it if he were here, and that is give your boys and girls a good education."[47]

Joshua knew he had to bow to her wishes. He also knew how much that money would help Margaret. The General had left thousands of acres of land but almost no money. Joshua had saved his earnings throughout the years and felt a duty to the Houstons for allowing him to work for wages. His skills in blacksmithing had been widely sought after, and Joshua had been frugal. The fact that he now had more money than his former mistress was an ironic twist of fate, but a fate that Joshua felt would not have been possible had it not been for the generosity and kindness shown by the General and his wife Margaret.

As Joshua traveled alone back to Huntsville, he knew that danger lurked. He was probably making plans to spend the rest of his life providing for his own family. Even though Houston had "freed" him, a war was still being waged that had the power to decide his fate for him, along with that of his friends and family. And, as always, he was faced with being captured by some vigilante. False charges could be brought against him, and he could be lynched by a mob on a moment's whim. But Joshua seems to have spent little time

worrying about the what ifs. He spent more of his time on plans for what
to do when real freedom came. His concern was not just for himself, but for
those like him who had been forced to live in servitude by a system which
separated them because the color of their skin was not white.

NOTES

1. Roberts, p. 290.

2. James M. Smallwood, *Time of Hope, Time of Despair* (Port Washington, NY:
Kennikat Press, 1981), p. 17.

3. Seale, p. 200.

4. Seale, p. 198.

5. Roberts, p. 297.

6. Seale, p. 207.

7. Roberts, p. 298; Seale, p. 207.

8. Roberts, p. 300.

9. Hamilton/Hunt, p. 78.

10. Ibid.

11. Hamilton/Hunt, p. 79.

12. Braider, p. 313.

13. Seale, p. 211–13.

14. Seale, p. 213.

15. Seale, p. 212.

16. Seale, p. 212–14.

17. Seale, p. 218.

18. Seale, p. 220.

19. Seale, p. 214.

20. Roberts, p. 309.

21. Roberts, p. 311.

22. Seale, p. 216.

23. Seale, p. 217.

24. James, p. 419.

25. Seale, p. 218, mentions Sam's trip. Because Sam and Margaret were together
during most of this time period, there are fewer letters in which to document their
own and Joshua's whereabouts. We have had to assume that the family's patterns of
behavior would remain reasonably stable.

26. Seale, p. 219.

27. Goree, p. 149.

28. Seale, p. 221.

29. James, p. 421.

30. Seale, p. 221.

31. McComb, p. 74.

32. James, p. 425; Hamilton/Hunt, p. 84–85.

33. Hamilton/Hunt, p. 85–86.

34. Seale, p. 223.

35. Hamilton/Hunt, p. 98–99.

36. Hamilton/Hunt, p. 100.

37. Hamilton/Hunt, p. 101.

38. Randolph B. Campbell, *An Empire for Slavery: The Peculiar Institution in Texas, 1821–1865* (Baton Rouge: Louisiana State University Press, 1989), p. 207.

39. Hamilton/Hunt, p. 117–118.

40. Hamilton/Hunt, p. 115.

41. Hamilton/Hunt, p. 116; Seale, p. 224.

42. Hamilton/Hunt, p. 38.

43. Roberts, p. 322.

44. James, p. 432; Seale, p. 231.

45. Hamilton/Hunt, p. 123.

46. Roberts, p. 350.

47. Hamilton/Hunt, p. 123–24.

CHAPTER FOUR

1865–1868

"Free at Last"

Nearly two years passed before all Texas slaves joined Joshua and became free. Freedom bells began ringing on 19 June 1865, when General Gordon Granger stood on the balcony of Ashton Villa in Galveston and read General Order Number Three: "The people of Texas are informed that in accordance with a Proclamation from the Executive of the United States, all slaves are free."[1] The ex-slaves in the crowd went wild. Their shouts of "we'se free," "Glory be" and "free at last" were nearly drowned out by hand clapping, finger snapping, singing and dancing in the streets.[2]

The grapevine telegraph was swift—the word about freedom spread like wildfire. Federal troops went from town to town in Texas reading the proclamation. But the news traveled faster than the troops, so celebrations by ex-slaves had already started by the time they arrived in most towns.[3] The promised land they had prayed for finally seemed about to arrive on earth, and they would no longer be confined to dreaming about a freedom to come in heaven. For the moment it seemed like every day would be a jubilee—the land of the free and the home of the brave would be for black-skinned people too.

Former slave owners could not believe their eyes or ears. Their worst nightmares were coming true right before them. Some slave owners tried to squelch the news at least until after the crops were harvested, but most were unsuccessful. The irony was that in reality, all slaves had been ordered freed by President Abraham Lincoln more than two years earlier when he issued his Emancipation Proclamation, but this order had simply been ignored by most.

Joshua probably had no words to describe what he felt as he witnessed the crowd gathered in Huntsville. The proclamation was read in the First Methodist Church by General E. M. Gregory, assistant commissioner for Texas.[4] Ex-slaves were no doubt jumping for joy and singing songs as they were in other Texas towns. And whites, if in attendance at all, were no doubt watching in shock. The tide had turned and slavery was against the law. Neither Texas nor the South would ever be the same again.

Joshua may have been thinking of how he felt the day General Houston assembled all his servants and announced they were free. Too bad that Sam Houston could not witness the celebration in the courthouse square. Joshua knew that many of the General's wishes were coming true: the war was over, the south would be back in the union, and slavery had been declared illegal. Houston's grave site was just a few blocks away and Joshua might have paused for a moment in reverence to the man who had made a vast difference in his life and in that of Texans of every color.

Joshua no doubt wondered if all men would now be free and equal. His own life had not been drastically altered during his two years of freedom, since he still had to abide by the special rules that governed the lives of free blacks. He was unable to vote, own property or travel as freely as a white man. But Joshua had kept himself busy even with all the restrictions placed on him. He had continued his work as a blacksmith and wheelwright, working for the owners of several Texas stagecoach lines in and near Huntsville, including those in Anderson and probably Crockett.[5] Before the war ended, there was quite a lot of work for a man with his skills. Huntsville had remained a major stagecoach center to Texas.

Fortunately, Joshua had worked for these stagecoach owners for many years so they were well acquainted with him and his work. Also, most of his employers, including Colonel George Grant, had known General Sam Houston and respected Joshua because of his relationship with his former owner.[6] The community's knowledge of this relationship probably allowed Joshua the freedom to make his own purchases for tools, supplies and merchandise from merchants like the Gibbs brothers of Huntsville, who had gotten used to dealing with him when he ran errands for the General. Joshua was probably allowed to lodge with these men while he worked for them. His biggest problem would have been traveling from city to city. With the General dead and the Civil War going on, Joshua was continually in danger.

Joshua may also have received support from the small (300 or so) group of free blacks in Texas,[7] like William Goyens of Nacogdoches whom he had met during his travels with the General. Most of the free blacks, like Joshua, were artisans. Others were hairdressers or barbers who provided services for

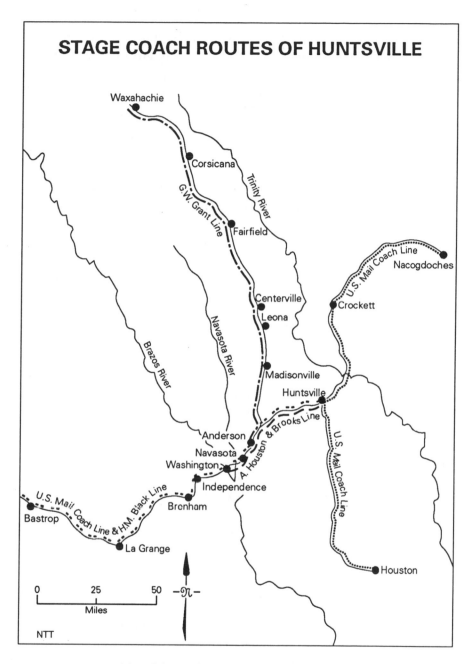

Map of stagecoach routes near Huntsville, Texas.
Joshua would have traveled many of these roads.
Courtesy Nancy Tiller.

white patrons.[8] But the few Negroes who had been free before Emancipation were in no position to help the other 182,566 Negroes in Texas who had been cursed with a life of servitude and were now for the most part illiterate.[9] Even when freedom finally came, the effects were virtually incomprehensible to most ex-slaves, who had spent a lifetime in poverty and oppression and had no place to go. Freedom came as a mixed blessing because they often had no means to feed or clothe themselves or their children. They owned no property and had few if any possessions, and most had neither money nor a marketable skill.[10] For this vast majority of blacks, the freedom road would not be the easy street they had dreamed of for so long. So after witnessing all the excitement of ex-slaves walking away from their homes, Joshua witnessed many heading right back down the same roads. They returned to the only food and shelter they knew. As oppressive as the slavery system had been, it was now all many of them had to fall back on. Unfortunately, there were plenty of unscrupulous former masters willing to exploit such desperate workers.

Ironically, many former slave owners were as unprepared for the sudden changes as the slaves were. They had never cooked, cleaned, harvested crops, taken care of animals or learned artisan skills.[11] It was a time of turmoil for all.

An account dictated by two freed brothers in 1937 sheds light on the situation in Huntsville during the Reconstruction years. The McAdams brothers had lived on a plantation in Walker County. Andy McAdams recalled his own experience:

> When that war was over, Massa, he called me there to his back door and told me that I was free and I could do just as I pleased, so I thanked him and went down to Huntsville, Texas. Negroes, they were plum thick hollering and shouting cause they were free, but that merriment did not last long as there was a white man came down through that bunch of people on a horse fast as he could go with a rag tied over his face and rode by a Negro woman, just leaned over in his saddle and cut that Negro woman nearly half in two and just kept riding. Something like an hour passed and a covered wagon came by with two men with rags over their faces, got out and picked her up and put her in that wagon and that was the last I'se ever heard of the Negro woman or the white people either. And, ever' last one of us Negroes that was left, we went home and went in a hurry cause we did not know how many more of us would be done just like that Negro woman.
>
> Then after we had been there at home three or four days without anything to eat, we begin to wonder what we were going to do and begin to

ask Massa because we were already getting hungry. Massa he told us he did not know what we were going to do as he was not responsible for us any more but we finally persuaded him to give us work or something to eat and we went to another place and got us a farm on the halves. So I went right on to Mr. Joe Larry and went to work for him that year and the next we farmed for him on the halves. Then we came up in Madison County and took us some land to farm and here I'se been ever since.[12]

Andy's brother John had a slightly different experience. He had gone to war with his master, to "tend his horses and keep his guns cleaned up good for him." When the war was over John's master told him he was free but he should "get home." John recalled what he thought about as he walked home:

I began wondering what I was going to do after I got home as I thought well, massa did not own me anymore and was he going to let me stay there with him after we was free. That was exactly what he done; he give us work there with him the rest of that year at $2 per month, and so I stayed on there in the old quarters and worked for massa all that year, and the next. Then I farms for another, Mr. Charlie Savage, his farm joins massa's.[13]

Both Andy and John expressed their disillusionment with what they had thought freedom would be. Andy felt betrayed by the new system:

I'se didn't exactly expect part of massa's land but they was plenty of land here that they could have given us a tract of. . . . we were worse off under freedom than we were during slavery, as we did not have a thing—could not write or read. Under slavery we were taken real good care of, plenty to eat, good clothes to wear and a doctor when we got sick. But after freedom all this was stopped, no one to look after us and we really had a hard go of it after we was turned loose like a bunch of dry cattle to rough it through.[14]

John McAdams used the same analogy to describe how he felt about the way they were treated:

I expected different from what I got out of freedom I can tell you. I knows one thing, I was not expecting to be turned loose like a bunch of stray cattle, but that is exactly what they done to us. . . . they hardly gave us work to do. Then half of them would not pay us when we worked because they knew they did not have to. . . . Our wages were so low that it was almost impossible for us to live on what we got. I have worked hard for ten cents a day. Sir that Reconstruction of the Negro was hard as we did not know a thing [and] could hardly buy our own groceries.[15]

The McAdams brothers' experiences were typical, but some ex-slaves suffered even harsher treatment. Many, like the unnamed woman in Andy's story, were maimed or killed. Within six months of the war's end, Texas authorities had issued 500 indictments for the murder of blacks by whites, unfortunately with no resulting convictions. From today's vantage point, the violence seems almost casual, with whites having no apparent motive except to chastise blacks, who were guilty of nothing more than trying to exercise their new freedom. One Texas county had a gang of white men who would "kill a nigger" for seventy-five cents. Furthermore, many white men still believed they had the right, exercised during the antebellum period, to sexual exploitation of black women.[16]

Within this climate, ex-slaves survived as best they could. Three examples from Huntsville—the Watkins, the Nevils, and the Hightowers, families which Joshua probably knew—reveal stories of determination and self-reliance which blacks needed in order to endure such difficult times.

The Watkins family is one example. During slavery Jefferson and Rachel were slaves on Colonel Watkins' plantation. Jefferson was plantation foreman and manager and, like Joshua, whenever his master traveled, he was regarded as the man-in-charge by the colonel's wife and children. Rachel was a house servant. Their five children, Joe Kimball, Frank, Walter, Rachel and Mattie, were pampered by the unusually lenient daughters of Colonel Watkins. Reportedly, their favorite was Walter, who was quite bright and preached his first sermon at the age of twelve. Some time after the war, Walter became the father of fifteen children, six of whom became ministers. Another son, Joe Kimball, had helped his father with farming and repair work during the war. During Reconstruction, he managed to receive the equivalent of a third grade education. He became one of Walker County's leading black farmers, eventually owning a 1000-acre farm. All this the family accomplished because they were able to subsist during Reconstruction on money earned by farming and other hard work, including the making and selling of cigars.[17]

The head of the Nevil family is believed to have been a scout for the Confederacy while he was still a slave, because he traveled throughout the southern states during the Civil War. He was light-skinned and probably could have passed for white. When he left Huntsville during the war he told the mother of his two daughters, Viola and Mary Ann, to take good care of them. The

Joe Kimball Watkins. Pictured above with his sister Ethel and grandson Richard, Joe Kimball Watkins came out of slavery to become a successful land owner and highly regarded politician. His brother was Walter "Watty" Watkins.
Courtesy the Watkins family.

Reverend Walter "Watty" Watkins. Reverend Watkins, who began to preach at the age of twelve and as an adult often preached in Latin, performed the marriage ceremony for Samuel W. Houston and Hope Harville on April 28, 1915.
Courtesy Reverend Curtis Watkins.

mother became very ill during the war, and just before she died she asked her mistress to care for her two daughters. When the war ended, the mistress and her husband considered the girls their wards and kept them enslaved. Relatives of the girls decided to rescue them, so in the middle of the night stole them away and drove off in a wagon. They were then raised by Monroe Liles, not far from Huntsville in an area known as Mt. Zion near Dickey Spout, an area with springs that bubbled up and provided an abundance of fresh water.[18]

Another Huntsville family which survived the Reconstruction experience was that of John "Tip" Hightower, a blacksmith. After slavery, while making his living as a blacksmith and sharecropper, John and his wife decided to take advantage of the Texas law which permitted citizens to survey land belonging to the state, then maintain and pay the taxes on the property in order to acquire the land. In order to raise enough money to do that, Hightower sold soft coal that he made by cutting pine timber and placing it in a kiln, which he then covered with sand to regulate the amount of oxygen available in the woodburning process. The resulting soft coal was excellent for warming homes, particularly rooms without fireplaces. It was also used inside irons as a heat source to iron clothes. He found a ready market in Huntsville and was able to raise the money needed to buy the land.[19]

What made Joshua different, and gave him an advantage over his fellow ex-slaves, was that he had already experienced "freedom" before Emancipation. Also, he could read and write, and he knew and was known by nearly everyone in town including leaders, ex-slaves and their owners. As a free man he had taken the last name of Houston. He was known as "Uncle" Joshua to at least some of the ex-slaves.[20] Many no doubt envied Joshua's position and believed him an "uppity nigger" who thought he was better than they were. Respected or envied, Joshua was in a unique position to help Huntsville, particularly its black community, through some turbulent times.

Huntsville, like other Texas towns, was having to restructure its government. A. J. Hamilton was appointed provisional governor of the state, and one of his first duties was to start the procedure for amending the Texas Constitution to reinstate its former relationship to the federal government. By August, Hamilton had also appointed officials for Walker County, including a Chief Justice, County Clerk, Sheriff, Treasurer, Justice of the Peace and four county commissioners.[21]

All of these officials were white men, and many were the same officials who had held office prior to the end of the Civil War. Hamilton made similar appointments throughout Texas, probably in an effort to maintain law and order

Brothers Jim and John "Tip" Hightower. "Tip" Hightower, like Joshua and the other freedmen, fervently sought to acquire land. To earn extra money toward this goal, he made what was called "soft coal" and sold it to the women in town for their irons. Tip's brother Jim Hightower had escaped his Huntsville master and gone to Oklahoma before the end of the Civil War. This photo of the two brothers, taken about 1875, records the only time Jim ever returned to Huntsville after Emancipation.
Courtesy Maggie Williams and son Cecil Williams.

and a structure of normalcy.[22] Many families, both white and black, were be-
wildered as their worlds were turned upside down. Land was worth next to
nothing, the crops were in the field with no labor to harvest them, Confederate currency was worthless, and transportation was disrupted. Newly freed
slaves were trying to locate family members they had lost during slavery years,
and hundreds of orphaned children and homeless old folks had no way of con-
tacting their relatives. Hunger was rampant, and added to the existing health
problems. Rapes, murders and other atrocities occurred almost daily, and in
some instances, blacks continued to be enslaved.[23]

In this climate, Joshua was able to make a bold move. He had been able to
accumulate some money while a slave of the Houstons, and he had no doubt
added to it during his three years of "freedom." On 15 January 1866, Joshua,
along with Hiram Bowen, purchased a tract of land on 10th Street in Huntsville just north of the courthouse, for the price of $120. The land was sold
to them by Micajah Clack Rogers, first mayor of Huntsville. Thus Joshua became one of the first blacks to purchase land in Huntsville. As more blacks
became able to buy land, many of them purchased it in the same area, which
became known as Rogersville.[24]

Nevertheless, lawlessness prevailed all around Joshua. In order to address
these problems quickly, some southern states held their constitutional conventions beginning in the fall of 1865.[25] It was November when Provisional
Governor Hamilton called for the selection of delegates to the Texas Constitutional Convention. When it convened in February, 1866, all of the delegates
were white. The new Texas constitution which they ratified denied equality to
blacks by prohibiting them from voting, holding office or serving on juries. In
addition, the document established a system of segregated public education
and guaranteed only minimal civil rights to freedmen.[26]

In the fall of 1866, the Eleventh Legislature of Texas further restricted the
freedom of blacks by prohibiting their service in the state militia and passing
the first Jim Crow railroad law in the south, stating that Negroes could not
be seated by white passengers while traveling. On 2 March 1867, the Congress of the United States intervened through a series of Reconstruction Acts
and demanded that Texas grant full legal and political rights to blacks. Eleven
unreconstructed southern states, including Texas, were placed under military
rule, and the commanders of each military district were given the power to
appoint state officials. Congress also ordered the states to call further constitutional conventions to write laws that denied no one equal rights.[27]

The federal government also intervened by establishing the Bureau of Refu-

Micajah Clack Rogers. The first mayor of Huntsville, Rogers sold Joshua his property on 15 January 1866. Joshua built his home and a wood shop on the property and established his blacksmith shop across the street. The area surrounding Joshua's property soon became known as Rogersville.
Courtesy City of Huntsville.

gees, Freedmen and Abandoned Lands. It soon became known as the Freedmen's Bureau because its mission was to help newly freed slaves. A chief
commissioner was appointed along with ten assistant commissioners. Colonel
E. M. Gregory was appointed assistant commissioner for Texas, but he did
not reach Galveston until September, 1865.[28] It was another year, October of
1866, before Captain James Devine finally arrived in Huntsville to set up its
branch of the Freedmen's Bureau.[29] Devine was most assuredly not welcomed
by most whites, but ex-slaves flocked to him. He had difficulty in obtaining a
room and furnishings, but by October 1 opened the Bureau's Walker County
office.[30] He rented office space from Carey and Birdwell Company located in
the Carey Building on the courthouse square in Huntsville. Mr. Birdwell was
mayor at the time.[31]

Joshua may have been one of Devine's most reliable sources of information.
He would have been able to tell Devine which farmers were willing to work
with the Bureau and were treating freedmen fairly. He could also have helped
Devine determine which free men were artisans and available for work and
how to obtain supplies from boats and barges on the Trinity River or from
stagecoaches and wagons.[32]

Devine was besieged by freedmen who complained that they had not been
paid for work performed in the previous year. He immediately set about resolving disputes between planters and freed slaves, most of whom worked
as sharecroppers or wage laborers. Those who worked as sharecroppers were
supposed to receive between one fourth and one half of the crop, depending on what agreement was made with the planter. One of the functions of
the Bureau's agents was to insure that labor contracts between planters and
freedmen were equitable. This was supposed to be accomplished by having all
contracts submitted to the subassistant commissioner for approval.[33]

A contract drawn up and agreed to by W. W. McGar and a freedman named
McGar in Walker County in the fall of 1865 is a good illustration of what
Mr. Devine was trying to accomplish during his first few months in Hunts-
ville. The contract provided the following:

1. Freedman McGar promises to bind himself to work for W. W. McGar
   for the year 1866 for $5.00 a month.
2. He is to do good and faithful work conforming to all rules and
   regulations of W. W. McGar, doing any work that he may order or
   direct.

3. W. W. McGar is responsible for feeding and clothing and paying medical bills except when a physician is sent for.

4. In that case, Freedman McGar is to pay the physician.

5. Freedman McGar binds himself to take all necessary care of the stock, tools and vehicles placed in his care and to do all kinds of work of any kind or nature that he is called upon to do.

6. W. W. McGar is to furnish good and wholesome rations at the rate of ½ pound of bacon per day or its equivalent in pork or beef and one peck of corn meal per week.

7. Furthermore Freedman McGar promises and agrees to hold himself responsible for all stock and articles of whatever kind and value.

8. W. W. McGar binds and promises Freedman McGar to protect and defend him in all legal rights of freedmen according to the laws of the Freedmen's Bureau.

9. The Freedman McGar is to account for all loss of time except for real illness at the rate of 25 cents per day.[34]

Many planters simply ignored Devine. Some of the ex-slaves had refused to return to their former masters and sought refuge in the city. They had heard that the government was going to take care of them, providing them with "forty acres and a mule." They flocked to the Freedmen's Bureau expecting to find food, clothing and shelter. What they got was mostly disappointment. Devine had not been provided the staff or the money to take care of all the homeless, jobless freed slaves.[35]

But there were also reports of positive progress among the negative. For instance, the courts did authorize payments to some whites for keeping paupers. One example was Colonel George W. Grant, who was paid $7.50 a month for keeping and taking care of Jenny Lightsey, a freedwoman described as "indigent and not able to make support."[36]

Grant was one of the white citizens of Huntsville known for assisting blacks.[37] During slavery Grant had tried to befriend his own slaves. He had even taken one slave, Dick Grant, to Mexico to help set him free. But Dick refused to stay in Mexico and returned to Huntsville with Colonel Grant.[38] He had also hired slaves Richard Williams and Joshua Houston as blacksmiths in his stagecoach business. After slavery he established Grant's Colony five miles from Huntsville as a "model farming colony" (possibly consisting of all freedmen). He continued to add to his land holdings and finally held over 6000 acres in the colony area. He was also one of the first to establish the tenant system of farming, with freedmen and their families living in his houses and paying him in cotton and corn as their share of the crops. His colony was prosperous enough to have a cotton gin stand as well as a gin engine in its Pine Valley community. Colonel Grant even approached the new Freedmen's Bureau agent in November of 1866 requesting help in establishing a school for freedmen's families at the Colony.[39]

In a letter to General J. B. Kidd dated 8 November 1866, James Devine described Grant as:

> . . . an old resident of the County . . . [who] has succeeded in establishing a colony and has happy families residing on his place. He wants to establish a school. . . . [h]e has 30–40 children in his settlement and wants help in constructing a proper school house and to furnish teachers and clothes for the children. . . . I recommend him as a person of integrity and kindness to industrious and intelligent freed people. . . . I would suggest you . . . give him letters to one of the charity aid societies.[40]

Another positive sign that Devine witnessed in Huntsville was the establishment of religious services by freedmen. They had begun to meet in one anothers' houses right after Emancipation. Such worship ceremonies were known as recess prayer meetings, and they prevailed until provision could be made for building a church. A Sister Rolling (known also as "Mother Rolling") had been an inspiration to many of the newly freed men, women and children. She held reading classes in her home, using the Bible to start them on the road to education.[41]

On 20 October 1866, Devine reported on the overall status of Huntsville:

(1) There is a white lady teaching school.
(2) The white churches have Sunday School–Sabbath Schools to help the freedmen to read.
(3) The cavalry has been here for a short time.
(4) We need troops here.
(5) This is a bad lot of people.
(6) The freedmen will not get help without troop protection.
(7) Whites will not testify either.
(8) Other counties in the area have bad reports.
(9) The freedmen are innocent and ignorant.
(10) The prison is being filled with freedmen.
(11) There is unequal sentencing for crimes.

(12) There are minor orphaned children to be taken care of.

(13) The vagrant laws are being used for a lot of purposes.

(14) Send troops.[42]

Two days later, Devine wrote again, this time requesting a mounted guard because he was anticipating trouble: "Please hurry. . . . [I am] expecting to be arrested." On October 24, he wrote, "all quiet . . . can get along without troops." Devine's letter of November 5 reported that a Lieutenant LeGrep had arrived, and on November 7, Devine sent a list of freedmen who were incarcerated in the Huntsville penitentiary. On December 4, a letter pointed out his attempts to regulate cotton shipments and asked for help in preventing "unprincipled planters from controlling the Freedmen's portion of the crop."[43]

But the most detailed record of events in Huntsville was included in Devine's year end report for 1866. In it he pointed out: "It is so close to Christmas, all I can do is pay attention to 1866 claims and let 1865 claims go." Devine recorded that two-thirds of employers did not pay their employees. He reiterated earlier reports that planters were ignoring him in an attempt to make him seem less important to the freedmen and thus encourage ex-slaves to deal directly with their former masters. Devine also noted that the County Clerk had approved eighty-eight freedmen marriages, with the only requirement being that proof be furnished that the husband had no other wife.[44]

The reasoning behind this single requirement can be seen in the example of Harre Quarls, a freedman who lived just north of Huntsville in Madison County. His problem typifies the situation faced by many ex-slaves. During slavery many owners not only allowed, but encouraged, their male servants to visit female slaves on other plantations during their leisure hours. As a result, many slave men had children by several different women. Quarls was one of these. His master had even given him week-long passes to go and visit his various families. After Emancipation, Quarls had three distinct families, but by law could only live with one. He felt that this was a grave injustice, as he cared for all the children he had fathered.[45]

Joshua probably faced a similar dilemma. He had been forbidden by law to marry any of the mothers of his children born before Texas slaves were emancipated on June 19, 1865. He had continued to support his family in Crockett at Hall's Bluff. His second wife, Mary Green, had died shortly after the birth of Joshua, Jr. Shortly thereafter he had married Sylvester Baker[46] and by the time the Freedmen's Bureau was set up, their son Samuel W. Houston was a

Sylvester Baker Houston. Sylvester became Joshua Houston's wife around 1863–64. They were prominent citizens of the community and leaders in the First Baptist Church. Courtesy Mrs. Hazel Houston Price and family and Samuel W. Houston, Jr., and family.

toddler.[47] Joshua's older children who were born during slavery[48] were now grown and starting lives of their own. His daughter Ellen, born 15 January 1856 to Joshua and Mary Green, now lived in Huntsville.[49] His three children by Anneliza, a woman of Irish-Indian descent who married another man after the Civil War, all lived in Crockett.[50] Julie had married shortly after Emancipation and was living with her husband Coleman Wagner.[51] Lucy was another daughter who lived in Crockett.[52] Joshua's son Joe had a family and was living on land in Crockett that Joshua had helped him acquire.[53] Joe's farm was located in Hall's Bluff, a major cotton shipping community located on the banks of the Trinity River. The farm had both a syrup and a grist mill operation.

But at least Joshua knew where his family members were located. Other freedmen had to go to great lengths to locate family members who had been sold away from them. One Huntsville freedman, Ed Houston,[54] separated from his wife and daughter Caroline for three years, knew only that they had been sold to an owner in Alabama. He worked his way there and found her. Their passage back to Huntsville was paid by her former owner, Mr. Walker.[55] At least one black woman avoided the problem of being separated from her children by not having any. Mary Gaffeny recorded in an interview in 1937 that her master had put her with a man she hated. When she wouldn't let him touch her, she was whipped by the master. So the next time she was with the man, she reports, "I let him have his way, but I cheated the massa. I never did have any slaves to grow and massa wondered what happened. . . . I tell you . . . I kept cotton roots and chewed them all the time so I never have had a child as a slave. After freedom I had five."[56]

Joshua and his friends were very concerned about the education of both freed children and adults. James Devine reported in October that a white school teacher was teaching about twenty black students. He also reported that the Methodist, Baptist, and Presbyterian churches were conducting Sunday Schools in order to help the education efforts. These churches were averaging thirty-five pupils each. Devine also claimed that the "intelligent portion of the community seem[ed] to be willing to cooperate in promoting mental and moral well being." Devine was able to give a few select freedmen the necessary authority to collect money for the purpose of building a church and school house for their community.[57]

Although Devine does not list the names of these freedmen, it is likely that Joshua was one of them because of his unique position in the community. Joshua and his two friends William Baines and Strother Green (known before the war as Strother Hume) went out into the community and raised money for the school.[58] Devine wanted to help so he put a contribution box in his office and later commented that the white people also contributed generously to the effort.[59]

In his Year End Report for 1866, Devine summarized the general lawlessness existing in Huntsville and Walker County, which was especially bad after the cavalry departed. Devine complained that: "Freedpeople have no protection," and thus "their gatherings and weddings are disturbed and fear of consequence keeps them from reporting it. . . . nearly every night some outrage is committed." Devine was aware of reported outrages committed against U. S. soldiers sent to keep the peace, but he added, "under threat of burning out and killing they will not testify."[60]

His report described the prisons, which were "being filled with free persons whose only fault was to incur the anger of a [former] master or being found guilty by a bitterly prejudiced court or grand jury." He noted a bit of progress in that no freedmen had been sent to prison in the month of October, and that he had "set aside the proceedings of a Justice Court and convened the Grand Jury to guard the interest of the freedpersons." The report also included information on the many orphan children, adding that he had "not indentured them for more than one year."[61]

Joshua, concerned with the rights of freedmen, probably did his best to mediate between white and black leaders, especially with regard to education and religious issues, which he saw as important steps toward true freedom. Even though blacks continued to make progress in those two areas, the overall climate in Huntsville and surrounding towns and counties was composed of violence, fear, mistrust and lawlessness. It must have been hard for Joshua not to become discouraged in the face of the many atrocities committed by whites on both ex-slaves and the whites who tried to help them, particularly when the crimes went unpunished.

For example, a Mr. Wilson, a Baptist preacher endeavoring to open a school for freed children, was taken from his bed one night and hanged several times just to the point of unconsciousness. He was then "escorted" across the county line by an armed detachment and ordered never to set foot there again. In Trinity County, Phillip Sublett shot a freedman named George Stubblefield, who then had to be operated on. Mr. Sublett had to pay the $200 doctor's bill, but was not charged with any crime. The Brent family, without a trial, hanged a freedman accused of raping a white woman. No action was taken against the Brents. Frank Wingate and Abe Smith both killed freedmen without suffering any consequences. A "yankee" woman's house was continually being vandalized. A private from the cavalry unit sent to help keep the peace was attacked by several men. A "free girl [named] Lizzie Ellen Ball was assaulted and beaten by Lydia Smith. . . . [The] case [was] tried and the *freed* girl fined . . . about $23 in all." All of these incidents were reported to Devine, who in turn complained to his superiors that one "Union lady here told [me] she will not testify until I have [military] force." The Civil authorities did little or nothing against the many lawbreakers.[62] Devine commented:

> Justices of the Peace attack and seize property of free men that under State law is exempt. Sheriffs serve writs, make arrests, seize crops for rents . . . [and] excite the community by preaching "bayonets," etc. [We] need bayonets backed by loyal troops to stop outrages.[63]

In an attempt to garner more respect for the law from his office, Devine issued a circular stating that "No contract between planters and freedmen is settled unless it has a certificate signed by Jas. C. Devine," and he also issued a notice that to "ship cotton from or through this county requires written permission from this office. Violation is subject to arrest and fine and cotton liable to seizure." Devine sent this circular to Galveston to keep the planters from being able to sell their cotton through the port without his approval. He also sent it to the prison in Huntsville, a large purchaser of cotton, in order to prevent their resale of it without his authorization.[64]

The reaction to this circular was very strong among the planters. The *Huntsville Times* on 16 November 1867, reprinted the following sentiments:

> The Bureau has ceased to be only a nuisance laying an occasional tribute of blackmail. It has become a fearful and terrible engine of diabolical oppression. . . . so outrageous are the orders issuing from that nasty receptacle of feculence and corruption that a great many men have determined to cease farming operations on anything like a large scale rather than subject themselves to the tyrannical and illegal orders of the irresponsible despot that may chance to hold the reins.[65]

In such a climate of extreme action and reaction, it is no wonder that most black agricultural workers could not prosper. A majority of them entered each year owing money to their landlords, who, if they were lucky, supplied them with food, tools and supplies. When wages were paid, they ranged from $2 to $15 a month for male field hands and $2 to $10 for females. Children who worked received less money, depending on the type of job and the speed of their labor. Most freed people had to supplement their food supplies by hunting and fishing.[66]

The scenarios that Devine reported were well known to Joshua and the other ex-slaves, who shared every bit of information they could with one another. The grapevine telegraph that had worked so well during slavery was still their main source of news as freedmen. Most still could not read, so news traveled as it always had, by word of mouth.

One of the most important elements in the lives of many freedmen was the need for spiritual freedom. Religion had sustained them through the horrors of enslavement, when many of them had been forced to slip away from their masters' property to worship together in the woods.[67] Now at least they did not have to have their meetings in secret. Joshua and some of the other more progressive freedmen were making plans to build a place of worship which they would own and control. Since so many of them had been carpenters or other types of artisans, they felt confident that they could construct a church building. However, finding land on which to build was a major hurdle, since so few of them had yet been able to acquire land.

Joshua's influence with the white community was to be a major factor in the acquisition of land for a church. On 27 April 1867, Joshua Houston, William Baines and Strother Green, "Freedmen of the county and state and trustees for the Freed people's church in the Town of Huntsville," purchased property from Baptiste Courtade for $50. The property was located in a central location in downtown Huntsville just a few blocks west of the courthouse square. The church that was eventually built there, a fifty foot by thirty foot frame building, became known as the Union Church. It served both Baptists and Methodists, with each denomination leading the services on alternating Sundays.[68] This became the first institution in Huntsville owned collectively by ex-slaves and thus subject to their control. It became much more than a religious institution. Freedmen often met there to share information about how to protect themselves and their families. The church also became an education center where both children and adults began learning to read the Bible and the few other books that were available to them.[69]

The three original trustees for Union Church were no doubt considered leaders among the freedmen. Strother Green was described as a "large, yellow Negro" and was known for his blacksmith skills. He and Joshua were unofficial brothers-in-law, as Strother's sister was Mary Green, mother of Ellen and Joshua, Jr. During the Civil War, while Huntsville was short of white male labor, he and several other slaves had carried on almost all of the manufacturing in town. William Baines was also described as a "big, yellow Negro." After Emancipation, he helped M. H. Goddin in organizing the Loyal Union League in Huntsville.[70] "The League," as it was called, had been founded by northern whites during the Civil War as a benevolent society, and afterward became established in the south where it recruited Negro members. One observer who lived in Huntsville during and after the war stated that, "Every Saturday the Negroes from the surrounding country came to town and, with those that lived in town, would march over all the streets . . . to the music of a kettle drum and fife, and that night attend the Loyal League exercises, whatever they were." The observer, who was white, considered the league a "secret society of Negroes, northern carpetbaggers and southern renegades."[71]

Memphis Allen, Joe Mettawer, Simon Crawford, Barney and Emeline Carter, and William "Billy" Murray were other early black leaders in Huntsville who were involved in the Union Church,[72] and therefore were probably friends of Joshua's. Memphis Allen had grown up on the Hodge plantation north of Huntsville, where he was taught by the Hodge children to read and write. Mettawer was a barber who came to Huntsville as a free man during the early 1860s. Crawford had been a slave on the Wynne plantation. The Carters were both former slaves, he for the Kittrell family and she for the Goree family. Murray had been purchased by the Murray plantation at the age of ten. When slavery ended, his former owners gave him a cow, a calf, a sow, horse and saddle, five pigs and $15.00.[73]

Part of the reason these people were better able than some others to overcome the climate of Reconstruction was that they had owners who were both kind to them during slavery and helpful to them afterwards. Another reason, for some of them, was that they had learned, illegally, to read and write. All had acquired skills which allowed them to earn a living as freed persons. It is revealing of their faith that their first unified step toward living a freer life was the founding of a church.

The union of the ideals of freedom with those of religion is evident in the fact that Union Church soon became the site of the annual "Juneteenth" celebrations.[74] Every year after 19 June 1865, blacks in Huntsville and all over Texas held large picnics to commemorate the day they were officially freed. Celebrations started with meal preparations the day before. Giant barbecue pits were dug for smoking pork, beef, goats and other meats. The meat and other types of food, including a type of "red sweet drink" and watermelons, were an important part of the yearly celebration, but Juneteenth was also celebrated with emotional speeches by dignitaries, as well as prayers of thanks for being free and a reading of the Emancipation Proclamation. For recreation, there were games, and the celebrations often ended with dances.[75] Joshua undoubtedly took part in these celebrations.

Juneteenth celebrations gave freedmen a chance to socialize and also to remind themselves of their progress even in the face of adversity. Although they were occasionally marred by violence, nothing could prevent these important public gatherings from taking place.

The number of obstacles put in the freedmen's way must have seemed overwhelming, even to someone like Joshua who had more advantages than most. James Devine's reports to the Freedmen's Bureau officials described the many changes that were taking place in Huntsville. Meanwhile, there were changes taking place in the bureau itself. In early 1867, a new commissioner was appointed for Texas. When Major General Charles Griffin arrived in Galveston he discovered that less than half of the freedmen's population had been reached by the bureau, so in May the state was divided into fifty-seven subdistricts in charge of sixty-nine agents, thirty-eight officers, and thirty-one civilians, stationed so as to provide protection to even the most distant areas of the state.[76]

Devine's reports on Huntsville and Walker County continued to record abuses of the law. In March, 1867, he reported that a Mr. Mynhaus was still holding a freedman in bondage, nearly two years after Emancipation had been declared in Texas. Devine was finally able to free the man and demand reimbursement for the work he had done. He also reported that more contracts had been signed and that two freedmen had left town without fulfilling their contracts. These two men were apprehended and returned to Devine.[77] In April, Devine left his post and was replaced by James P. Butler, a native of New York and a former captain in the U. S. Army.[78] Like Devine, Butler seemed genuinely concerned about the condition of freedmen in the county. His first report, dated May 25, informed the Freedmen's Bureau headquarters that education continued to be a problem, stating that "the freedmen were still quite poor and there was little chance they could afford to erect a school building anytime in the near future."[79] Butler did report four schools operating in Walker County although he counted only ninety students.

Butler's May 31 report cited two civil cases. Pinckney Lightey had assaulted freedman Silas Putman, who filed a complaint with the justice of the peace. The white man was found guilty and fined one cent plus costs. In another case a white woman assaulted a freedwoman and was fined three dollars. Butler wrote that the proper fine for such a crime was twenty dollars.[80]

Butler's reports, like Devine's, included both positive and negative news. In June, Butler claimed that 4000 people had attended the Juneteenth celebration and that he had addressed the crowd about the importance of education and building schools and churches. He reported that the group had conducted themselves in an orderly and credible manner.[81] Butler also wrote this time about the general lawlessness in Huntsville and asked for troops. He had previously asked the Mayor for police protection in case any troublemakers showed up at the Juneteenth celebration.

The progress being made was also evident in this report. He noted that the County Court was in session on the first of the month and that all cases were tried by a "loyal colored jury." Unfortunately, he did not name the members of the jury. He mentioned this jury again in his July report, stating that it only tried cases where freedmen constituted both parties.[82] More encouraging news was that $131 had been collected to aid in the building of the freedmen's church. Butler gave more detailed information on the current schools for freedmen in the Huntsville area. One with twenty scholars, on the Trinity River, was taught by John Rogers; another one with fifteen scholars at Stubblefield's Mill was taught by Sarah Whitman; one with twenty scholars in Huntsville was taught by a Mrs. or Miss Tanner.[83]

Butler wrote that there was only one soldier helping him and that he needed troops to take care of a "few lawless young men and arrest some planter who refused to settle last year." He further noted that "heavy rain would likely damage the cotton crop" and that "the Trinity River overflow had drowned a number of plantations." He also described a bad corn crop which would yield only half of the usual harvest, placing further hardships on all freedmen who worked for shares of crops.[84]

Across the South reports of the outrages against the freedmen were being sent to Washington by agents like Butler. In March 1867, the Congress of the United States intervened through a series of Reconstruction Acts and demands that Texas grant full legal and political rights to blacks. Texas was placed under military rule and the military commander of each district was given full power to remove and appoint state officials.[85]

The 4th of July 1867, signaled a new involvement for freedmen in Walker County and elsewhere. The new Reconstruction Act had provided for the registration of qualified voters and the holding of elections for the purpose of electing delegates to the constitutional conventions. The Texas Republican convention was held in Houston July 4 and 5. Twenty-seven counties were represented by 20 whites and 150 blacks.[86] Governor Pease presided over the Convention and George T. Ruby, a black and former Freedmen's Bureau agent, was the vice president. It is very likely that Joshua Houston attended this convention and was possibly one of the delegates. This convention laid the groundwork for blacks to begin voting.

The number of black delegates to this convention outraged many whites. Things got so bad that Butler's life was in jeopardy. His July 16 report described a mob which had drawn pistols on him in the presence of the Mayor and City Marshall with no repercussions on them. Butler and several other men signed a petition requesting protection.[87] Butler also noted in this report that schools had adjourned for an indefinite period.

On the positive side, he described the "fine building under construction and almost completed for church and school purposes," which was due to be ready by 1 September. This most assuredly was the Union Church building.[88] His next report expanded on the description, saying the school building had accommodations for 500 scholars, and that night school would be provided for over 200 more. Among his other notes were that eight troops were stationed in Huntsville to help protect freed people. Butler said Civil officers were no help whatsoever, and recommended they be removed from duty.[89]

By mid-August, all activities of the Bureau were at a standstill.[90] A yellow fever epidemic had struck Walker County, many families had fled in panic and the schools were closed down. Hardly a house in Huntsville was unaffected by the fever. At least one doctor, Joshua A. Thomason, accepted the then popular belief that a poisonous night atmosphere known as a miasma was the cause of the sickness, so he burned smudge pots continually.[91] Even the mail was suspected as a potential contaminant. Mail deliverers put mail in the boxes with tongs and the recipients baked the letters in ovens before opening them.[92] Meanwhile, Agent Butler was having a difficult time. He came down with the fever and could not take care of his sick soldiers. Mr. Courtade, a dry goods merchant on the square, closed his store and nursed the ill soldiers. Most were far from their homes and had no one to care for them. Since Agent Butler had no funds, Courtade paid the $15 apiece burial costs for those soldiers who died, and also made all the burial arrangements. It was difficult to get this done since almost everyone had left town.[93]

When the yellow fever epidemic ended, more than 130 people had perished in Huntsville alone.[94] James Butler was one of the lucky ones who recovered after being stricken with the fever.[95]

Very little evidence exists that any of the freedmen, including Joshua or any one in his family, died during the epidemic. In fact, it seemed at the time that the majority of them were immune from yellow fever. Some of the freedmen who had maintained good relationships with their former masters may have been involved in caring for them during the epidemic.[96] Such was certainly the case at Margaret Houston's household in Independence, where Margaret was desperately ill.[97]

When Joshua got word that Margaret had died from the fever, he was probably devastated, particularly since she died so quickly. Her former slave (and Joshua's friend) Bingley had dug her grave in the middle of the night. Because of the contagious nature of her illness, she could not be brought back to Huntsville to be buried by the General, so her body was put to rest beside her mother's grave in Independence.[98]

It was due in large part to the kindness of the Houstons that Joshua had achieved so much in his life, and Joshua had proved his loyalty to them time and time again. He was probably confident that with Eliza's continued presence among the family, the orphaned children would be cared for. Eliza, unlike Joshua, had never wanted to be separated from Margaret, even when the General had freed her. She even wanted to be buried near her former mistress.[99]

During the panic of the epidemic most of the violence against the freedmen had stopped, but after the epidemic passed, it began again. In November, 1867, Butler reported that a white man, William Gilbert, had murdered freedman Ben Edward with no civil action being taken. Butler also reported an incident wherein four white men attempted to murder M. H. Goddin, an agent of the Freedmen's Bureau in Polk County, adjacent to Walker County.[100] This incident was fully described in *Flake's Semi-Weekly Bulletin* in Galveston:

> No sooner was Mr. Goddin announced in the Bulletin as superseded by the merging of Polk County into adjoining Bureau districts, than he was assaulted by a mob and compelled at the muzzles of their shot guns and under threats of instant assassination, to remit a fine which, as Agent of the Bureau he had imposed upon the leader of the party. He was paraded through the county as a prisoner by his captors, who had the air of men engaged in a very laudable transaction.[101]

The rumor that had been reported earlier in the year in the *Union Republican* newspaper had been correct. Texas had been placed under military rule and each commander was given power to remove and appoint state officials.[102] In Huntsville this proved to be a direct turning point in the life of Joshua and, indirectly, in the lives of other freedmen. Joshua was appointed a city alderman.[103]

This appointment came during a chaotic time in Texas, one filled with political intrigue. The Republicans were concerned that the Democratic office holders were not complying with Reconstruction policies. General Sheridan, commander of the Fifth Military District—which included Texas and Louisiana—was given the power by General Grant to remove civil officials and fill the offices with appointees of his choice. On 8 August 1867, he removed the elected Governor of Texas, J. W. Throckmorton, and appointed E. M. Pease in his place.[104] Sheridan authorized General Charles Griffin in Texas to begin removing local and state officials, but Griffin had just begun this job when he contracted yellow fever and died. Meanwhile, the Republicans found out that Sheridan was due to be replaced by Major General Hancock, a Democratic sympathizer. Governor Pease and Major Joseph Reynolds (Griffin's replacement) had the month of November in which to act before Hancock's scheduled arrival in his New Orleans headquarters. In that short time, Reynolds removed 400 Democrats from office and appointed 436 Republicans.[105] The recommendations for most of these names came from Freedmen's Bureau agents, like Butler in Walker County, and from fellow Republicans across the state.[106] The appointments had been completed just as Hancock arrived in New Orleans to take command of the Fifth District on 28 November 1867.[107]

Joshua's appointment was one of these. It was the first time in Huntsville's history that a black man had held public office. It seems natural that such a distinction would have gone to Joshua, since he had been recognized as a unique resident of the community even during slavery, and had proved himself a trustworthy leader after Emancipation. This was Joshua's beginning as a statesman.

He joined several other appointees in Huntsville, which was designated District Thirty. The *Union Republican* reported their names: Honorable J. B. Burnet, Judge; Hon. W. E. Horne, District Attorney; W. B. Rome, District Clerk; M. Butler, Sheriff; A. J. Rape, Surveyor; Dr. W. C. Oliphant, Treasurer; and M. H. Goddin, Mayor. Joshua was one of six city aldermen, including at least one other black, John Clark.[108]

Joshua's responsibilities had now broadened considerably. Not only did he have a family to provide for, a business to run, and church and school affairs to lead and participate in, but he was now involved in helping to govern a very emotionally divided community. Having M. H. Goddin as Mayor probably made Joshua's life a little easier than it would have been otherwise. Goddin had served as a Freedmen's Bureau agent in nearby Polk County, and was a member of the Loyal Union League. These qualifications would not have made him popular with most of the white community, however.

Another appointed official with whom Joshua was no doubt acquainted was M. Butler, who had been appointed sheriff. He came down with yellow fever and after three weeks recovered. He then resumed his duties as registrar of voters. Along with freedman Joseph Dixon and other members of the Registration Board, Butler began registering voters 23 September 1867, and continued until 28 September. That same evening, he suffered a relapse of yellow fever, and died before he could make a supplemental report. This extension of time to enable more freedmen to register infuriated whites all across Texas.[109]

Good news for the freedmen came near the end of 1867. On November 11, a contract was signed between Agent Butler and George W. Benchley which paved the way for the completion of the school.[110] So by the end of the year, Joshua could reflect with pride on the building of the Union church and school. He had seen many of his friends begin a journey toward financial stability and gain hope of educational progress for both adults and children. Only the efforts toward creating an atmosphere of safety and harmony had proved nearly futile.

On 31 December 1867, the conflict between Agent Butler and the civil authorities almost resulted in his death. As Butler was passing along the public square in Huntsville, Joseph Burges, the county sheriff, came out of a store in broad daylight, presented a loaded and cocked derringer at Butler's head and told him "if he had anything to say, say it quickly for in one minute he would be a dead man." Luckily, Burges was disarmed and lodged in jail under guard, but he was soon released. Butler must have taken immediate action, because by January, Burges was notified in writing that he had been suspended from office.[111]

February 1868 signaled an important political turning point for Texas freedmen. They were allowed to vote in a statewide election calling for a convention that would create a new constitution. They hoped to make this one more fair. The first constitution after the Civil War had denied to freedmen many of the rights which would have made them fully participating citizens, and now they wanted to change that. Whites stayed away from the polls, not wanting to take the oath of allegiance to the Union and not wanting to stand in line with the freedmen.[112] Over 35,000 freedmen went to the polls on election day, and by a statewide vote of 44,689 to 11,440, a new convention was required. The voters selected ninety delegates to the Constitutional Convention and, although blacks cast seventy-six per cent of the statewide vote, only nine of the delegates were blacks. The election was nevertheless a milestone in terms of blacks' participation in the political process.[113]

The vote aroused passions on both sides. Many Anglos were afraid their power structure was slipping away from them, and many freedmen were excited at the thought that their full rights as citizens of Texas would finally be granted. Charles Taylor Rather recalled the reaction in Huntsville:

> The first election I have any recollection of was held soon after the war closed, and the voting was done at the small courthouse, situated in the southwest corner of the courthouse yard. Voters had to approach the ballot box through a line of Yankee soldiers with bayonets.[114]

An article in the *Huntsville Times* on 29 February 1868, reveals some of the tactics whites were using to try to lure freedmen away from the Republican party:

> Attention Freedmen: You voted in the last election and expected to get your 40 acres and a mule that you had been promised by the Radicals [Republicans]. . . . where is it? You are slaves today. They will not feed or clothe you. They swear you to vote their way, drive you up to the polls like dumb brutes, vote you like automatons, then turn you loose to starve or beg and steal from old masters. How long will it take you to learn that you are being used as tools by political demagogues who really care nothing else for you? [115]

The organization that was credited with getting blacks to the polls was the Loyal Union League of Texas.[116] What role Joshua may have played in the League is not known, but it is assumed he would have been active in any organization so dedicated to obtaining civil rights for blacks. It is likely, also, that Joshua knew the League's president, George T. Ruby, a free-born black who had come to Texas as a Freedmen's Bureau agent.[117] Working through the Loyal Union League, Ruby became active in organizing the "Party of Lincoln" (Republican party) in the state, to which most freedmen belonged.

The opinion most whites had of the Loyal Union League, and about the

ability of blacks to take part in the political process, is evident in an article
published in the *Huntsville Times* just after the February elections.

> We learn that the Loyal League, alias African Midnight Conclave, . . . is
> becoming quite popular with the white men about Huntsville, and that
> about 25 or 30 men, heretofore regarded as respectful, have actually entered
> the African League and attended their secret midnight meetings under the
> curtain of secrecy and hoping thereby to "run with the hare and yelp with
> the hounds." . . . If the report is true we in our Dark Corner think it the
> stepping stone to miscegenation or the intermarriage of the white and black
> races. . . . In our neck of the woods we want to know their names: some we
> are told are lawyers, some doctors, some merchants. . . . We have to deal
> with all professions, and the reason why we want their names published is,
> if they are of the dark conclave, we may make our selection when . . . we
> need their services. . . . Since the election was held 10–14 Feb., 1868, blacks
> who went to Huntsville to vote have all returned. I have not found one
> who would tell me for whom they voted. . . . We were told that they were
> directed to go to Strother [Green] to get tickets. All did so and went and
> handed them in to the managers and their great work was done without
> their knowing anymore about the Great Farce. With very little training a
> lot of monkeys could have performed the same grand feat with equal politi-
> cal judgement. I mean no offense to our black population. It is not their
> fault that they have no political capacities to perform the duties assigned
> to them by their Radical masters, and the more, and the longer they are
> permitted to exercise a political franchise, the more miserable the condition
> of both races.[118]

It is easy to imagine the humiliation Joshua must have felt as he read these
newspaper accounts. Here he was a forty-six-year-old family man, able to read
and write, a leader in both religious and educational matters, capable of earn-
ing his own living and now able to vote and hold a political office. Yet still his
progress in life was being hindered by those who opposed him on the basis of
skin color.

Evidence of anti-black sentiment was not confined to newspaper articles.
There were rumors that a group of white men were organizing a vigilante
group in Texas known as the Ku Klux Klan. Already there were reports that
they had donned white sheets and posed as "ghosts" in attempts to scare blacks
away from the polls.[119] One former slave, Rosa L. Pollard, many years later
described the atrocities:

The KKK used to make the Negro hop cause them there ghosts would never let the Negro vote, and if he hired a man he better stay right there and work. If he didn't, the KKK would come to see him the first time and take him out and stretch him over a log, hit him fifty times with a red poker, and put tar and feathers all over him. The tar was hot and would take all the hide off that Negro.[120]

After February, political activity among both blacks and whites in Huntsville increased. The new constitutional convention was due to convene in June. Walker County's delegate was James P. Butler, the Freedmen's Bureau agent with whom Joshua was well acquainted. Those elected from nearby counties included C. B. Horn of Grimes, Walker and Madison; James McWashington, a black, from Montgomery, and M. H. Goddin from Polk.[121] All were Republicans. It is likely that Joshua began making his views known to them following the election.

Meanwhile, Butler continued his duties for the Freedmen's Bureau. His March 30 report to his superiors lodged more complaints against civil officers in Huntsville. One officer who particularly irked him was a justice of the peace described as "not only a rebel but a bigoted, superannuated old fool and not in any way competent to perform his duties." An incident in April 1868, further revealed the unwillingness of the civil authorities to protect the freedpeople. William Raney was a freedman employed by H. M. Elmore. Sent by Elmore to work in the woods, Raney returned after a short time to get a tool. Elmore claimed that Raney had already taken it. When he denied it, Elmore beat him. The freedman, his head badly cut and one of his fingers broken, told Butler of the incident. Butler sent him to the civil authorities, and in the county court Elmore pleaded guilty to the charge of assault and battery. The court found him guilty and fined him one cent plus costs, prompting Butler to comment with irony, "such is the way of Southern chivalry!"[122]

When Butler departed the service of the Freedmen's Bureau in June of 1868, he recorded his discouragement and disillusionment in his final report.[123] However, he chose to remain in Huntsville, from which place he attended the constitutional convention.[124]

When the Constitutional Convention convened in Austin on 11 June 1868, Joshua Houston was among the attendees.[125] Although not a delegate, Joshua was able to observe firsthand the political process and climate of Texas. Seven years previously, Joshua had witnessed pre-Reconstruction political turmoil in Texas politics as servant to General Sam Houston, when he was being deposed as Governor. He had left Austin as a slave, driving the Houston family down Congress Avenue, and now he was returning as a free man and a voting citizen of the state of Texas.

The first major conflict of the convention drew the dividing lines between groups. The nine black delegates were generally in favor of obtaining civil and political rights for blacks and for free public education. However, they were not unified on all votes. Although most of the resolutions, declarations, and bills introduced by the black delegates suffered defeat, some managed to pass, proving that contrary to expectations on the part of whites, many of the freedmen's ideas had merit. Black delegates generally seemed to show concern for both the problems of blacks and the state of Texas as a whole.[126]

Joshua had probably already met most of the black delegates, but being at the convention gave him a chance to become better acquainted with them. They came from varying backgrounds, but George T. Ruby perhaps stood out the most by virtue of his training and his position as president of the Loyal Union League of Texas. He was a native New Yorker educated in the state of Maine. He had taught in Louisiana before coming to Texas in September of 1867 as a Freedmen's Bureau Agent and now, at the age of twenty-seven, he was a delegate to the Republican National Convention. James McWashington was a representative for Montgomery County, where blacks outnumbered whites by 250 people. He came to Texas as a slave just a couple of years after Joshua arrived. The delegate from Harris County, C. W. Bryant, a minister, had been an agent for the Freedmen's Bureau in Texas. Benjamin Franklin Williams was also a minister and served as vice president of the Loyal Union League. At least three delegates were blacksmiths like Joshua. Shephard Mullins had been a slave, arriving in Texas from Alabama eleven years before Emancipation. As a freedman he had continued his blacksmith work and had acquired land in Waco and McLennan County. Benjamin O. Watrous, a wheelwright and property owner, had been in Texas nearly a decade before Emancipation. Mitchell Kendall, a blacksmith from Harrison County, was probably the wealthiest of the black delegates, with assets valued at $2400. Among the other delegates were Ralph Long, farmer; Stephen Curtis, carpenter; and Wiley Johnson, shoemaker.[127]

When Joshua returned to Huntsville after the close of the first session of the convention, he had probably renewed his hopes for equal civil and political rights for blacks. Still, another session was scheduled for December, and Joshua had witnessed the hostilities to which the black delegates were subjected.[128] A bright spot for Joshua had come late in the convention when

M. H. Goddin introduced the following resolution concerning General Houston.

> Whereas no suitable monument marks the resting place of the hero, statesman and father of Texas, General Sam Houston, therefore be it resolved by the people of Texas in convention assembled that a committee of thirty-six be appointed by the president of the convention to receive subscriptions by themselves on thoughts to erect a monument and appoint a Committee of Style and Inscription in the erection of said monument.[129]

Joshua, perhaps more than anyone else present, knew the significance of the resolution. He had long been concerned about Houston's final resting place, and, out of respect for the General, had built a small fence around the grave and kept it maintained.[130]

As the convention was over before the Juneteenth celebrations for 1868, the convention and its implicit promise of new political strength among freedmen was no doubt a major topic of discussion at the festivities. For the first time, freedmen not only had land where they could hold the celebration but also had a church structure to which they could point with pride. And, in spite of all of the atrocities and other efforts to impede their progress, they now had some physical evidence of progress, including a school.

A likely addition to the Juneteenth festivities this year was the appearance of a band organized by Joe Mettawer, a well-known musician who had come to Huntsville as a free black during the Civil War. The story is that he came to town with some horse traders but was taken into custody and jailed for several months until he could prove that he was a free man. Once out, he established himself as a barber with a white clientele. He became known as a splendid banjo player and could often be heard performing in his barber shop. His decision to create a band may have been welcomed by all of Huntsville, but the freedmen were especially proud to have this band to help liven up their separate social events.[131] However, with no agent for the Freedmen's Bureau in Huntsville, any freedmen gatherings, even Juneteenth, had to be celebrated with caution.

The most encouraging developments in 1868 were proposals for other freedmen schools in and near Huntsville. On 9 September, plans were well underway for a school at Grants Colony, the farming settlement created for freedmen by Colonel George Grant after Emancipation. Six trustees requested land from Colonel Grant for a school and church for the "common benefit of all citizens of Grants Colony." The trustees—all freedmen—were Richard

Williams, Joseph Morris, Allen Justice, Green Justice, Sam Sims and Anderson Bates. Grant, who had been involved in education efforts in Huntsville for many years, deeded two acres to the trustees for this purpose.[132]

During the summer of 1868, the appointment of Reverend Joseph Welch as superintendent of Texas schools seemed to breathe new life into Negro education.[133] By September the Freedmen's Bureau reported there were at least forty-seven schools, forty-five teachers and more than 1550 students in all of Texas.[134] And although that was not a sizeable percentage of the freedmen population, it signified steady growth from the year before, when there were only four schools reported. The school in Huntsville was thriving with a new teacher, very possibly Miss Lizzie Stone, a white woman from the north, as were most teachers in the freedmen schools right after slavery.[135] There had not yet been sufficient time to train teachers from the freedmen ranks.

There were no reports from Huntsville filed to the Freedmen's Bureau until agent N. H. Howard arrived there sometime near the end of the year. His December report echoed the pleas of agents before him, claiming that "the respect and efficiency of my operations as Agent would be materially increased by the mere presence in the office of a detail of two or three soldiers daily."[136] Since those troops were not forthcoming, it is safe to assume that, for all practical purposes, the power of the Freedmen's Bureau was over by the end of 1868. Because the government would not or could not send federal troops, the bureau could not maintain the momentum they had gained during 1866–1867. Still, progress had been made. The educational programs they established were the beginning of black education in Huntsville and the rest of Texas.

NOTES

1. Patricia Smith Prather, "A Celebration of Freedom," *Texas Highways*, June 1988, p. 2.

2. T. R. Fehrenbach, *Lone Star: A History of Texas and Texans* (New York: Collier Books, 1985), p. 395.

3. Prather, p. 2.

4. P. R. Thomas, *Outline History of the First Baptist Church, Huntsville, Texas* (Huntsville: published privately, 1923), p. 6.

5. Walker County Genealogical Society & Walker County Historical Commission, *Walker County, Texas: A History* (Dallas: Curtis Media Corporation, 1986), p. 6. [hereinafter abbreviated to WCGS & WCHC]

6. Hamilton/Hunt, p. 10.

7. Smallwood, p. 5.

8. Cary D. Wintz, *Blacks in Houston* (Houston: Center for Humanities, 1982), p. 6–7.

9. Smallwood, p. 8.

10. Smallwood, p. 29.

11. Crews, p. 8. John W. Thomason says in his essay "Huntsville," published in this book: "My grandfather Captain Thomas J. Goree, late a field officer of the staff in the First Corps of the Army of Northern Virginia, plowed his land at Raven Hill (near Point Blank, fourteen miles east of Huntsville) with his own hands, while his yellow body-servant—reportedly a good and faithful slave—went to the state legislature."

12. Andy McAdams, Madisonville, Texas; WPA Interviews, "Slave Stories," p. 6–7. (Dist 8, A-12, Archives Box 4H360, Barker History Center, Austin, Texas.)

13. John McAdams, Madisonville, Texas; WPA Interviews, "Slave Stories," p. 10, (Dist 8 A-12, Archives Box 4H360, Barker History Center, Austin, Texas.)

14. Andy McAdams, p. 7–8.

15. John McAdams, p. 3.

16. Smallwood, p. 33.

17. WCGS and WCHC, p. 778; also Jane Monday interview of descendant Richard Watkins in November 1992.

18. Joseph Ross (a descendant), interview with Jane Monday, 25 July 1992.

19. WCGS and WCHC, p. 450.

20. Hamilton/Hunt, p. 124.

21. Smallwood, p. 5.

22. Smallwood, p 5.

23. Smallwood, p. 27; also James Devine, Year End Report for 1866, Freedmen's Bureau Records, Walker County, Texas. Microfilm Reel 3393, Archives Division, Texas State Library.

24. Walker County Deed Records, Walker County Courthouse, Huntsville, Texas, Volume F, Page 604.

25. Merline Pitre, *Through Many Dangers, Toils, and Snares: Black Leadership in Texas, 1868–1900* (Austin: Eakin Press, 1985), p. 5.

26. Pitre, p. 6.

27. Ibid.

28. Smallwood, p. 39.

29. James Devine, letter to General J. B. Kidds, 6 October 1866. Freedmen's Bureau Records, Estelle Owens Collection, Texas State Archives, Austin, Texas. Microfilm Reel 3386. Hereafter, all letters and reports from Devine are from the same source unless stated otherwise.

30. Ibid.

31. Mae Wynne McFarland Collection, Peabody Library, Sam Houston State

University, Huntsville, Texas, Box 34. (See Note #1 in Chapter 7).

32. In one of his letters, Devine says he "gathered together some of the intelligent freedmen and talked to them about raising money for a school and church." Joshua became a trustee of that school and church, so we assume he was one of the people participating in that discussion. He was also appointed city alderman in 1867, so we have assumed he would have been a source of help for Devine from the very first.

33. James Devine, letter to Headquarters, 6 October 1866.

34. Contract between W. W. McGar and Freedman McGar, Laura E. Hill Papers, Mae Wynne McFarland Collection, Peabody Library, Sam Houston State University, Box 34.

35. James Devine, Year End Report 1866, Reel 3393.

36. Ibid.

37. James Devine, letter to Headquarters, 8 November 1866, Reel 3386.

38. McFarland Collection, "Negroes" notebook.

39. WCGS and WCHC, p. 75.

40. James Devine, letter to Headquarters, 8 November 1866, Reel 3386.

41. P. R. Thomas, p. 6–7.

42. James Devine, letter to J. B. Kidds, 20 October 1866, Reel 3386.

43. James Devine, letters to J. B. Kidds, dates as listed in paragraph, Reel 3386.

44. James Devine, Year End Report 1866, reel 3386.

45. Harre Quarles, Madisonville, Texas, 12 February 1937, "Slave Stories," WPA Interviews.

46. We have found no written documentation of their marriage, but have assumed because of the family stories that they did officially marry at some point.

47. Assumed from the birthdate given on his gravestone, Oakwood Cemetery, Huntsville, Texas, and the 1870 census. There are conflicting dates, but the authors, after reviewing all the evidence, feel that 1864 is the most realistic birthdate because it best fits the documented sequence of events in his life.

48. An affidavit signed by Samuel W. Houston in the Walker County Courthouse, dated 5 September 1940, lists Joshua's wives and children as follows:
"Joshua was married twice, to Mary Green first and Sylvester Baker second. Joshua Houston and Mary Green were married, or at least termed themselves husband and wife, sometime prior to 1856 and they had born to them the following children, to-wit: 1. Ellen Houston, who was born in 1856 and who died about 1925. Ellen first married Sam Dillard and after Sam's death, married Ed Spears. 2. Virginia Houston who was born about 1858, having died in her early teens without ever having married and without leaving any issue surviving her. 3. Joshua Houston Jr. who was born in the year 1860 or 1861 and who died in 1920. The said Mary Green Houston died shortly after the birth of Joshua Houston, Jr. and several years prior to January 15, 1866. Within two or three years after the death of the said Mary Green Houston, Joshua Houston married Sylvester Baker; the marriage taking

place during the latter part of the Civil War, and probably in the year 1864 or 1865. There were born to this union the following children to-wit: 1. George Houston who was born in the year 1868 or 1869 and died in infancy when about one or one and a half years of age. 2. Sam W. Houston who was born on the 22 day of February 1874 [authors' note: see previous endnote]. 3. Minnie O. Houston, who was born in the year 1877 and who is now the wife of Ben Dillard."

On the same day, Dave Williams also signed an affidavit that Joshua had first married Mary Green, who he said was a sister of Strother Green, and that Mary had died about 1861 or 1862 and that Joshua had married Sylvester about 1864 or 1865, or at least prior to January 15, 1866.

These documents are filed in the Walker County Courthouse in Huntsville, Texas, as "No. 88, Sam W. Houston to the Public," and "No. 89, Dave Williams to the Public." It appears that these affidavits were made to establish claim to the land Joshua bought on 15 January 1866, and therefore Samuel felt the need to omit mention of the Crockett family: Anneliza, Joe, Julie, and Lucy. Subsequent interviews with descendants reveal the Huntsville family's knowledge of the Crockett family members.

49. Marriage Records, Walker County Courthouse, Huntsville, Texas, Book C–D Colored. Ellen Houston's marriage certificate had an unsigned note attached to it apparently written by a former owner, attesting to the fact that he had her birth date recorded as 15 January, 1856 and that she was indeed eighteen, so of legal age to marry.

50. Houston County Historical Commission, *Houston County History 1687–1979* (Tulsa: Heritage Publishing, 1979), p. 608.

51. Ibid; also Georgia Mae Wagner Jolly and Desdamona Fobbs (descendants), interviews with authors in 1992 in Crockett, Texas.

52. Houston County Historical Commission, p. 359. Also same interviews as stated in previous endnote.

53. Houston County Historical Commission, p. 416. Also same interviews mentioned in previous endnote.

54. No known connection to Joshua Houston.

55. Scott E. Johnson, interview with Jane Monday in Huntsville, 1992.

56. Mary Gaffeny, 20 October 1937, "Slave Stories," WPA Interviews.

57. James Devine, Year End Report 1866, Reel 3386.

58. Crews, p. 81.

59. James Devine, Year End Report 1866, Reel 3386.

60. Ibid.

61. Ibid.

62. James Devine Report to Commissioner in Galveston, "Outrages Against Freedmen in Walker County," Reel 3393.

63. Ibid.

64. Ibid.

65. Ibid.

66. Smallwood, p. 43–44.

67. Silverthorne, p. 166.

68. Crews, p. 81.

69. Smallwood, p. 69–70.

70. McFarland Collection.

71. Crews, p. 129.

72. Wilson, p. 25.

73. Wilson, p. 4–15.

74. Crews, p. 82.

75. Prather, p. 2.

76. Harrell T. Budd, "The Negro in Politics in Texas, 1867–1898," Master's thesis, University of Texas at Austin, 1925.

77. Devine, Monthly Report, 1 March 1867.

78. McFarland Collection.

79. Butler, Monthly Report to Galveston, 25 May 1867, Reel 3394.

80. Paul Sugg, "The Freedmen's Bureau in Walker County," Master's thesis, Sam Houston State University, 1990, p. 10–11.

81. Butler, Monthly Report to Galveston, 30 June 1867, Reel 3385.

82. Butler, Monthly Report, July 1867, Reel 3385.

83. Butler, Monthly Report, 30 June 1867, Reel 3385.

84. Ibid.

85. Pitre, p. 6.

86. Pitre, p. 85.

87. Butler, Monthly Report, 16 July 1867, Reel 3385.

88. Crews, p. 82.

89. Butler, Report, July 1867, Reel 3385.

90. Sugg, p. 12.

91. Crews, p. 235.

92. Goree, p. 149.

93. McFarland Collection.

94. Crews, p. 207.

95. Sugg, p. 12.

96. Crews, p. 207.

97. Hamilton/Hunt, p. 127; Roberts, p. 358.

98. Roberts, p. 358.

99. Ibid.

100. Sugg, p. 13.

101. "Violence in Polk County," p. 4, col. 5, *Flake's Semi-Weekly Bulletin,* Galveston, Texas, 30 October 1867, Archives Division, State of Texas, Reel 3385.

102. McFarland Collection.

103. List of Local Officials 1870–73, Election Registers, City of Huntsville, State of Texas, Reel 5.

104. William L. Richter, *The Army in Texas During Reconstruction, 1865–1870* (College Station: Texas A & M University Press, 1987), p. 111–12.

105. Richter, *Army,* p. 112–24.

106. McFarland Collection; Sugg, p. 12.

107. Richter, *Army,* p. 124.

108. McFarland Collection. The authors found conflicting information about the racial backgrounds of some of the other aldermen. They are listed as black, or mulatto, or white on various records. Clark is the only one consistently referred to as black.

109. McFarland Collection; Richter, *Army,* p. 105.

110. Butler, Monthly Report, November 1867, Reel 3386.

111. James Butler, Report against Joseph Burges, Sheriff of Walker County, 31 December 1867, Military District Reports, State of Texas, Box 401–1000.

112. Budd, p. 14.

113. Pitre, p. 7–8.

114. Crews, p. 140.

115. *Huntsville Times,* 29 February 1868, "Newcomb Papers: State Newspapers," 2F115, Barker History Center, University of Texas.

116. Budd, p. 4.

117. Pitre, p. 8.

118. *Huntsville Times,* 29 February 1868. Strother had changed his name from Strother Hume to Strother Green. He had been a slave of the Humes and had run the blacksmith shop on the square for them. After the War, Strother had bought the shop from Mrs. Hume and continued to run it on the square. Strother's sister Mary was "married" to Joshua before she died, so the two men would have been, in effect, brothers-in-law for at least a short time.

119. Smallwood, p. 145.

120. Rosa L. Pollard, 30 October 1937, "Slave Stories," WPA interviews.

121. Pitre, p. 18.

122. Butler, Monthly Reports for 30 March 1867 and April 1867, Reel 3386.

123. Butler, Monthly Report, June 1868, Reel 3386.

124. McFarland Collection.

125. McFarland Collection.

126. Pitre, p. 12–13.

127. Pitre, 8–10.

128. Pitre, p. 15.

129. McFarland Collection.

130. John W. Berry, Walker County District 6, Points of Interest, WPA Project for Walker County, 4H109, The Center for American History, The University of Texas at Austin.

131. Wilson, p. 15.

132. Crews, p. 75.

133. Claude Elliott, "The Freedmen's Bureau in Texas," *Southwestern Historical Quarterly* 56 (1952): 17.

134. Elliott, p. 17.

135. Crews, p. 84.

136. N. H. Howard, Monthly Report, December 1868, Reel 3386.

CHAPTER FIVE

1869–1870

"Didn't My Lord Deliver Daniel?"

The newly drafted Texas constitution offered renewed hope for freed black Texans. The constitution recognized the equality of all persons before the law, as well as proposing that office-holding and jury service be open to blacks and that equal educational opportunities and general civil rights be granted them. The educational article provided for the opening of state-supported schools on an equal basis, regardless of color or previous condition of servitude.[1] The convention, which ended 6 February 1869, gave black delegates experience in politics, particularly the law-making aspects. Although there was no consensus even among the nine black delegates concerning what provisions to include in the constitution (two of them even refused to sign the completed document[2]), the experience was a valuable one for all involved.

Ironically, while there was a struggle at the state level for legislating the right of freedmen to hold public office, Joshua had already experienced that right in Huntsville, having been appointed city alderman beginning in 1867.[3] When Joshua returned to Huntsville, he probably thought that it would not be long before other freedmen could join him in public office. His report on the convention to Union Church members would have been enthusiastically received, for things looked hopeful at this point.

Still, political activity in Texas remained volatile. Once it became clear that Texas was moving toward reorganizing its state government and rejoining the Union, state leaders began positioning themselves for state office. The Republican party divided into two factions during the summer of 1869. George T. Ruby, also president of the Loyal League, led the Radical Republicans. They backed E. J. Davis for governor. The Loyal League assessed its members twenty-five cents each to raise money to support Davis. The Moderate Republicans, on the other hand, supported A. J. Hamilton for governor.[4]

The Loyal League in Huntsville would have had no reason to go against its state leaders, so it is assumed that Joshua and the League members there contributed to Davis's fundraising efforts. There can be little doubt that Joshua was well aware of the activities of the Loyal League, since he was a friend and associate of M. H. Goddin, who had been active with the Loyal League early on.

On 11 August 1869, the Loyal League (also called the Union League at times) sent a circular around the state officially supporting E. J. Davis for governor and urging all its members to work hard to elect him.[5] Freedmen throughout Texas, including Huntsville, were registering to vote under the League's encouragement. Election Day in Texas was scheduled for 30 November 1869. Because it was to be the first time freedmen could vote for candidates to represent them in state government, both excitement and tension increased as the day approached.

Joshua would have been even more excited than many other freedmen, because his participation in politics had begun during the years he served Sam Houston, one of the greatest politicians that Texas had ever produced. It had continued when, shortly after the end of the war, he had been appointed to serve as city alderman in Huntsville. But this added knowledge and experience also made it possible for Joshua to be more fearful of what might happen on election day. Even with state troops to guard the polls, election day promised to be violent.

In his later years Andy McAdams, a Walker County man whose life was more typical of an ordinary freedman's than Joshua's was, told the story of his attempt to participate in the election:

> I voted one time there in Huntsville when the Federal Governor Edwin J. Davis sent them soldiers up there to guard us Negroes when we voted 'cause he was one of my great friends. They were that time, if you remember, three or four days holding the election and they guarded us while we voted, and . . . [some were] begging us Negroes to go home and stay away from that election. . . . [They] told us Negroes that the padderollers would get every last one of us for that voting we done, but all us Negroes we thought that Governor Davis would protect us, but oh . . . them padderollers they went to catching Negroes the first thing we knew, but thank the Lord, they never did catch me cause I went right to the Trinity River

bottom and stayed there until they quit whipping Negroes before I came out again. That was the last time I'se ever voted, yes sir, that was enough for me.[6]

At least part of the reason whites were angry with the voting process is explained by McAdams' claim that he "did not know who [he] was voting for or even what they was holding that election for." Because the educational level of the freedmen was still so low, the soldiers often did the voting for them. As McAdams explained: ". . . some white soldiers they did the voting while I just touched the end of the feather until he got through, then he told me I could go, and that was exactly what I done."[7]

The experience of Andy's brother John typifies the reaction of many other freedmen who felt so threatened that they avoided the voting process altogether: "I did not ever try to vote 'cause I saw one Negro that tried to vote and the KKK got hold of him and like to have beat that poor Negro to death. They put hot tar and feathers all over him. . . . that Negro never did try to vote anymore."[8] An incident reported in the *Austin Republican* on 6 December 1869, reveals another example of the tragic consequences some freedman paid for voting: "In Bryan, Texas, a Negro went to the polls and voted for the conservative Hamilton and was applauded by the whites around the polls and sneered at by the Negroes. The next day he was found dead."[9] There was no speculation as to whether blacks or whites had committed the violence.

Obviously the threat of violence did not deter all freedmen from voting. But it proved that their newly-granted political power was more tenuous than they had thought. The perception that Negro strength was growing probably fueled the atrocities and other actions that threatened their advancement. The most obvious evidence to substantiate that fact was the growing activity among the Ku Klux Klan and other groups dedicated to keeping the newly freed men and women in their places of servitude.

Nevertheless, in spite of all the efforts to keep freedmen from voting, the election results provided them with representation from their own ranks in state government. Huntsville citizens helped elect ex-slave Richard Williams to represent the Fifteenth District (comprised of Madison, Grimes, and Walker Counties) in the Texas legislature.[10]

In the midst of all the setbacks in efforts towards gaining political power, the freed men and women of Huntsville must have been heartened by the smoother process of their attempts at exercising religious freedom. Attendance at Union Church's religious, educational and social activities had grown so much that the various denominations decided to build their own places of worship. The African Methodist congregation built a church several blocks east of Union Church, while the Baptist congregation (in which Joshua and his family became members) built in the section of Huntsville known as Rogersville.[11]

The Methodist Episcopal members remained in the original church building and kept the same trustees. The Union Church trustees—Joshua Houston, Strother Green, William Baines, William R. Fayle and William H. Sinclair— sold the land back to John Courtade for $301.50, and he then sold it to the Methodist Episcopal Church on 6 August 1869. The agreement stated that the church would be used for both "Divine Worship and for school purposes."[12]

The $300 purchase price for the church came from the white Bishop of the Methodist Episcopal Church, who wired the money from Austin while holding his first Texas Conference. The Union Church then became known as the St. James Methodist Episcopal Church. The first board of stewards included John Clark, who was also the local exhorter, Barney Carter, Lawrence Hightower and Solomon Jones. The original stewardesses were Martha Clark, Nancy Jones and Mary Baines. The preachers were Reverend Loggins and Presiding Elder Reverend Kingston, a white man who was to preside over the "colored" Methodists for many years before being succeeded by black presiding elders. (Richard Williams, the state legislator, later became a pastor of St. James.[13]) Members of the white Methodist church, as a rule, were very helpful to the members of St. James.[14]

The early teachers of the school located in the St. James building were whites from the north: Lizzie Stone, Texana Snow, and three people with the last names of Ausbourn, James, and Brown. The blacks who later became teachers were Joseph (a.k.a. Jacob) F. Crozier, O. A. C. Todd and Mollie Flood, all of whom were surely acquainted with Joshua and his wife, Sylvester, since they at one time went to the same church.[15]

Joseph Cozier was from the West Indies.[16] One of his students was Memphis Allen. When Allen became an elected official in 1886, he recalled how he and his friend William Goode would come into town to attend night classes and learn arithmetic from Cozier. For Allen and other freedman, the steps toward becoming educated began with learning to read, and then with learning arithmetic. Because so many blacks were already adults by the time they had an opportunity to become educated, they had to juggle the demands of work and family responsibilities with those of getting an education. It took

Memphis Allen. Like Joshua, Memphis Allen was an early property owner and served as a county commissioner in Walker County. He was a strong supporter of Bishop Ward College, founded in 1883 in Huntsville, only eighteen years after the end of slavery. Courtesy James Patton and the Walker County Historical Association.

*First Baptist Church. Located in Huntsville, this church was founded in 1869. Joshua and
Sylvester Houston were prominent members of First Baptist Church.
Courtesy Samuel Walker Houston Cultural Center—Huntsville, Texas.*

a great deal of commitment, but eventually this effort paid off for freedmen
like Memphis Allen, who later helped shape the history of Huntsville.[17]

Although the black community in Huntsville was large, because of the per-
secution which they all suffered at this point in time many of its members
probably knew of one another. Along with the church leaders of the Methodist Episcopal church, some other black leaders who were probably at least
acquaintances of Joshua's were Jake Skelton, Sam Montgomery, Gus Holt,
Washington "Wash" Dillard, Simon Crawford, "Mother" Sarah Dillard, Ellen
Herndon, Lucinda Jimison and Melinda Beecham, all stewards of the African
Methodist Church.[18]

Reverend J. J. Rhinehardt, first pastor of the First Baptist Church, is even
more likely to have been Joshua's friend. When Rhinehardt came to Huntsville in 1869 he already had much in common with Joshua, including a love
for learning and an appointment to a city office. Rhinehardt was a progressive pastor who had in 1867 established the first Race Church in Navasota,
Texas. He had an excellent education, including a familiarization with Latin,
Greek and Hebrew. He had been appointed a member of the first city council

in Navasota when it was under martial law, although he had refused to hold office at that time.[19]

"Mother" Sarah Rolling, who assisted Rhinehardt at the First Baptist Church, is also likely to have been a friend of Joshua and his wife Sylvester. Rolling had been one of the first to take newly freed slaves into her home to help them learn to read. She gave liberally of her time and money to First Baptist and once contributed $100 "that the struggling cause might live," according to P. R. Thomas, historian for First Baptist Church. Clark Rolling, Joseph M. Mettawer, Jasper Sims and Houston Rolling were deacons of the First Baptist Church along with Joshua, and so were likely included in his social circle.[20]

The Rogersville area where the new First Baptist Church was located was being settled by many of the members of that church.[21] Joshua's family was one of the first; the land he purchased on 15 January 1866 for $120 was in the same block as the church.[22] He bought the land with Hiram Bowen, who owned wagons which he used to haul freight from Huntsville to Houston and other communities.[23]

The house that Joshua built on that lot was later described by Constance Houston Thompson, one of his granddaughters, as a

big, two-story house located on 10th and O Streets. It had a porch across the entire front with two doors. One door led to the parlor and the other to the bedroom. There were four windows across the front. It had a bathroom with a tub, and a dining room. The house had a fence.[24]

Her description of the house resembles the description of the one Joshua had built at Raven Hill for General Samuel Houston in the 1840's, leading to speculation that he might have used the same design when building his own house. Thompson also remembered that four sycamore trees were on the property, and that Joshua's blacksmith shop was near the house, although she could not recall how it looked.[25] However, at least one other old Huntsville resident claimed that the blacksmith shop was located diagonally across the street from Joshua's house, on the southeast corner. Joshua later sold the property across the street on the southwest side to his sister, Virginia Wilson.[26]

Evidence also exists regarding property acquisition by the First Baptist Church in 1872. The site was purchased for $40 in gold by Clark Rolling, John James and York Henderson, trustees of what was then known as the Colored Baptist Church of Huntsville.[27]

Property ownership was a major goal of the newly freed slaves. Like education, acquisition of property was considered essential if they were to begin to prosper in an environment that had held them captive for several generations. Before Emancipation, even the few free blacks who owned property almost lost it when the Texas Congress passed a law in 1840 giving all free Negroes within the Republic the choice of either leaving before the end of two years or being sold into slavery.[28]

Another early property owner was Joseph Mettawer, a barber, who built his two-story home just south of Rogersville on 12th Street near the Courthouse Square. Mettawer was a well-known musician, a deacon, and a teacher in the First Baptist Sunday School.[29]

First Baptist Church quickly became the center of Rogersville religious and social activities. Membership in the church grew to two hundred within a short time after its formation.[30] A special feature of the church program was the annual Sunday School picnic in May at Nelson Creek, nine miles north of Huntsville. It was attended by persons living throughout the county and young men engaged buggies from livery stables weeks in advance of the occasion.[31] (See photo on p. 194, Chapter 7.)

Joshua's entire family was actively involved in church affairs. Joshua himself was a deacon. His importance to the church can be judged by the tribute to him in the history of the First Baptist Church published in 1922.

> A citizen of Walker County, he had few peers among the white or colored ranks. He took part in all movements of the county, which aimed to better the general conditions of the country, politically, socially, industrially and religiously. Firm, outspoken, honest, industrious, a staunch leader, he commanded the respect of the citizenry, white and colored. Was County Commissioner and member of the City Board of Aldermen for years. A good husband, a loving father, a true friend, a devout Christian, a hard worker, always engaged in church work—church treasurer, deacon, trustee, in his time, a pillar and tower of strength of First Baptist Church.[32]

Joshua's wife Sylvester was an active member of the Church Aid Society. These societies had a vital role in early African American churches. Members administered to the sick (at a time when hospitals were unavailable to blacks), they provided food for the poor, and they took on a variety of other necessary tasks to assist their community.[33]

Ellen Houston, Joshua's daughter, was among the first Sunday School teachers at First Baptist. She had been born during slavery, but as a young

*Aunt Jane Ward at Juneteenth Celebration. Aunt Jane Ward (with flag) was an early
leader of the annual Juneteenth Celebration, as well as a leader in church affairs and one of
the strong supporters of Bishop Ward College.
Courtesy R. H. Williams family.*

woman could read and write. The Sunday School teachers taught reading and
writing as well as religious instruction, and were obviously popular, with an
average of seventy-five to a hundred pupils. The other early teachers were
Johnnie James, Wash Sullivan and Ella Fisher Gray.[34]

First Baptist members continued to join with other churches in the area for
the annual Juneteenth celebrations. These celebrations were spearheaded by
Jane Ward. Before the church split, the celebrations had been held on Union
Church grounds. Under Jane Ward's direction, they were held on a little hill
two blocks from the site of First Baptist Church, near the corner of Pleasant
Street and Old Madisonville Road.[35] In order to keep up interest and excitement about Juneteenth through the years, Jane Ward would gather the boys
and girls and have them march through town with flags flying.

She had come to be called "Aunt" Jane Ward by nearly everyone not only
because of her work on the celebration, but also because of her care for the
sick and indigent. She owned a ten-room boarding house on 11th Street in

Huntsville, where she rented rooms for fifty cents a night, with no limit on the number of inhabitants. She also owned two small houses in back of the boarding house, in which she allowed elderly people to live until they died.[36] Since there were no hospitals which would care for sick blacks, Jane Ward's work was crucial to the community. She used home remedies such as Sassafras tea for fever and blood cleansing. In order to provide nourishing food for her boarders and patients, she would get soup bones from a Mr. Northerton's meat market. The soup she made was usually served with corn bread, biscuits, or hoe cakes.[37]

Having a community such as Rogersville helped the recently freed families in a number of ways in addition to that of religious unity. By living close together they could watch out for one anothers' safety in an environment that was fraught with violence against them. They could also share precious goods like food and clothing. The few who had businesses, like Joshua, could provide training for young residents or at the very least serve as models for others to emulate. They surely could offer the young black people of Rogersville hope for a better life than their parents had suffered under slavery.

But tensions between the freedmen and their former owners continued to run high in Huntsville. One historian recalled a family story which illustrates that problems still existed:

> Mr. W. L. Adair moved to the home of his brother-in-law Magruder Wynne after his son rented the Williamson place and contracted several freedmen to farm it. Once three freedmen rode up on horseback, [one] with a pistol strapped on his belt. They asked to see Uncle Weyman who was down in the field plowing and grandfather either went or sent for him. When going through the open hall from the back gallery to the front Uncle Weyman made a point of letting the freedmen see him place his pistol on a table before he went out to talk to them. During this conversation on the front gallery grandfather and Uncle Ras Wynne, with shotguns ready for use, tensely watched from the inside, prepared to shoot if Uncle Weyman were attacked. The conference was peaceful and the colored men left in a short while. Papa sat on the banisters during the talk—he was not afraid but he felt the tense situation.[38]

NOTES

1. Pitre, p. 6.
2. Pitre, p. 19.
3. McFarland Collection, "Negroes" notebook.
4. Budd, p. 13.
5. George Ruby, letter to J. P. Newcomb, 11 August 1869. J. P. Newcomb Papers, Barker History Library, Austin. Box 2F109.
6. Andy McAdams, "Slave Story," WPA Transcripts.
7. Ibid.
8. John McAdams, "Slave Story," WPA Transcripts.
9. *Austin Republican,* 6 December 1869. Newcomb Papers. Box 2F115.
10. Pitre, p. 8.
11. P. R. Thomas, p. 7–8.
12. Crews, p. 83.
13. Elnora Hudley (St. James Methodist Episcopal Church historian), interview with Jane Monday, December 1992.
14. Crews, p. 83–84.
15. WCGS and WCHC, p. 150.
16. McFarland Collection, "Negroes" notebook.
17. Wilson, p. 8.
18. Wilson, p. 9.
19. P. R. Thomas, p. 10–11.
20. P. R. Thomas, p. 11.
21. Scott E. Johnson, interviews with Jane Monday, 1992.
22. Deed, 15 January 1866, Walker County Court House, Huntsville, Texas. Vol. F, p. 604.
23. Felder Jones, interview with Jane Monday, January 1993, Huntsville, Texas.
24. Constance Houston Thompson, interview with Jane Monday and Patricia Smith Prather, 1992. The deed which records the sale of the lot does not mention a house, so we assume he built it.
25. Ibid.
26. James Patton, (County Clerk of Walker County), interviews with Jane Monday, January 1993.
27. P. R. Thomas, p. 10–11.
28. H. N. P. Gammel, *The Laws of Texas, 1822–1889.* Austin: Gammel Publishing, 1898.
29. P. R. Thomas, p. 10–11, 23.
30. P. R. Thomas, p. 11.
31. C. W. Wilson, p. 21.

32. Thomas, p. 23–26.

33. Thomas, p. 23.

34. Thomas, p. 21.

35. R. H. Williams (grandson of Aunt Jane Ward), interview with Jane Monday, 1992.

36. Ibid. The authors have a copy of the floorplan of this house.

37. Ibid.

38. McFarland Collection, "Negroes" notebook. The names are confusing in this story but we have recorded it exactly as given in the notebook.

"There are few distinguished Texans of the period 1840 to 1860 whom Josh[ua] does not distinctly remember," according to former president of the Sam Houston Normal Institute, Harry Estill.

Adolphus Sterne. Joshua accompanied Sam Houston on many of his visits to his close friend Adolphus Sterne. Sterne also came to Huntsville several times, including a trip in 1851 for the dedication of Austin College across the street from the Woodland home where Joshua would have seen him again. Courtesy Archives Division—Texas State Library.

E. M. Pease. Governor E. M. Pease appointed Joshua city alderman for Huntsville in 1867, making Joshua one of the earliest black leaders of the Reconstruction era.
Courtesy Archives Division—Texas State Library.

Dr. Ashbel Smith. Smith was a close friend of Sam Houston. When Margaret became ill with a breast tumor, it was Joshua who rode through the night to get Dr. Smith to attend to her.
Courtesy Archives Division—Texas State Library.

Edmund J. Davis. Governor Davis declared martial law in Huntsville, Texas, in 1871, after
a freedman was killed and a shootout occurred at the courthouse. While Joshua was
a city alderman, the city's citizens were fined to pay for the expense of sending
the troops in to restore law and order.
Courtesy Archives Division—Texas State Library.

A. J. Hamilton. Provisional Governor A. J. Hamilton, appointed following the end of the Civil War, attempted to restore order in the violent and unstable years of early Reconstruction, while Joshua and other freedmen were struggling to meet the challenges of freedom.
Courtesy Archives Division—Texas State Library.

CHAPTER SIX

1871–1880

"Deep River"

A landmark day for blacks in Texas history came on 8 February 1870 when the Twelfth Legislature opened in Austin with two black state senators and eleven black state legislators. Walker County freedmen were no doubt rejoicing that they had helped elect one from their own ranks. The election of Richard Williams as state legislator representing Walker, Grimes, and Madison counties was cause for celebration. Free men, just five years previously slaves themselves, had elected another ex-slave to represent their county in Austin.[1]

As prominent black citizens, Joshua and Sylvester may have honored Williams and his family with some sort of celebration in their home. Joshua and Williams were well acquainted. Their relationship predated the Civil War when both were blacksmiths and both worked for Colonel George Grant, owner of one of the stagecoach lines.[2] Fate, hard work and luck had made a difference in both their lives. Although both had been slaves, each had belonged to a family that treated him with more civility and kindness than the ordinary slave could expect.

Williams, born in South Carolina,[3] belonged to the McGar family in Huntsville when he was hired out to work blacksmith jobs with Colonel Grant.[4] After Emancipation, Williams had moved to Grants Colony, made up of mostly freedmen, and become very active with its development. In 1868, Williams requested that Colonel Grant donate land to the freedmen for a school and church. When the request was granted with a donation of two acres of land for the "common benefit of all citizens of Grants colony," Williams became one of six trustees of the school and church.[5]

Williams was later described by one man who remembered him as a "tall, big, rawboned Negro, who was all Negro and made no pretensions to more than he was."[6] He was fifty years old by the time he was elected to the state legislature, just a couple of years older than Joshua.[7]

Texas was re-admitted to the Union by 30 March 1870. Newly-elected Governor E. J. Davis did not begin his official duties until after the fourteenth and fifteenth amendments were ratified. Davis, a native of Florida who had studied law in Corpus Christi, became a Texas elected official beginning in 1850. During both the 1866 and 1868 Texas Constitutional Conventions, Davis led the so-called radicals. Among their proposals were disfranchisement of all supporters of the Confederacy. Davis was considered an ally to freedmen and no doubt received a large percentage of their vote.[8]

However, the newly-elected freedmen found that discrimination was as obvious in Austin as it had been in their hometowns. They were not invited to the State Ball in January, nor were they invited by Governor Davis to the executive mansion.[9] Nevertheless, they took an active role in state government. A major issue early in the session, which convened on 28 April 1870, was racial turmoil. The Republicans proposed creation of a state police and the re-establishment of the state militia. These bills passed the House after numerous heated discussions, but faced an uphill battle in the Senate. The two black senators, George T. Ruby and Matt Gaines, were instrumental in pushing them through.[10] Gaines was from Washington County and cited personal experience with violence in his efforts to push the bills through:

> I owe a duty to my constituents whose interest I have at heart and that duty compels me to cast my vote. . . . In my own county there are men today riding around stealing horses and shooting blacks, and yet I am told that we do not need a militia system in this state. I also know that bands of men are in my county not only ready to kill the niggers, but to shoot down the damned hated Yankees. . . . And I know if some of our democratic friends had seen the Ku Klux Klan as I have seem them, there would be less opposition.[11]

On 4 June 1870, several Republicans, both blacks and whites, established the Radical Republican Association for the purpose of "supporting the present administration and of successfully carrying party measures through the legislature." The members swore an oath of secrecy.[12] Richard Williams from Huntsville was a member of this new organization, as were all but two of the other black legislators. As secretary, freedman Richard Allen from Houston administered the oath to Williams and the other members. Meetings were

Richard Williams. Williams, from Walker County, was elected to the House of Representatives in 1870. He represented Walker, Grimes, and Madison Counties in the Twelfth Legislature just five years after slavery ended. He was re-elected to the Thirteenth Legislature. He and Joshua were both blacksmiths and had worked for Colonel Grant's stagecoach business while they were still slaves.
Courtesy Archives Division—Texas State Library.

held on Mondays and members were fined twenty-five cents for each absence unless they were sick or could prove some other satisfactory reason.[13]

Richard Williams also remained active in the civic affairs of Huntsville. On June 17, he became a trustee on a new deed "to establish a site for a school house to be used for the education of freedmen and children irrespective of race and color." This deed was in lieu of a previously filed deed to comply with the requirements of the Freedmen's Bureau, which was still operating a few schools in Texas.[14]

The establishment of public schools became an issue in the Twelfth Legislature, particularly with respect to having black and white children in the same schools. When a representative introduced an amendment to forbid any mixture of races, Richard Williams countered with an amendment to table the previous one, though it failed by one vote. The Free School Bill of 1870 passed, calling for a Superintendent of Public Education and for children of both races to attend classes at least four months of the year. It also established a school fund in which blacks would share equally with whites. But the bill would not stand the test of time. In the second session of the Twelfth Legislature, advocates of segregation repealed the bill. The Free Bill of 1871 was interpreted as a justification for segregated schools.[15]

Joshua and other Huntsville leaders would not have welcomed the news of segregated schools, although their Union school had been separate from white schools from the beginning. Other disheartening news to reach Texas was that Freedmen's Bureau schools would be officially discontinued when the Bureau itself closed operations on 30 June 1870.[16] Fortunately, the Huntsville school for freedmen was well established and would be able to carry on without Bureau support. Two of Joshua's children, Samuel W. and Joshua, Jr., were of the age to be enrolled in school, but because no attendance records exist, it is impossible to know for sure that they were students there. Both the Union school and the Freedmen's schools had to charge tuition, so the day had not yet arrived when black children in Texas would receive the same free education as white children did.

Meanwhile, other events around Huntsville were affecting the lives of freedmen. By July, Walker County had been included in the Thirtieth Judicial District and a special tax was levied to build a county jail. On 12 August, Huntsville was selected to be connected to Hempstead via the Eastern and Western Trunk Railway, and the next day a time limit was given to the Brazos Branch Railroad to build a line from Navasota to Huntsville.[17] The building of both a county jail and railroad opened up job possibilities for freedmen, as well as other Huntsville citizens.[18]

Huntsville received new local officials on 21 September 1870, when Cyrus Hess was appointed as mayor along with aldermen A. T. McKinney (who soon resigned), J. Lyle Smith, Richard Phillips, and Solomon Jones (a black man). Joshua was again appointed as Huntsville alderman. Rapid turnovers and brief terms reflected the political chaos that was occurring throughout the state.[19]

There was still plenty of political activity, both positive and negative, among members of the Union League. On 17 June a request for another Texas Union League Charter had been received for Montgomery County.[20] And on 8 September 1870, a dispute erupted in nearby Grimes County over the appointment of a Mr. Horn as Union League of America deputy.[21] This dispute was not settled until December, when Sheriff J. M. Gibbs wrote to Secretary of State J. P. Newcomb that Mr. Horn's appointment had been upheld. Meanwhile, membership in Anderson, Texas, was estimated at between 750 and 800 freedmen, which Sheriff Gibbs told Newcomb would assure the election of the Republican candidate John Wilson for Justice of the Peace of Precinct One there.[22] A circular from the national League headquarters was printed in October of 1870, and it clearly shows the kind of rhetoric being used to keep the League's members from sliding into passivity.

> Brothers—The contest is upon us! The glorious army of the Union League, upon whose banner is written the record of so many brilliant victories, is called upon once more to face the old enemy. . . . Get into your Councils all who have lately come of age. . . . Let your Councils meet in perpetual session from this time until the sun goes down on election day. Let none of the devices of the adversary win you away from your sacred allegiance to the Union League. . . . For if we secure an unmistakable triumph, we need have little fear of [the Copperhead Democratic] party of misguided men and traitors again being heard of as a national party. . . . Rouse, then, and strain every nerve, shrink not at any honest sacrifice! Let the claims of your own private business stand aside, and spend a few days for your Country. . . . On election day be at the polls at sunrise, and work every moment for success. Have your challengers ready for duty, and appoint a vigilance committee to be in attendance at every poll. See that teams are ready so that even the lame, and halt, and blind may help in the good work. . . . Let all your preparations for the election be conducted with profound secrecy, and be sure to

obtain your ballots from the Council only. This advice is especially needed in localities where treachery of any kind may be feared. . . . [23]

This directive had special meaning in Texas, because according to the 1870 census, over thirty per cent of the 818,597 Texans were blacks.[24] Their voting strength was important to the Republicans, who got nearly all the freedmen votes. In some counties—known as black belts—the percentage of black voters was higher than that of whites. Huntsville was one of these counties, since the voting population averaged more than five blacks to every white.

By 19 December Huntsville had new local officials, with Mayor Hess being replaced by Mayor Mortimer H. Goddin, with whom Joshua had served previously. Also, Solomon Jones, W. C. Oliphant and John Courtade were elected as city aldermen along with Joshua.[25] Courtade was the man who had sold land to Joshua and the other freedmen to use for their church. Mortimer H. Goddin was a colorful figure who was not well liked by the whites, but he had been loyal to the Republicans and active in the Union League. Born in Virginia in 1828, he was nevertheless a long-time Texas resident who had property and influence in several counties between the Trinity and the Sabine valleys. Goddin had served as sub-assistant commissioner of the Freedmen's Bureau and as justice of the peace, and been a delegate to the state constitution convention of 1868–1869 before being named mayor of Huntsville.[26] The 1870 elections resulted in increased representation for the freedmen and their allies. However, despite this representation, violence was common and freedmen lived in constant fear for their lives.[27]

In January 1871, a sensational trial took place in Walker County. Historian Mae Wynne McFarland records that "a Negro named Sam Jenkins testified before a grand jury that he had been flogged by some white men." A few days later his body was found, "bearing evidence that he had been murdered."[28] Captain L. H. McNelly was sent to Huntsville with a squad of police to ferret out the criminals and in a short time he arrested four men and brought others in for preliminary examination before Judge J. R. Burnett. Last names of the attorneys for the defendants were Baker, Maxey and Hightower. The trial for Nat Outlaw, Joe Wright, Fred Parks and John McParish lasted three days, with friends of the prisoners making threats that they would carry out if the men were sent to jail. Eventually, the defendants were found guilty, but somehow their friends managed to slip them at least two six-shooters. On his way to take them to jail, Captain McNelly was shot, as was Tom Kesee, one of the state policemen, but they also managed to wound some of the prisoners before they were met by their Confederate friends armed with shot-guns. Mounted on horses, shooting off their pistols and yelling like savages, the prisoners and their friends got away.[29]

Charles Taylor Rather, an eyewitness whose sympathy obviously lay with the Confederates, gave his account years later:

> There was a Negro killed out in the country a few miles. He was reported to be one of the leaders under "Carpetbagism" rule and made himself ob-noxious to white people generally. . . . Judge J. R. Burnett, an appointee, I think of Edmund J. Davis, the Carpetbag Governor at that time, pre-sided at the examining trial and, when he announced the case unbailable, the boys rose up shooting. Captain McNelly, with several members of his state police force appointed by E. J. Davis, w[as] in the courthouse at the time, and a general battle took place. Parish escaped with bullet wounds in his arm and shoulder, Nat Outlaw was knocked down and captured, and Joe Wright escaped with Parish. Captain McNelly was wounded in the leg and one of his men named Kezee was wounded in the neck. Judge Burnett is said to have saved himself by falling over behind the platform on which he sat and presided. The smoke of battle had scarcely cleared until I was on the scene. Captain McNelly was guarding the foot of the stairway leading up into the courtroom where the fight took place and where Nat Outlaw was then a prisoner. I asked Captain McNelly if I could go upstairs and he told me I could. I then made bold to ask him if he was hurt, and he said yes, that one of his boots was then full of blood from a wound in his legs. Very shortly thereafter Nat Outlaw was brought down and the state police, accompanied by Captain McNelly on horseback, carried Outlaw to the penitentiary, where he was imprisoned for safekeeping. Horses, saddled and bridled, were conveniently placed for the boys to make their getaway. One of the boys was having difficulty in untying his horse and called on someone to cut him loose. My father chanced to be close by and performed the act. He drew a hundred dollar fine for assisting a prison escape.[30]

McNelly ordered the sheriff to summon a horse and pursue the prisoners. He later made out a written report that only two citizens could be found who were willing to be part of the capture. Confederates with cocked pistols pre-vented two policemen on the stairs from helping. An attempt was made on the Judge's life by ex-sheriff William H. Stewart. The District Attorney at the time, W. E. Horne, wrote that the prisoners were guarded by thirty to forty well-armed friends who defied arrest and threatened to kill Captain McNelly.

According to Horne, "so many helped [the prisoners], I rather state those who didn't: Judge Jeff Benton, Col. Abercombie, Sanford Gibbs, Macgruder Winn [sic], Dr. Rawlins, Mr. Bush and Mr. Kelly, county commissioner."[31]

Joshua, as a city alderman, was involved in the aftermath of this. He watched some of his fellow officers, like the mayor, get removed from office because of what happened. Other freedmen would also have been aware of these events, as newspaper reports contained all the details and everyone in town was talking about it. In addition, the fiasco resulted in Governor E. J. Davis declaring martial law in Walker County on 15 February 1871. Special Order #18 directed the Chief of Police of Texas, Colonel James Davidson, to

1. Proceed to Walker County.
2. Proclaim Martial Law dated January 20, 1871.
3. Assess County or parties implicated for expenses.
4. Use General Court, or Military Commissioners for trial if better [than] Civil Courts.
5. Be prompt so troops can return home.
6. A strong squad of police must be left in Walker County or leave a detachment of Militia or State Guard under a good officer to hunt down and bring justice to the offenders.
7. Court Martial in Grimes County any militia men who refused service in Walker County.[32]

The Governor issued another Special Order on 22 February for the court martial of Cyrus Hess, former mayor of Huntsville. On 27 February, a military commission was set up for the trial of some twenty persons. Some were fined, and one was sent to the penitentiary for five years. The expenses of the proceedings were paid by a levy of twenty-five cents on each $100 of all taxable property in the county.[33]

While McNelly was convalescing he was interviewed by a reporter from the *Galveston News*. He declared that the sheriff could have prevented the trouble by searching the people who entered the courtroom. McNelly also said he did not think martial law was necessary, as shown by the fact that just eight or ten men were collecting the tax, and he intimated that it was imposed for the money it would bring.[34]

Martial law was an extreme measure, and the white citizens were very upset. Their hostility toward it is evident in a *Daily State Journal* newspaper article for 17 March:

Norman Kittrell declared that the people did not resist martial law because they had been dominated five years by the carpetbagger, scalawag and Negro . . . . [Kittrell said] "As I look back on the day when I was but little more than a youth, [I] went with a committee of citizens to protest against the tax levy and martial law [and noticed how] contemptuously the petty tyrant Davidson treated the committee. I wonder that the people had not risen in a body and whipped him and his roving band of buccaneers off the earth. I always regretted that they did not.[35]

These activities probably spurred the organizing efforts of the Union League, but it also resulted in an internal fight within the League. On 12 June, members of the Union League of America requested of A. J. Hamilton an official charter for the Walker County League, which had apparently been operating on an informal level up to this time.[36] The next day a letter from A. J. Bennett to J. P. Newcomb, Secretary of State, complained of a conspiracy against him within the League, organized by Stacy, Contrade [could be Coutrade], and Talbot. Bennett requested that a new charter be sent to league president M. H. Goddin. A clue as to the other men's dissatisfaction with him may lie in Bennett's assertion that he had "made more money for the state by convict labor than any other men."[37] Bennett wrote another letter to Newcomb on 16 June, indignant in regard to his name being linked with Moore and Hall. He asked that copies of his letter be sent to him to use as proof of his standing in the League.[38] On 21 June, Goddin himself wrote to Newcomb asking for receipt of a new charter of the Union League, saying he "would recognize Governor Davis as leader of the party."[39]

The tense situation in the community and around the state continued. In July of 1871, the Walker County Commissioners Court allowed money to be paid to men for guarding the ballot box during the elections.[40]

When the state Republicans held a meeting in Houston on August 3 and 4, the black leadership divided in thirds over the candidacy for United States Congress from the Third Congressional District, which was over forty per cent black. One third supported black candidate (and current State Senator) Matthew Gaines; one third supported black candidate Lewis Stevenson; and the others supported William T. Clark, a white candidate. Governor Davis supported Clark, and tried to keep black delegates from being seated until after Clark's nomination. Gaines protested against Stevenson and Clark by saying, "Irish and Dutch are good in their places but [white folks view] blacks [as somebody who] is always there to vote for the white man. Expel me from the party, but I'll never be a Clark man." It is almost certain that Joshua attended this meeting, as he was both a local official and a member of the Republican Party. Two Huntsville freedmen, Nathan Haller and Richard Williams, are documented as active participants in the convention.[41]

A prominent organizer of the Union League in several black belt counties, Lewis Stevenson and six of the delegates who supported him walked out of the convention before it adjourned. Along with other delegates who were barred from entering the "Clark Padlock Convention," these dissidents called a rival convention in a nearby hall, where one of the black candidates, Israel S. Campbell, withdrew his name in favor of Stevenson, whom the groups then unanimously nominated for Congress. Nathan Haller, a black from Walker County, served as the secretary of the rival convention. When called upon to endorse Stevenson, he said that he was sure attempts had been made by the Clark men to buy delegates, because he had received an offer himself. Contending that he had never been "for sale since his shackles as a slave had fallen from his limbs," Haller urged blacks to stand true and support Stevenson. Another outspoken Walker County black at this convention was Richard Williams, the state representative who lived in Huntsville. Williams said he supported Stevenson because he believed nine-tenths of the black people in his district were behind him. A Grant and Stevenson Club was formed with Richard Williams and Nathan Haller named vice president and secretary, respectively. It appears that Walker County was well represented at this rival convention, since Williams and Haller had been early Republican Party leaders (along with Joshua) in city, county and state affairs.[42]

Amidst all the political turmoil in Austin, it was easy to lose sight of the progress being made on the local level. Back in Huntsville, more and more blacks were being educated in spite of the fact that the Freedmen's Bureau was no longer there to help. Even though the schools had to charge tuition, local blacks were filling the schools in order to learn to read and write, many in an effort to become teachers. The schools the freedmen had once run "immediately became overcrowded with blacks. . . . Where it was impossible to lease buildings, blacks offered their churches," according to one historian.[43]

Another note of progress for black education in Texas was taking place in Galveston, where Barnes Institute, the state's first "normal school" (a school for training teachers) for Negroes, was established with a five-hundred-book library.[44] Galveston also had office headquarters for the National Colored Labor Union. Unfortunately, neither institution lasted very long.[45]

Yet another positive sign in education was that prisoners were being taught.

This effort was led by Colonel George Grant, who had always been among Huntsville's educational leaders.[46] His efforts in the prisons were especially significant for freedmen, who made up a large percentage of the prison population.[47] Prisoners had been an important source of labor for nearby landowners, who were able to hire them at very low wages,[48] so any effort towards educating them was a step in the right direction.

The prison also supplied many necessary community services with its furniture plant, textile mill, iron foundry, brick kilns, and wagon works.[49] In 1871, in an attempt towards correcting the abuse of prison labor, the Texas legislature required the state's prison management to be leased out for ten years. But that decision was to prove detrimental to the inmates. Between 1871 and 1876, the death rate for prisoners doubled and, in response, escapes increased from 50 to 381.[50]

Even though across the state only one in a hundred blacks owned land, in Huntsville conditions seemed more favorable for allowing them to acquire it.[51] A few, like Joshua, owned property in town, but most freedmen owned farm land out in the county.[52] Life was not easy for these families. The six years since achieving freedom had been tough ones. They had been forced to provide for themselves with few skills and little opportunity to earn money.

Most of the freedmen were sharecroppers living on their ex-masters' land. So freedmen like Joshua, Memphis Allen and a few others were the exception. Allen accumulated between five and six hundred acres of land just west of town, which was worked by sharecroppers. He also owned a cotton gin. John "Tip" Hightower first accumulated 147 acres of land and continued to add to it through money he made blacksmithing, repairing wagon wheels and oxen yokes, making household tools, and selling soft coal he made himself on the farm. This coal he sold in town to the ladies to burn in irons for ironing their clothes.[53]

Both landowners and sharecroppers had a ready supply of wood for housing material in the surrounding forests of East Texas. They cut down the pine trees, leaving stumps that served as blocks to hold up their houses. (Union Chapel in Hall's Bluff, where Joshua's family attended, was built using this technique. See photographs on page 145 and 146.) To secure their fireplaces they mixed a particular kind of soil they called "chimney mud."[54]

Day to day existence for most freedmen consisted of working hard just to provide food for the table. Two former slaves, Lizzie Atkins and Harriet Barrett, revealed in an interview for the WPA in 1937 that they would have starved to death had they not killed wild game in the woods. Sometimes they

Union Chapel, 1992. Located outside of Crockett, Texas, in the Hall's Bluff community,
Union Chapel church stands as an example of the freedmen's efforts to build churches and
schools immediately after emancipation. Joshua's Crockett family attended this church.
The floor of this building rests on tree stumps.
Courtesy Chester Hines.

would steal chickens and potatoes to eat, but then the KKK would come and
there was no one to protect them. They seldom had money even when they
worked, because they were not always paid the fifteen to thirty cents per day
they earned picking cotton. There was a limited supply of clothing, also, and
most could not afford the tuition or the time for an education. In most families, the women took care of the sick or injured and delivered the babies, as
no other means of health care was available. Many of their treatments had
been handed down from prior generations during slavery.[55] Harriet Barrett,
who served as a midwife in Walker County, talked about some of her basic
treatments:

(1) charcoal, onions and honey for little babies, (2) camphor for chills,
fever and teeth cutting, (3) Red Oak bark boiled to make a tea for fevers,
(4) a rabbit foot tied around the neck to protect from chills and fevers, and
(5) cactus weed roots to make tea for fever, chills and colic.[56]

Church foundation. This view from underneath the Union Chapel shows the tree stumps on which the building rests. This innovative technique was utilized by the early freedmen. Courtesy Chester Hines.

A slightly different version of black life during that time was explained by Champ Anderson, whose father Tom had started out as a sharecropper on 125 acres of the nearly 8000-acre Spells-Scales Ranch. He later became foreman and his wife Rachel became a cook. The Andersons grew cotton, corn, and a type of bluish-skinned sweet potato usually fed to the cows and horses. When they got hungry, the family would bake the potatoes in sugar and eat them. When Tom and Rachel would go to Huntsville for supplies, a two-day trip, they would take a wagon and four yoke of oxen. Even with that, the streets of Huntsville were often so muddy that another team of oxen would have to be rented to pull the wagons through town. Champ Anderson remembers that they would camp by the springs at Crab Prairie at night.[57]

In January 1872, an exchange of church property in Huntsville took place which, when viewed today, reveals much about what blacks had to go through to purchase property, even for their churches. Colonel George W. Grant agreed to sell the property at the corner of Avenue I and 11th Street to the African Methodist Episcopal Congregation, through James A. Baker as trustee.[58] Colonel Grant stated in the deed:

Whereas Mary Hightower from a sense of duty and a desire to furnish at her own expense a lot of ground for a church edifice for the use and benefit of the African Methodist Episcopal Church at Huntsville, Texas, has procured and induced James A. Baker to advance and pay me in gold $50.00 for the lot of ground hereinafter described. . . .[59]

The deed also said the congregation was to have the use of the property and that when Mary Hightower had repaid the purchase price, plus ten percent interest, title would be granted to the African church congregation. It was further stated that if Mary Hightower left the service of Mr. Baker while he was paying her reasonable wages or if she died before the debt had to be repaid, the congregation would be responsible for the balance of the purchase price and interest. If the debt had not been cleared in three months [sic], then Mr. Baker was authorized to sell the property at public auction to the highest bidder.[60]

The year 1872 brought progress for blacks in other areas as well. In March, for instance, Negroes were first appointed to the grand jury. This was also the year that the first train arrived in Huntsville.[61] A ceremony was held and an address given by William Walter Phelps, member of Congress from New Jersey.[62] The celebration also included a banquet and ball at the courthouse.[63] As city alderman, Joshua would have taken part in the planning of the celebration, though he would probably not have been invited to the banquet or the ball.

More importantly, he would have helped coordinate the easements for the railroads and welcomed their coming as a source of employment for city and county residents.[64] Many blacks were later able to use wages made from the railroad to purchase land. Several towns sprang up near Huntsville along the railroad's route: specifically, New Waverly, Dodge and Riverside. The construction of the railroads also attracted immigrants to the area. For example, a group of Polish Catholics settled in New Waverly.[65]

Huntsville was a busy cotton market by 1872, so it was not long before a cotton wharf was established at the railroad shipping point.[66] Also, beginning in 1870, the sawmill in Elmina (near New Waverly, just fifteen miles from Huntsville) was established, and soon employed over three hundred people.[67] Many of the Negroes would go to Elmina to work after their crops were harvested, to earn extra money to purchase land and necessities.[68]

Richard Williams was re-elected in 1872 to represent Walker, Madison and Grimes County in the Thirteenth Legislature. Because his election was contested, he was not able to take his seat until February 1873. This time he would be joined by seven other blacks in the House. Both George T. Ruby and Matthew Gaines would be returning to the Senate, so the Thirteenth Legislature would open with three fewer blacks than had the previous one.[69] Only two of Williams's colleagues from the Twelfth Legislature returned to Austin: Henry Moore from Harrison County and Richard Allen from Harris County.[70] However, Williams's own district gained another black, James H. Washington, a freeborn black from Virginia who completed his higher education at Oberlin College. Washington had moved to Navasota, Texas, in 1870, where he organized a chapter of the Union League and worked as principal of the school.[71] In this same 1872 election, Colonel George Grant was elected sheriff, which was the same as County Judge,[72] and so Joshua again had at least two close associates in important political positions.

Although they suffered a number of defeats, black delegates in the House and Senate continued their efforts for a statewide system of free public schools which would include blacks. Richard Williams, for instance, introduced a bill to establish a normal school at Harmony in Walker County, but it did not pass. For the most part, black legislators voted against bills to provide railroad subsidies, one reason being that they were forced to sit in separate coaches on railroad cars even though they paid first class fares.[73]

Another issue which continued to be of importance to black legislators was prison reform, with Richard Williams playing a lead role because the state penitentiary was located in his district. Williams introduced a resolution asking for aid to the town of Huntsville in the form of job restoration to those citizens whose jobs had been taken by prisoners. He supported his resolution by reading petitions and memorials from citizens of Walker County. One such petition asked for "relief against convicts" in and around Huntsville. Another asked for passage of a law authorizing certain apartments in the Huntsville penitentiary to be used as a common jail. When Williams introduced a bill to authorize Walker County to levy a special tax to repair the jail and the courthouse, the bill passed without difficulty. Gaines then took up the prison issue in the Senate and introduced a bill urging inspections and reports, not only on the conditions of the jail, but also on the condition of the prisoners. This bill passed and became law.[74]

Even as such progress was being made by blacks involved in the political process, such white supremist groups as the KKK continued to rally against them. Beginning about 1868, some Texas blacks were forcibly removed from their offices, as well as their homes, because of what klansmen called their "obnoxious conduct"—too much interest in politics. The number of blacks who were beaten, flogged and/or murdered for even attempting to vote may never be known.[75]

This might explain why the Union League of America was so successful in organizing chapters and registering black Republican voters. The organization probably served as another form of protection for freedmen who, by working together as a group, could look out for one another and plan strategies for safety at the polls and elsewhere.

By July of 1873, a "statewide convention of colored men" was called by Norris Wright Cuney. Cuney was a young man of twenty-seven who had already started his rise in the Republican Party. He had been born a slave on the Waller County plantation owned by his white father. He was freed before the Civil War, attended school in Pittsburgh, and later studied law on his own. After the war, he moved to Galveston, where he became head of the Loyal Union League. George T. Ruby was his mentor.[76]

Cuney called the meeting to order in Brenham to discuss the moral, commercial and political interests of the black race in the wake of their growing disillusionment with the Republican Party. Altogether, there were 156 delegates from twenty counties at the convention. Joshua was probably among these delegates, as were most of the elected and appointed blacks in Texas. James H. Washington and N. H. Haller, both from Walker County, were also there. Although the convention eventually endorsed the Republican Party, they refused to endorse the candidacy of E. J. Davis for governor, some believing that it was not the intent of the convention to do so.[77]

The elections of 1873 again changed the proportion of blacks in the Texas House and Senate. Both Ruby and Gaines were defeated as senators and the total number of black representatives decreased to six. Walker County elected one black representative, Thomas Beck, but both Richard Williams and James H. Washington were defeated.[78] Beck was a thirty-four-year-old farmer when he was elected to the Fourteenth Legislature. Huntsville farmers were probably especially pleased with Beck's election, believing that they finally had a man who could speak for their needs in Austin. In the same election, M. H. Goddin was elected Justice of the Peace, defeating Colonel Grant. Nathan Haller and Reverend George Orviss were both elected as county school directors.[79]

Joshua and other blacks would have received news by word of mouth and via their church pulpits of progress in the field of higher education for freedmen. Two colleges for Negroes were now open in the state of Texas, both

Norris Wright Cuney. In 1888, Joshua Houston and Norris Wright Cuney were both Texas delegates to the national Republican Convention, at which time Benjamin Harrison was nominated for the presidency of the United States.
Courtesy Archives Division—Texas State Library.

private. In Austin, Paul Quinn had been founded in 1872 by a small group of circuit-riding preachers of the African Methodist Episcopal Church (AME), which had been in existence since 1787 when a black Philadelphia minister named Richard Allen organized a revolt from the Methodist Church in response to its policy of segregation. Paul Quinn's stated purpose was "to train the newly emancipated Negro slaves to assume the duties and responsibilities of citizenship," and to develop clergymen. Opened in Marshall in 1873, Wiley

College was a project of the Freedmen's Aid Society of the Methodist Episcopal Church, organized after the Civil War to assist blacks attempting to gain an education. By 1869, this society had created fifty-nine elementary schools, spread over nine states, with 105 teachers and 2000 students.[80]

On 18 March 1874, railroad service was extended to the communities surrounding Huntsville. One train went from Dodge to Riverside on the Trinity River and then backed up to Dodge and turned around. Another went to Riverside and backed up to the Trinity and turned around and went to Palestine. Its passengers were then ferried across the river to Riverside, which had a large hotel where they could stay until the next train came.[81]

Joshua's blacksmith business no doubt flourished with the railroad business in Huntsville. And by this time his son Joshua, Jr., was old enough to begin his apprenticeship at his father's business. Joshua's other young son, Samuel W. Houston, was eleven years old and in all likelihood enrolled in one of the schools in Huntsville. The year 1875 brought Joshua (then fifty-three) and his wife Sylvester (aged forty-two), the birth of a daughter Minnie.[82]

The next year, 1876, was an important one politically for Joshua and his associates. Two of Joshua's close friends, General George Grant and N. H. (Nathan) Haller, were elected to positions of power within Walker County. Grant was chosen as county judge and Haller was elected county commissioner.[83] Haller had been born a slave in Charleston, South Carolina, on 8 July 1845, and moved to Walker County with his master. After Emancipation, Haller started farming. He married Miss Paralee Jordan of Huntsville and their two sons were Jackson and James. He was married again, after his first wife died, to Miss Annie Butcher, and three more sons were born: J. M., Joe, and Monroe.[84]

Joshua had also entered the race for county commissioner for Precinct One, but lost by nine votes to E. A. Harper. The vote was 269 to 260. Richard Williams was re-elected to the Texas House of Representatives by garnering 879 votes.[85] So even though Joshua lost his first race for county office, three of his close associates were elected, a fact which created a useful network and foundation for blacks' involvement in county and state politics.

One of the most significant events of 1876 for black Texans came when W. H. (William) Holland, a black legislator from Waller County, questioned the legitimacy of using federal monies for the establishment of A & M College for whites only. In connection with this, he introduced legislation "to establish an agricultural and manual school for colored youths of the state."

Nathan H. Haller. Haller was the first black elected a county commissioner in Walker County. He was elected in 1876, when Joshua lost his bid for commissioner by nine votes. He was elected again in 1878, and this time Joshua was elected to serve with him. Later, he moved to Brazoria County, Texas, and was elected to the house of representatives. Courtesy House of Representatives Printing Division, Texas Legislature, Austin, Texas.

Holland monitored every aspect of this bill and at the same time distributed hundreds of copies of it as souvenirs. When it passed, he became known as the "Father of Prairie View." Prairie View Normal and Industrial College (called at first the Agricultural and Mechanical College of Texas) would be the first public school for higher education of blacks in Texas and one of the two oldest public universities in the state.[86]

At the national level, 1876 was the year when Reconstruction came to an end, which drastically affected the lives of blacks all through the south, including Texas. When Rutherford B. Hayes was elected in 1876, he promptly made plans to withdraw federal troops, reasoning, along with the Democratic Party, that after ten years, the South should be able to rule itself without Northern interference or Negro influence.[87] Texas blacks from that point on had to fend for themselves without the protection of federal troops.

An important event signaling some progress among blacks was the 1876 meeting of the State Convention of Colored Farmers Association in Huntsville. In attendance were 150 delegates from eleven counties.[88] This meeting was important not only to farmers but also to Joshua and other black leaders in Huntsville, who would have helped with preparations for and then participated in the activities of the convention. The farmers themselves were aware of the successes blacks had experienced in the political arena, and the convention was no doubt an effort to ensure some successes of their own. One vital lesson that ex-slaves had learned during their first decade of freedom was that they had to stick together in order to accomplish anything.

But the whites had learned some of the same lessons and were working feverishly to regain control of Texas by preventing Republicans, particularly blacks, from voting or holding office. For instance, in Harrison County, which had a black population of seventy per cent, the Democrats organized a "Citizens Party." The stated purpose of the party was "that no colored voters be allowed to vote in the primary election, unless the judge had positive information that the applicant had heretofore voted the Democratic ticket."[89] In 1878, the Citizens Party in Marshall, Texas, captured Republican votes for its own candidates by using the same color ballots as the Republicans. In prior elections, the Republicans had used blue-backed ballots so that illiterate blacks would be able to identify them. The confusion about ballot color caused many in this election to unknowingly vote for the Citizens Party nominee. This party soon became known as the White Man's Party and it began to spread to other counties in Texas.[90]

In many counties the White Man's Party and other groups kept blacks from voting by the use of violence. In one place, masked men entered the polling place while the ballots were being counted and started shooting, wounding three blacks severely. In another, a coffin carrying the names of four black leaders was put on display. And in another, word went out that there would be some "dead niggers" if the polls opened. When the polls opened there, a shootout occurred—but this time the blacks shot back, wounding one man and killing another. This incident led to the lynching of three blacks.[91]

There can be little doubt that some people in Walker County also made an effort to keep blacks from voting, as this was a statewide effort on the part of the Democratic Party in 1878. The efforts were either minimal or did not pay off, however, for Joshua received enough votes to be elected as the second black county commissioner of Walker County. Joshua had continued his work in the community and was obviously determined not to let the anti-Negro sentiment discourage him from running for office. His determination to represent his people in the making of county-wide decisions paid off when the voters favored him by thirty-nine votes over his opponent R. S. Heflin. He joined ranks with Colonel George W. Grant, who remained as County Judge, and Nathan Haller. The other two commissioners elected in 1878 were T. A. Sylvester and J. A. Hill.[92]

Walker County also elected a black representative, Thomas Beck, to the state legislature in 1878. But he would be the last black to represent Walker County in Austin. After 1878, the number of blacks serving in the state legislature began a steady decline.[93]

Although black men in Texas were taking some steps backward, especially in state government, they were making some progress in other areas. For example, on 11 March 1878, eight young Negroes became the first of their race to enroll in a state-supported college in Texas. The college had been established by the Fifteenth Legislature as the Agricultural and Mechanical College of Texas for Colored Youths, in response to the bill presented by W. H. Holland. It soon became known as Prairie View Normal School, and within two years of opening it had enrolled sixty students. Many of these early students were being trained as teachers to fill the classroom needs throughout Texas.[94] Joshua Houston, Jr., was among the early enrollees in Prairie View.[95]

On another level, some blacks were beginning to organize their own fraternal organizations. John Hope Franklin wrote of this phenomenon as "another manifestation of the Negro's struggles to become socially self sufficient."[96] In Texas, the first black group of the Grand Order of Masons began its annual meetings in 1875.[97] The first black group of the Grand Order of Odd Fellows was organized in Texas sometime prior to 1879.[98] These organizations were secret societies but they had some common goals. They offered insurance against sickness and death, aided widows and orphans of deceased members and gave opportunities for social intercourse.[99] Presumably, the all-black organizations based their operations on the same goals.

At some point, Joshua was made a member of the black Grand Order of Odd Fellows, which had a chapter in Huntsville.[100] Joshua's involvement in the community was spreading from the church and school to the courthouse, and from the business world to a fraternal organization. He had been able to establish his blacksmith shop partly because of General Houston's legacy, but without his continued honesty and hard work, he could not have continued to be successful. Also, his associations with community leaders like Colonel Grant, Sanford Gibbs, John S. Besser, J. R. Smithers, Judge B. R. Randolph and Colonel L. A. Abercrombie kept him in the middle of all aspects of Huntsville and Walker County business.

Social outlets for Negroes in Huntsville were expanding. Their St. James Methodist Church had started a reading society as one of its many efforts to advance the education of church members. Records indicate that on 30 March 1878, the reading society subscribed to the *Golden Ceuser,* a publication for which they paid five dollars and twenty cents.[101] At First Baptist Church, Joshua's wife Sylvester was an active member of the Women's Missionary Society and also listed among those women who were engaged in the literary profession.[102] This probably meant that they were teachers either in the church or in the local schools.

Because the black legislators had been unsuccessful in their attempts to have state schools integrated, Sam Houston Normal Institute was established in Huntsville in 1879 with its doors opened only to white students.[103] The school was located across the street from General Houston's and Joshua's former home, the Woodlands. Joshua could not have avoided seeing the school being built, and as he watched he must have hoped that his own and other black children would one day have the opportunity to go there. On a positive note that same year, David Williams became the first black in Huntsville to take the school board examination and be granted a teacher's certificate. His first teaching assignment came on 31 October at Grants Colony at the Harmony Grove School.[104]

Williams, just eighteen years old, had come a long way since his birth as a

David Williams. Professor Williams was one of the freedmen who came out of slavery, went to school as an adult, and became a teacher. He was also an outstanding musician and helped to form the community band that played for many social occasions.
Courtesy Samuel Walker Houston Cultural Center—Huntsville, Texas.

slave in Alabama on 1 January 1861. Sometime before he was two, his family moved to the Cleveland Larkin Plantation near Raven Hill. He attended the "colored school" at St. James Methodist Church at an early age, and later recalled that his teachers had been white with the exception of Jacob Crozier, a "West Indian Negro." After his father deserted the family, David was bound out to the home of Colonel and Mrs. Besser, but he decided to run away. He walked the seventy-six miles to Houston, where he found work first as a bootblack and then in the cook's gallery of the Steamboat *Diana*. When he returned to his mother and the Huntsville cottonfields, he decided to continue his studies, probably at one of the night schools. It was his music teacher, Professor O. A. C. Todd, who encouraged him to apply for a certificate from the school board of education.[105]

Joshua and his wife Sylvester continued to be very active in the First Baptist Church. Joshua was still a deacon there, along with other eminent black men of Huntsville including Houston Rolling, Emmett Johnson, J. M. Mettawer, Madison McKinney and Jasper Sims. Sylvester continued her work with the Women's Missionary Society, along with Sarah Rolling, Mrs. M. Mettawer, Millie McKinney, Ella Gray, Jane Rolling and Jane McLeemore.[106] Joshua's children in Huntsville at this time ranged in age from four-year-old Minnie to twenty-three-year old Ellen, who had married Sam Dillard on 20 July 1874.[107] Samuel W. Houston was about fifteen years old, and Joshua, Jr., was also around that age.

By 1879, the church had a new pastor, the Reverend George B. Orviss, who according to church history "was held in high esteem by his example of his teaching by both races."[108] The Orviss and Houston families became fast friends. Reverend Orviss was remembered in later years by Champ Anderson, who grew up in the Hopewell community not far from the Orviss home. He described Orviss as between 5'6" and 5'8" with reddish, light-colored skin, sandy hair, and weight between 175–180 pounds. He had mixed, or what Anderson called "thrifty" blood, but was thought of as black.[109] Voter Registration records listed him as mulatto.[110]

Orviss had pastored a church in Navasota (Grimes County) before coming to Huntsville. He owned a farm of about 600 acres, on which he employed a number of people in growing cotton, corn, sweet potatoes and watermelons. He also had a syrup mill and grinders for corn, and he kept cows. The two-story Orviss house, located about a half mile from the post office, was the nicest house in the Hopewell community. It had been built before the

Reverend George B. Orviss. Reverend Orviss was minister of the church Joshua attended,
First Baptist Church, from 1879–1888. A wealthy landowner and farmer in the Hopewell
community, he became Joshua Houston, Jr.'s, father-in-law in 1898.
Courtesy Constance Houston Thompson and the Sam Houston Memorial Museum—
Huntsville, Texas.

Civil War with lumber planed by hand. It had square white columns at the
entrance, with large double doors. The roof was domed. There were at least
six rooms, with the girls sleeping upstairs and the boys downstairs.[111]

The Orviss and Anderson children went to school at the Hopewell Church,
which was a two-mile walk for the Andersons and a four-mile walk for the
Orvisses. Champ Anderson's description of the school gives clues as to what
the normal educational experience for black children might have been. He re-

Mary Orviss. Mary, the wife of Reverend George B. Orviss, raised seven daughters and one son in a large two-story farmhouse in the northwest part of the county in the Hopewell community.
Courtesy Constance Houston Thompson and the Sam Houston Memorial Museum—Huntsville, Texas.

lates that school was held in a small house behind the church. It had one room with a common planked desk for the teacher and benches and desks for the children. School would start at 9:00 a.m. and let out at 4:00 p.m. The penalty for lateness was a whipping, by belt for the boys, and by hand for the girls. There was a fifteen-minute recess in both the morning and the afternoon, and an hour for lunch which was eaten outside. Lunch was often cornbread, bacon and syrup. Time was allowed for chores both before and after school.[112]

Sundays at First Baptist Church must have been very special for the Orviss, Anderson and Houston families, as well as the others who attended. They would ordinarily arrive early for Sunday School dressed in their best clothes and stay until the main service ended. The Baptist hymns no doubt included some of the Negro spirituals that had grown out of slavery days when songs were composed in the cottonfields. Words like those to "Go Down Moses" would have reminded them of the days they longed to be free of the shackles of slavery. Some of the songs viewed death as the only salvation, like "Soon I Will Be Done with the Troubles of the World"; while others were happy songs like "Hallelujah." Songs like "Steal Away" had carried a message during slavery days when they wanted to communicate a planned runaway. Some of the other songs were, "I Want Jesus to Walk with Me," "We Are Climbing Jacob's Ladder," "My Lord What a Morning," "Amazing Grace" and "Great Day." [113]

The Colored Men's Convention for 1879, held in Houston, dealt with an issue that concerned all blacks—church members or not—the Landlord and Tenant Law. There was growing tension in Texas and elsewhere among landlords and tenants. One speaker at the convention complained of the high rents landowners were allowed to charge as a result of the oppressive law. The speaker went on to note that these factors restricted the Negroes' opportunity to become owners of small farms, by retaining them in the tenant system.[114]

One of the leading black landowners in Walker County was Jesse Baker. His mother, Emma, had been a slave on the Curtis plantation and his father was from a prominent Huntsville family. When the Ku Klux Klan had found out about the child, his father became afraid they would harm him or the mother, so he arranged for Emma to leave and for the boy to be raised by the Courtneys, who were friends of the family living in Huntsville. The father continued with financial support to the family and when Jesse grew up he worked long hours to establish his own family and eventually ended up owning several farms. He would buy land or squat on it and pay the taxes. He bought land for about $4 an acre and sold the timber for logs, firewood and pulp wood. He also had a number of people working for him making syrup from sugar cane, which he would sell for cash. Jesse had a number of other enterprising ways to make money. He herded wild "prairie" horses from Houston to Huntsville, broke them and sold them. He also owned a number of mules that he used in cutting timber. When the railroad came, he leased those mules for use in clearing land for the tracks.[115]

Goree Hightower was another early landowner. When his family needed money, he would slaughter a beef, cut it up, put it on a wagon, cover it with hay and carry it from house to house to sell.[116] Goree worked hard from early morning until late night in his fields. In 1976, Goree was taped talking about his life. One story in particular is revealing of how hard life was back then.

Jesse Baker. Baker was a major landowner and influential politician. Like Joshua, he became a financially successful leader in the community. Many of the students at Samuel W. Houston's school at Galilee worked on Jesse Baker's large farm, doing both field work and canning.
Courtesy Woodrow and Jessie Wilson and the Baker family.

He relates that one day he was working in the field and cut himself very badly. They took him to a nearby house where the lady packed the wound with cobwebs to stop the bleeding. By the time he got home the bleeding started again, but they were a two or three hour ride away from any doctor. Meanwhile, a friend stopped by and told them to pack the wound with flour, which they did. It saved him from bleeding to death.[117]

Along with Tom Anderson, Jesse Baker, and Goree Hightower, at least two of Joshua's close friends were accumulating land. Memphis Allen had a farm along Robinson Creek which was between five and six hundred acres. He had a number of sharecroppers working on the farm. Many of the surrounding farmers used his cotton gin. And John Tip Hightower was continuing to add to his 147-acre farm that he got through squatter's rights after the Civil War. His work as a blacksmith, supplemented with money from the sale of soft coal, earned him enough to purchase additional land.[118]

Joshua joined the ranks of the farmers when he purchased fifty-four acres of farm land in 1880 from Mrs. E. C. Smithers. The land was located just northwest of his homestead and blacksmith business.[119]

But 1880 also brought bad news for Joshua. On 1 November, he lost his bid for the office of county commissioner of Precinct One by just three votes. He received 240 votes to W. F. Cotton's 243. His friend Nathan Haller also lost the race in Precinct Two, by just four votes. Haller received 207 votes, and A. S. Wilson 211 votes.[120] Joshua and his people were used to defeat, so the natural thing to do was to begin laying the ground work for the next election in two more years.

The year 1880 was a more positive one for another of Joshua's friends and fellow members of First Baptist Church, Professor B. F. Carter. He began teaching in Walker County at the Pine Grove School. According to P. R. Thomas, historian for the First Baptist Church who was one of Carter's early students, "he came from one of the best families of Walker County, emerging from farm life boyhood he rose to the [position] of teacher of the common Public Schools of Walker County."[121] Apparently the demand for education among blacks was growing statewide, because at least three new colleges opened in Texas this same year. Bishop College in Marshall, Texas, was founded by the American Baptist Home Mission Society and became the first Baptist college for blacks in the southwest. Tillotson Collegiate and Normal Institute in Austin opened its doors to students in 1881. It was founded by the American Missionary Society, which had founded several other colleges for blacks including Hampton Institute. Another college founded that year was

Hearne Academy, named for the city in which it was located.[122] These institutions offered learning at the elementary, secondary and college levels because often they were the only educational institutions around. For the most part, their purpose was to train teachers to improve the literacy of fellow blacks. By now, Negroes formed the largest ethnic minority in Texas and had the majority population in eleven counties.[123]

By 1881, Paul Quinn College had moved to Waco.[124] An important private college for blacks opened outside the state of Texas this year, too. Tuskegee Institute was founded by Booker T. Washington.[125] Joshua would likely have heard of this, as it was a significant event in the black community of the south. To him, it meant that the dream of educating his own and other freedmen children was becoming more and more of a reality. The promise that he had made to Margaret Lea Houston, that he would use the $2000 in gold to educate his family, was being fulfilled. His son, Joshua, Jr., was about to enroll in Prairie View, and his son Samuel W. would soon be ready to choose a college.

On 2 November 1882, Joshua's preparation in the political arena paid off and he was again elected county commissioner of Precinct One. He beat two white opponents, F. O. Brown and William Switch.[126] His friend Nathan Haller, later described by Champ Anderson as a "brain man" because of his intelligence and leadership abilities,[127] won his bid for the office of Justice of the Peace in Precinct Seven. Memphis Allen was also elected county commissioner.[128] He and Joshua had known each other since they were both slaves in Walker County.[129] Allen was thirty-eight years old this year and Joshua was sixty.

Other Negroes were making progress in being able to make a good living. Joe Mettawer had been awarded the contract to build a fence and sidewalk around the jail.[130] Joshua Houston and Memphis Allen were firsthand witnesses to what was happening concerning the jail, as well as other county court business, since they were serving with County Judge J. M. Smithers.[131] On 16 December 1882 the minutes of the Commissioner's Court reflect that each commissioner present, including Joshua Houston, be paid a per diem of $3 for the meeting.[132] The court had allocated money to pay the sheriff to take prisoners from Lampasas to Huntsville and to and from other communities around the state. They considered the purchase of a fireproof vault for the courthouse. They authorized a county brand for Walker County to be placed on cattle that belonged to county residents, in addition to the owners' own brands.[133]

In spite of the growing numbers of blacks making a successful living, the fact remained that the masses of ex-slaves were still struggling to recover from a past that left them nearly helpless. Having leaders like Joshua Houston, Memphis Allen, Nathan Haller, Richard Williams, Thomas Beck, Joe Mettawer and the others at least held out a glimmer of hope that their children might have a better chance than they had. Efforts to achieve literacy for freedmen children was probably one of the foremost objectives of the black community, after filling basic needs of food, clothing and shelter.

NOTES

1. Pitre, p. 22–24.

2. Lede, *Samuel W. Houston,* p. 19.

3. Pitre, p. 24.

4. McFarland Collection, "Negroes" notebook.

5. WCGS and WCHC, p. 75.

6. McFarland Collection, "Negroes" notebook.

7. Pitre, p. 24.

8. Pitre, p. 12–24.

9. Budd, p. 37.

10. Pitre, p. 25.

11. Pitre, p. 26.

12. Pitre, p. 27.

13. Minutes of Meetings of Constitution of Radical Republican Association, 4 June 1870. J. P. Newcomb Papers, James Pearson Sr. Collection, Barker History Center, University of Texas, Box 2F109.

14. WCGS and WCHC, p. 75.

15. WCGS and WCHC, p. 150–51.

16. Elliot, p. 24.

17. County Legislative Acts Index, Walker County, Box 409, VI 413, 197 and 645. Barker History Center, University of Texas, Austin.

18. James Baker, interview with Jane Monday, July 1992, Huntsville.

19. Local Officials 1870–1873, Reel #5 Election Registers, City of Huntsville, Texas State Archives, Austin.

20. Letter to Hon. J. P. Newcomb, 17 June 1870, J. P. Newcomb Papers, 2F109.

21. Louis W. Stevenson, letter to "Friend" Newcomb, 8 September 1870. Newcomb Papers, 2F111.

22. J. M. Gibbs, letter to J. P. Newcomb, 4 December 1870, Box 2F111.

23. National League Circular, October 1870, J. P. Newcomb Papers, Box 2F111.

24. *The Texas Almanac* (Dallas: A. H. Belo Corporation, 1956), p. 115.

25. Local Officials 1870–1873, Election Registers, City of Huntsville, Reel #5, Texas State Archives.

26. William L. Richter, *Overreached on All Sides* (College Station: Texas A&M, 1971), p. 189.

27. WCGS and WCHC, p. 82.

28. McFarland Collection, "Negroes" notebook.

29. Court Martial Report to Governor E. J. Davis, 26 January 1871, Adjutant General's Reconstruction Records, Box 401–866, Texas State Archives.

30. Walker County Genealogical Society and Historical Commission, p. 139.

31. Court Martial Report to Governor E. J. Davis.

32. Special Order #18, 15 February 1871, Adjutant General Reconstruction Records, Box 401–866, Texas State Archives.

33. Special Order (not numbered), 22 February 1871, Adjutant General Reconstruction Records, Box 401–866, Texas State Archives.

34. McFarland Collection.

35. McFarland Collection. Norman Kittrell was the son of well-known physician Pleasant Kittrell, who attended Sam Houston and bought the Steamboat House after his death. Norman had been a member of Hood's Brigade during the war, and would have been a strong Confederate.

36. Members of Union League of America, letter to A. J. Hamilton, 12 June 1871, J. P. Newcomb Papers, Box F118.

37. A. J. Bennett, letter to J. P. Newcomb, 13 June 1871, Newcomb Papers, #F118.

38. A. J. Bennett, letter to J. P. Newcomb, 16 June 1871, Newcomb Papers, #F118.

39. M. H. Goddin, letter to J. P. Newcomb, 21 June 1871, Newcomb Papers, #F118.

40. Walker County Court Minutes, July 1871, p. 182.

41. Pitre, p. 94–95.

42. Pitre, 95.

43. Lede, p. 14.

44. Smallwood, p. 89.

45. Smallwood, p. 49.

46. WCGS and WCHC, p. 76.

47. James Devine Year End Report, December 1866, Freedmen's Bureau Records.

48. Wendell Baker, interview with Jane Monday, 1992, Huntsville, Texas.

49. WCGS and WCHC, p. 45.

50. WCGS and WCHC, p. 192.

51. Wilson, p. 2.

52. Cecil Williams, interview with Jane Monday, 1992, Huntsville, Texas.

53. Ibid.

54. Ibid.

55. Lizzie Atkins and Harriet Barrett, "Slave Stories," WPA Interviews, 1937.

56. Atkins and Barrett interviews.

57. Champ Anderson interview.

58. WCGS and WCHC, p. 84.

59. WCGS and WCHC, p. 85.

60. The deed says "months," but must have intended to say "years," since three years later, on 4 January 1875, James A. Baker transferred title to the Trustees of the AME Church. $15 was paid by Mary Hightower and the remainder of the $65 was paid in gold by the trustees, who included Washington Dillard.

61. Walker County Minutes, Box 4H109, Barker History Center, University of Texas.

62. Crews, p. 46; also McFarland Collection.

63. WCGS and WCHC, p. 46.

64. Cecil Williams interview; Wilson, p. 17.

65. WCGS and WCHC, p. 71, 77, 78–85.

66. McFarland Collection.

67. WCGS and WCHC, p. 72.

68. Cecil Williams interview.

69. Pitre, p. 37–41.

70. Pitre, p. 205–06.

71. Pitre, p. 39–40.

72. Local Officials 1870–1873, Reel #5 Election Registers, Walker County, Texas State Archives.

73. Pitre, p. 45.

74. Pitre, p. 46.

75. Pitre, p. 131.

76. Pitre, p. 188–89.

77. Pitre, p. 98.

78. Pitre, p. 206.

79. Walker County Election Reports, November 1873, County Courthouse, Huntsville, Texas.

80. Michael R. Heintze, *Private Black Colleges in Texas, 1865–1954* (College Station: Texas A&M Press, 1985), p. 21–25.

81. WCGS and WCHC, p. 46, 84.

82. Birth certificate of Minnie Houston, Houston, Texas.

83. WCGS and WCHC, p. 7, 9.

84. Pitre, p. 62; also J. Mason Brewer, *Negro Legislators of Texas* (Dallas: Mathis Publishing, 1935), p. 100.

85. Walker County Election Reports, November 1876, Walker County Courthouse. Huntsville, Texas.

86. Pitre, p. 67.

87. John Hope Franklin, *From Slavery to Freedom* (New York: Knopf, 1967), p. 332.

88. Rice, p. 179.

89. Pitre, p. 144.

90. Pitre, p. 149.

91. Ibid.

92. Walker County Election Reports, November 1878, Walker County Court-house, Huntsville, Texas.

93. Pitre, p. 207.

94. George Ruble Woolfolk, *History of Prairie View: A Study in Public Conscience 1878–1946* (New York: Pagent Press, 1962), p. 1.

95. Hazel Price, interviews with Jane Monday, 1992, Huntsville, Texas.

96. Franklin, p. 406.

97. Proceedings of the Eighty-First Annual Communication of the Free and Accepted Masons, Fort Worth, 1956.

98. Rice, p. 269.

99. Franklin, p. 406.

100. Information taken from his gravestone in Oakwood Cemetery in Huntsville.

101. Wilson, p. 25.

102. P. R. Thomas, p. 28.

103. Percy Howard, interview with Jane Monday, 1992.

104. Wilson, p. 17.

105. Ibid.

106. Thomas, p. 13.

107. Marriage certificate, Walker County Marriage Records, "Colored," Walker County Courthouse, Huntsville, Texas. A note on her marriage certificate, apparently written by a former owner, reads: "I hereby certify that one Ellen, now Ellen Houston, the daughter of Joshua Houston, was originally—before Emancipation Proclamation, my slave—that she was born January 15, 1856—as appears from the family [Bible] in my possession and is therefore over eighteen years of age."

108. Thomas, 13.

109. Champ Anderson, interview with Jane Monday, 1992, Hopewell, Texas.

110. Voter Registration Records, 1873–1896, Volume I, Walker County, Walker County Courthouse, Huntsville, Texas.

111. Champ Anderson interview.

112. Ibid.

113. Wendell Baker, interviews with Jane Monday, 1992, Huntsville, Texas.

114. Rice, p. 170.

115. Wendell Baker, James Baker and Jesse Baker, interviews with Jane Monday, July 1992.

116. Goree Hightower, oral history tape, 1976, Huntsville Public Library, Huntsville, Texas. This tape records some details about everyday life which are interesting.

He says that sometimes a family would buy a steak from him and not plan to eat it until the next day. They would throw it up on the roof, where it would stay cool and safe until the morning, when they would cook it for breakfast.

117. Goree Hightower interview, 1976.

118. Cecil Williams and Richard Watkins interviews.

119. Walker County Deed Records, 18 December 1880, Box Y-251, Walker County Courthouse, Huntsville, Texas.

120. Walker County Election Reports, November 1880, Walker County Courthouse, Huntsville, Texas.

121. Thomas, p. 42.

122. Heintze, p. 212.

123. Alwyn Barr, *Reconstruction to Reform* (Austin: University of Texas Press, 1971), p. 17.

124. Rice, p. 231.

125. Booker T. Washington, *Up From Slavery* (New York: A. L. Burt, 1900), p. 106.

126. Walker County Election Reports, November 1882.

127. Champ Anderson interview.

128. Walker County Election Reports, November 1882.

129. Wilson, p. 8.

130. Walker County Court Minutes, 5 November 1881, Book B, p. 51.

131. WCGS and WCHC, p. 7.

132. Commissioner's Court Minutes, 16 December 1882, Walker County Courthouse, Huntsville, Texas.

133. Walker County Court Minutes, 11 April 1883, Walker County Courthouse, Huntsville, Texas.

CHAPTER SEVEN

1881–1902

"Soon I Will Be Done with the Troubles of the World"

The year 1883 marked a major milestone for Huntsville. Joshua and thirty other Negro leaders from there made preparations to open a college. What a momentous occasion it must have been to these men, barely eighteen years out of the shackles of slavery. Bishop Ward Normal and Collegiate Institute opened its doors in September. It was housed in an eight-room, two-story brick mansion situated on fifty-four acres of land and located just northeast of Rogersville. It was located at a place on the north side of Pleasant Street between what became Highway 75 North and Old Madisonville Road, known as Smith Hill. The house was purchased from Mrs. S. R. Smith on 6 September 1883, for $5,500 to be paid partly in cash and the remaining in six notes. Joshua owned the adjoining property.[1]

In November, according to historian Mae Wynne McFarland, "the colored people [held] a 'jug breaking' in the courthouse . . . for the benefit of Bishop Ward School." The Board of Trustees was responsible for raising money for the school and for approval of the hiring of teachers. After talks by C. W. Porter, the jugs were distributed among members and donations and subscriptions were deposited in them. Prizes (a gold watch for first place and a gold chain for second) were offered for the two people with the largest contributions. Then there was a "jug breaking" ceremony chaired by Aunt Jane Ward. When the jugs were broken, the trustees counted $500. Memphis Allen matched the amount raised so he got the gold watch. The gold chain was won by Sylvia Mason.[2]

Memphis Allen had remained in the forefront of the fundraising efforts. The names of most of the thirty trustees have been lost to history, but those that remain include Alex Wynne, Will Mills, Strother Green (Joshua's former brother-in-law), John Wesley Wilson (Joshua's nephew), William Kittrell and Joshua Houston. The college was established by Elder C. W. Porter of the Methodist Episcopal Church. Porter presented plans to the blacks and convinced them that the key to upward mobility for their young people was education,[3] something Joshua already knew. Porter was made President of the Institute and R. P. Dorsey was secretary.[4] It may also have been Porter who suggested the school be named after Seth Ward, who had come south after the Civil War and become a Methodist Bishop.[5]

When a dormitory was needed, Memphis Allen and five trustees went to see Dr. J. A. Thomason, who loaned them money at ten per cent interest. Allen used his farm as collateral to secure the note.[6]

The ten faculty members included Professor C. W. Luckie from Georgia, who later went to Prairie View (and even later had a building named for him there). While he was at Bishop Ward College he taught Joshua's son Samuel and inspired him to go east to school to further his education. Other faculty members were "two Evans sisters from Georgia," Professor Johnson, Professor O. A. C. Todd (who taught music), Professor Spradling, Professor Hightower and Professor Jennings (who served as first principal). Jennings's wife was also among the faculty. Most of them had educations from Fisk University in Nashville or from Atlanta University in Georgia. There was no money for a library, so faculty members shared their own books with students.[7]

There were more than 100 students enrolled at the school. Joshua's daughter Minnie was of an age to be enrolled in the elementary courses, and his son Samuel would have been in advanced studies. C. C. Herndon was also a student, and he was destined to later become a teacher in Huntsville.[8]

The curriculum for upper elementary and high school was Latin, Greek, Math and Grammar, while that for the lower grades required the ABC's, numbers, writing and reading.[9] Almost certainly included in both were Bible study and Sunday School methods, since the school was founded by a religious order. One historian referred to some "courses in Women's Industries and theology."[10] This suggests that young women may have been encouraged to study cooking, ironing, sewing and cleaning. Other than teaching and agricultural work, these were about the only jobs women could find once they finished school.

Memphis Allen and Joshua Houston, in addition to their duties as school trustees, church leaders and county commissioners, both had their own businesses to tend to. Joshua had his blacksmith business and Allen had his farming and cotton gin.[11] In 1883, Joshua added to his land holdings by acquiring additional acreage on his farm, which gave him a total ownership of fifty-four acres.[12]

A major thrust toward establishing a network among black educators and institutions in Texas came in 1884 when the Colored Teachers State Association of Texas was formed by L. C. Anderson, Principal of Prairie View. He had risen from the rank of teacher shortly after the school opened. Among those attending the first meeting, held on the Prairie View campus in Hempstead, Texas, were E. L Blackshear, H. T. Kealing, David Abner, Jr., and I. M. Terrell, all of whom later became officers in the Association.[13]

It is likely that Joshua and/or other representatives of the Bishop Ward Normal and Collegiate Institute attended this historic meeting, as it presented a rare chance to network with black educators from around the state. Unfortunately, Joshua and the other trustees of Bishop Ward were having problems. The school was running short of funds. C. W. Porter, president of the school, traveled north to solicit aid. When he did not return on time, teachers' salaries were only partially paid. Joshua had a letter from Porter saying to "prepare Christmas turkey" for him, but still he did not show up. Memphis Allen received a letter stating that Porter would return with enough money to pay the demands, but a later letter from him claimed he could face "two court charges, wife desertion and larceny." Apparently the school never saw Porter again, and most believed that their president had absconded with all of the funds he collected.[14]

Meanwhile, educational advancement was proceeding in other parts of Texas. Guadalupe College opened in Seguin in 1884 with David Abner, Jr., serving as President. The building they used had been a Catholic school until purchased for five thousand dollars by the Negro Guadalupe Baptist Association. It was owned, directed, staffed, patronized and supported by blacks.[15]

In Walker County, Joshua and Memphis were able to influence education on the primary level in spite of their school's closing. In the commissioner's court, decisions were being made about where to draw the boundaries for the fourteen basic school districts. Several black men were appointed as trustees, presumably in those districts which included black schools. For instance, it was decided that "all territory belonging to Election Precinct No. One which lies west of the Wyser Ferry Road and the Danville Road outside of the corporate limits of Huntsville" be incorporated into School District No. One, with E. A. Harper, Columbus Kearse and N. H. Haller (a black) "appointed to hold elections in said district for trustees." The territory in Election Precinct No. One which lay "outside of the corporate limits of Huntsville, east of the Wyser Ferry Road and the Danville Road" was designated as School District No. Two. Richard Williams (a black), G. W. Grant and M. Hartnett were chosen to hold trustee elections for this district. School District Five lay "within the limits of Election Precinct No. Five," and L. A. Wynne, Alex Wynne (a black), and Albert Tucker were appointed to hold elections.[16] It is possible that Memphis and Joshua were the ones instrumental in getting so many blacks appointed to hold the school elections.

Some of the power that both men had was certainly lessened on 4 November 1884. They had both sought election as commissioner of Precinct One— but both were defeated by E. L. Parish, a white man. Apparently having two such qualified blacks running had split the black vote. Parish got 255 votes, Allen 220 and Joshua 215.[17] This marked the end of Joshua's career on the commissioners court. His direct involvement in politics had dated back to 1867 when he became a city alderman. His thirteen-year stint in public office spanned some of the most difficult times his race would ever experience after slavery ended. In spite of this defeat, Joshua continued his involvement in Republican Party politics at both the local and the national levels.[18]

Black education took a step backwards on 26 June 1885, when the trustees of Bishop Ward met at the Walker County courthouse and sold the school property back to the Smiths for $2,000.[19] There were no doubt a lot of sad faces as the trustees witnessed their dream for a local school of higher education for blacks end on the auction block. They knew that the students who had been enrolled and had not yet completed their degrees would have trouble finding another school, since they were not allowed in Sam Houston Normal Institute across town and would have to travel far to any of the other Negro colleges.

Around the rest of the state, however, some positive steps were being taken. By 1886, some of the first graduates of Meharry Medical College, an all-black college in Nashville, were setting up their medical practices in Texas. Twelve of these men met during the annual meeting of the Colored Teachers State Association of Texas in Galveston and formed the Lone Star State Medical, Dental and Pharmaceutical Society. It was the second such organization for Negroes in medicine in America.[20] One of the founding members was Dr. N. Hill Meddleton from East Texas.[21]

Another private college for Negroes opened in Texas in 1886, this one for women. The Mary Allen Seminary was located not far from Huntsville, in Crockett. Although enrollment records are unavailable, the school's proximity to Joshua's home makes it likely that some of his granddaughters went there, and his daughter Minnie and his future daughter-in-law Georgia Carolina Orviss certainly did.[22] Mary Allen was established by the Presbyterian Board of Missions for Freedom of the Presbyterian Church.[23] A leader in the establishment of this school was Reverend Samuel Fisher Tenney, who had operated a mission school for black children in the Crockett area.[24] Prominent Crockett citizens donated ten acres of land for the college.[25] Joshua's oldest son Joe might well have been one of those who contributed.

In 1887, The Texas Colored State Fair Association was formed with capital stock of $25,000 and was chartered by the state. A prime mover in this endeavor was William M. McDonald of Fort Worth, "who organized some of the ablest and most influential men of his race in his state," according to author William O. Bundy. Thousands of blacks took part in this effort.[26] Bundy described the first annual fair held in Fort Worth:

> The [black] farmers of the state sent their products. School children in all sections sent their works of art. Ladies vied with each other in the culinary as well as the sewing arts. Men and women in all parts of the state were aroused to the importance of the Fair. They saw the splendid opportunity to learn what colored people were doing and could do. Both young and old of our race and from all walks of life were greatly interested in the Fair. . . [which] opened October 15. Two days before the opening day it began to rain and continued for five days. Nevertheless, excursion trains came from all directions and Fort Worth had the largest number of colored visitors in all of its history.[27]

It is not known if Joshua or any members of his family participated in this fair, but it is quite likely that at least a few of Huntsville's black farmers and other citizens participated. The event was apparently well advertised through the churches, fraternities and other networks established by blacks at that time. The fair was opened with a lengthy and very complimentary speech by the Governor of Texas, L. S. Ross. Participating in a grand parade leading to the fair grounds, according to Bundy, "were city officials of Fort Worth, then the Texas Colored Militia, a band of music, then military companies, then many on horseback and many pedestrians, with four brass bands interspersed."[28]

Slavery had ended in Texas twenty-two years before the Fort Worth Fair was held, and although events like the celebration helped blacks to feel less isolated, they still remained in a tenuous position. Events such as statewide meetings were only brief interludes and they were only attended by those who could afford the travel. All black men and women remained under constant surveillance and knew they could be terrorized at a moment's notice, either physically or mentally. And most were still locked in the tenant farmer positions not a whole lot different from those of their slave ancestors.

On the national scene, the Colored Farmers' National Alliance and Co-operative Union came into existence in 1886, and was growing rapidly in all southern states.[29] According to historian Lawrence D. Rice, "agrarian discontent gave birth to the Farmers' Alliance movement, and [in addition] the white farmers association excluded Negroes." In Texas, the alliance came into existence on 11 December 1886 with the organization of a group in Houston County, which includes the town of Crockett. News of the organization must have been widespread, because a meeting of several county organizations was held at Weldon, Texas, on 29 December 1886, with the purpose of forming a statewide organization. The alliance was made a secret association, which appealed to many blacks.[30] Secrets were no doubt part of the survival arsenal gathered among ex-slaves to help protect them from being victims. Such atrocities as lynchings were still being recorded throughout the state, especially in the so-called black belt counties with large numbers of Negro citizens, and particularly around election time as a deterrent to keep blacks from voting.[31] Unfortunately, these scare tactics were having some effect; statewide there were only two Negro legislators in the Twentieth Legislature of 1887, one from Grimes County and one from Washington county.[32]

Blacks were, however, still active in the Republican Party, where many held leadership roles. Norris Wright Cuney, for instance, had served as chairman of the Republican Party of Texas and also served as vice president of the national organization.[33] Since Joshua remained active in this party also, he was no doubt already acquainted with Cuney when, on 24 April 1888 they were both elected (along with seven other blacks) as delegates to the Republican National Convention.[34]

The national convention would have been exciting for Joshua. Benjamin Harrison was nominated for President of the United States. He had been a strong opponent of slavery, and during the Andrew Johnson administration had supported the "Radicals" who wanted harsh treatment of the defeated South. Joshua probably supported Harrison wholeheartedly. In the election, Harrison defeated Democrat Grover Cleveland by an electoral vote of 233 to 168, even though Cleveland received 100,000 more popular votes than did Harrison.[35]

On the home front, Joshua was embroiled in a turf fight with fellow black leaders over the location of a new public school. The Andrew Female College, established in Huntsville in 1853 by the Methodist Church, deeded its building to the city of Huntsville for use as "a public school for Colored children." There was a major disagreement over where to move the building. Memphis Allen, Joe Mettawer and Joshua were to make the decision. Each man wanted the building near his home. Meanwhile the board of trustees for the public schools called for a bond issue in the amount of $15,000; $3,000 to purchase the land and $12,000 for the building. But as the battle raged, the allocated money began to dwindle. It was spent for other things that the white school needed. By the time they made the decision to locate the school on 10th street near Joshua's home, business and church, the funds had dwindled to $1800.[36] C. W. Luckie eventually became principal of the new school. He had been on the faculty of Bishop Ward Normal and Collegiate Institute since it opened.[37]

Given the emphasis that Joshua placed on education, his daughter Minnie may have been among the students at the new public school for Negroes. She was fourteen years old in 1889, and was the youngest of Joshua's and Sylvester's children. Minnie had entered a vastly different world from that of her parents and even from her older brothers and sisters. She was born free, ten years after Texas slaves were emancipated, into a generation of blacks not bound under the yoke of slavery. Joshua and Sylvester were able to provide Minnie with a home with two loving parents; an education; more than adequate food, clothing and shelter; and religious and social freedom—things that would only have been dreamed about during slavery.

Joshua would have told Minnie stories about slavery and about how his own experience with General Sam Houston gave him advantages which allowed him to prosper after the war. Like any good father, he probably emphasized the importance of becoming educated. Minnie would have witnessed or heard herself, on an everyday basis, things that Joshua could only have dreamed of during his years as a slave: her father coming home from work at his *own* business or from meetings with the commissioner's court, her parents conversing with community leaders—both black and white—on an equal basis, her pastor delivering a sermon about the importance of religious and educational freedoms, her teachers being able to openly teach her to read and write. She would have attended the Juneteenth Celebrations where her father and other former Houston slaves like Prince and Albert would lead the parade dressed in their "best frocks with top hats."[38]

Minnie also would have learned a lot from her older brothers and sisters.

"Colored" public school on Tenth Street. The Huntsville "colored" school pictured above was
finally located on Tenth Street after a dispute between Memphis Allen, Joe Mettawer, and
Joshua Houston, Sr., over its location. Joshua won the argument, so it was placed in his
neighborhood in Rogersville. Students and year are unidentified.
Courtesy Mrs. Lucy Mason Willis.

For example, Samuel could easily have brought her news about his experiences and travels after he returned from school in the East. This may have sparked her own interest in becoming a teacher, a dream she realized after attending Prairie View Normal.[39]

Joshua and Sylvester were working hard to provide for their children the educations that General Houston and his wife Margaret had sought for all children of Texas. Like any parent, Joshua probably compared the lives of his children to his own life, and he had to have been pleased with the results. He had come so far from his days of picking cotton as a slave of the Lea family in Alabama. He could not have envisioned that he would rise to the position of county commissioner or business owner, or even homeowner and landowner.

In 1889, the Farmers Improvement Society, another important statewide organization for Negroes, was launched. It was founded by R. L. Smith, who would in 1897 serve as the state's last Negro legislator of the Reconstruction period.[40] This organization had similar goals to the Alliance of Colored

Farmers of Texas group which had been formed a couple of years earlier and was still growing rapidly—that is, they were concerned with improving living and farming conditions for black farmers. But the new organization was concerned with the purchase of land and homes as well as cooperative purchasing and selling of farms, supplies, and equipment.[41] Both organizations were to continue into the next century and each attracted thousands of members. One historian noted that "no other organization in Texas did as much to better the social and economic welfare of the Negro" than did the Farmers Improvement Society of Texas.[42] The Colored Alliance even published its own newspaper for a while; the *National Alliance* was published weekly in Houston beginning in 1889.[43]

The significance of black farmer organizations in Texas becomes clear when one learns from historian John Hope Franklin that "seventy-five percent of the Negroes in the United States were still residing in the former confederate states in 1800 and [were] primarily engaged in agricultural work.[44] Franklin also notes specifically the importance of the Farmers Improvement Society of Texas in his claim that by 1891, the organization had instituted "a program of benevolent activities that extended in 36 towns in Texas."[45] It is likely that one of these programs existed in Huntsville, as most programs were located in towns where there were sizeable black populations. In addition, Huntsville had hosted one of the first statewide meetings of Negro farmers.

Reverend G. B. Orviss had left his post as pastor of the First Baptist Church in 1888. A number of church members withdrew after that to organize Friendship Missionary Baptist Church with Reverend Orviss serving as its first pastor.[46] The Wilson family, including Virginia Wilson, was among these founding families. Virginia was Joshua's younger sister, born in 1846. Not much is known about her childhood in Huntsville. She married George Wilson and their family became landowners in Walker County.[47] Virginia Wilson was the first president of the Women's Missionary Society, and her son Wesley became the first president of the youth organization of the church.[48]

Although he was getting older, Joshua continued to be active in local and state activities. In 1893, he attended the Colored Teachers State Association meeting in Brenham, Texas, along with Joe Mettawer.[49] And he still had contacts in the state legislature. Nathan H. Haller had moved out of Walker County after serving as county commissioner, and was elected in 1893 to serve as state legislator representing Brazoria and Matagorda.[50]

Another form of communication among Negroes began to take on importance as more of them learned to read. Several newspapers owned by Negroes

Virginia Wilson. Joshua's sister Virginia was a founder of Friendship Baptist Church. She was the mother of the Wilsons pictured in the wedding portrait on page 184. Many of her children, like John and Caddie Wilson, became teachers, and her son Wesley became the first black chaplain of the Texas Department of Corrections.
Courtesy Woodrow and Jessie Wilson and the Baker family.

were being published in Texas. David Abner, president of Guadalupe College, was part owner of three of them. In Houston, the *Texas Freedman* began publication in 1893, edited by Emmett J. Scott, who later became personal secretary to Booker T. Washington.[51]

The year 1894 welcomed another black school of higher education. This one, Texas College, was located in Tyler. The college was founded by the Colored Methodist Episcopal Church.[52] Several descendants of Joshua were to attend this college and one, Roberta Willie Gardner (descended from his daughter Lucy), would write and publish a book of poems.[53]

Fortunately, Joshua's children and the other Negro children of Huntsville were surrounded by educators who served as role models. Dave Williams had been teaching in Walker County since he had become the first black in the city to receive a teaching certificate some fifteen years earlier. He had remained in the school started by the Freedmen's Bureau in Grants Colony, at first under the tutelage of a Quaker from Ohio, Dr. E. H. Williams.[54] Dave Williams was just a few years older than Joshua's son Samuel W. Houston, who had been in preparation himself to become a teacher, studying at such eastern schools as Howard and Atlanta Universities. Both David and Samuel were destined to serve as school principals in Huntsville. Also, both men would be influenced by some of the same teachers, notably C. W. Luckie, who taught at Bishop Ward College in Huntsville, and B. F. Carter, who taught at the Pine Grove School beginning in 1880.[55] Several of Luckie's students became teachers, including P. R. Thomas, two members of the Holomon family, and C. C. Herndon, who also became a school principal.[56]

The fact that the city of Huntsville had always been progressive in educating its citizens—an effort led by General Sam Houston, Colonel George W. Grant and others—meant that its black citizens were exposed to this educational foundation also. Even during slavery, those who grew up on plantations where their owners provided some sort of educational opportunity, were among those who became the leaders of the black community once slavery ended. Joshua and Memphis Allen were prime examples of this pattern.

Meanwhile, the churches remained a critical link in the ongoing education efforts. First Baptist Church at this time was blessed with the membership of Richard Henry Boyd, who was widely known for his efforts in religious education. Boyd had been a slave in Brenham, Texas, and had accompanied his master to his Civil War battles. Following his marriage in 1869, he decided to become a minister. With no formal education up to that time, he secured the assistance of white friends in learning to read and write. Many believe that

Boyd became the first ordained Baptist minister of his race in Texas. After his ordination he spent two years at Bishop College in Marshall, and then began organizing churches in Texas. In 1894, he brought out the first religious literature published expressly for Negro Baptist Sunday Schools, and he later established the National Baptist Publishing Board.[57] One historian for the First Baptist Church in Huntsville would later refer to Boyd as the "Grand Old Man of the church," while another wrote that his "work in religious education was so extensive that its implications are still felt more than sixty-five years after his death." The presence of a role model like Boyd would have had a positive effect on Joshua, his family, and other members of the congregation. Many other church leaders followed Boyd's example, including W. M. A. Johnson, who attended Guadalupe College and then Chicago University, specializing in Hebrew and Greek. He would later return to Texas and have a profound effect on education.[58]

First Baptist Church was also lucky enough to have many of Huntsville's leading black educators serve as their Sunday School Superintendents during its early years. The list includes O. A. C. Todd, J. M. Mettawer, David Williams and C. C. Herndon.[59] A list of the duties and responsibilities of superintendents and teachers of First Baptist church gives insights into not only religious goals, but goals for everyday living as well. It is also of interest because Joshua, as trustee, might have been involved in formulating the list.

Always be on time, rain or shine.
Don't teach a few Sundays and drop out.
Attend church as well as Sunday School.
Keep a list of your pupils. Know each personally.
Greet your pupils on Sunday morning.
Recognize them when you meet them on the streets.
Give them special correspondence.
Visit them when sick.
Watch their contribution individually.
Be always prepared on the lesson.
Always observe good order in class.
Don't present the lesson so dry.
Don't be too full of play.
Tell the parent of the children's progress.
Treat all the pupils alike.
Read your Bible regularly.[60]

Joshua's son Samuel had been brought up under these rules. He may have utilized them as he went away to college and then later in his life, when he became a teacher. With the encouragement of C. W. Luckie, Samuel left Huntsville to attend school at Atlanta University. He later went on to Howard University in Washington, D. C.[61] Joshua and Sylvester must have felt, as their son left for school, that it was fitting that he should be the one named for the General. Their dream of providing a first-class education for their children—made possible by the General's generosity in allowing Joshua to keep his wages and by Margaret's wise refusal of Joshua's own generous offer, as well as Joshua's hard work and thrift—was coming true. Following Joshua's example of establishing a supportive network of like-minded black leaders in education, religion, and politics, his son Samuel was forming friendships which would help him become a black leader with many national connections.

About this same time, Booker T. Washington took the nation by storm by making a speech that would affect Negro education for years to come. When he had arrived at Tuskegee Institute fourteen years earlier he found a white community hostile to the idea of a school for blacks. In order to conciliate the whites, Washington believed, he had to convince them that the education of blacks was in the true interest of the entire South. His plan involved student cooperation in the necessary work to build and run Tuskegee, such as constructing the buildings, producing and cooking the food and performing innumerable other tasks. The community was given assurances that the students were there to serve, and not to antagonize. As Washington saw the salutary effect which his program was having on the white South as well as on his Negro students, he became more and more certain that this was the pattern for strengthening the position of southern blacks. He became the apostle of a form of industrial education that he saw would not antagonize the South and that would, at the same time, serve to educate and maintain a place of service for Negroes in their communities.[62]

The success of his plan, according to John Hope Franklin, led to Washington's speech at the Atlanta Exposition in 1895, where he told his audience:

> In all things that are purely social we can be as separate as the five fingers, yet one as the hand in all things essential to mutual progress. . . . To those of my race who depend upon bettering their condition in a foreign land or who underestimate the importance of cultivating friendly relations with the Southern white man . . . I would say, "Cast down your bucket where you are"—cast it down in making friends in every manly way of the people

of all races by whom we are surrounded. Cast it down in agriculture, in mechanics, in commerce, in domestic service, and in the professions.[63]

Washington, of course, faced opposition to his stance on industrial and vocational education, notably from black scholars such as W. E. B. DuBois.[64] But he also became a hero among the millions of blacks who had not progressed very far during the three decades since slavery ended. Washington's philosophy became known throughout America, and there is little doubt that blacks in Walker County—including the Joshua Houston family—were aware of it.

Along with the changes going on in education, religious matters in Huntsville were also in a constant state of flux. By 1896, yet another new church was formed. Joshua, Jr., along with four other trustees of the Grand United Order of Odd Fellows of Huntsville, Texas, sold land on November 20 for $175 to the trustees of Antioch Baptist Church, including Joe Mettawer, Walter Green and Jefferson Spillers. The church was located near the northwest corner of Avenue M and Thirteenth Street, on land which later became the site of the Huntsville City Hall.[65]

That the younger Joshua was an active member of the Odd Fellows shows that he too, like his brother Samuel, had become a part of the inner network of black leaders. At this time, Joshua, Jr., was making preparations to marry Georgia Orviss, daughter of George Orviss, pastor of First Baptist Church from 1879–1888, and his wife Mary.[66] The two young people had grown up in the church together, and their families had been friends for many years. By the time of their wedding, Joshua, Jr., had built and furnished (including a piano) a beautiful Victorian home, surrounded by a picket fence, for his bride-to-be. This home, located just west of downtown Huntsville not far from his blacksmith business, indicates both the taste and status of the Joshua Houston Family. Although the fence is long gone, the house still stands on the corner of 13th and N Streets.[67]

At 3:00 on 11 October 1898, Joshua Houston, Jr., and Georgia Carolina Orviss became man and wife. The Reverend R. L. Brooks performed the ceremony.[68] The wedding portrait from this date reveals a lot about the Houston family (see p. 184). There are eighteen people in the photograph. Sitting regally in the midst of everyone is the family patriarch, Joshua Houston, Sr., holding the cane that became his trademark during his last years as a statesman.[69] Except for his stark white beard he looks much younger than his seventy-six years, and he is dressed impeccably. To Joshua's right stand the

Home that Joshua, Jr., built in 1898. In its day a lovely Victorian home revealing the taste
and economic status of Joshua Houston's family, this house still stands today on the corner of
13th and N Streets in Huntsville.
Courtesy Charles W. Monday, Jr., 1993.

bride and groom, a picture-perfect Victorian couple, she in a high-necked
dress and he in a dark suit and bow tie. One of the bride's seven sisters,
Cornelia, is in the portrait, as is her husband-to-be, Samuel W. Houston. Two
of the women are sisters of the groom, Minnie and Ellen. The rest of the group
consists of the sons and daughters of Virginia Wilson, sister of Joshua, Sr.,
except for Reverend Brooks, who is also included.[70] Joshua's wife, Sylvester, is
absent. She may already have been ill with whatever sickness caused her death
just a month after the wedding.[71]

To be sure, the wedding of Joshua Houston, Jr., and Georgia Carolina
Orviss was not a typical black wedding in Huntsville. Although no written
record of the wedding exists, one can imagine that it was quite an event,
involving many of the leaders of the community, possibly followed by a re-
ception either at the First Baptist Church or at the new home that Joshua, Jr.,
had built for his bride.

Years later, Joshua and Georgia's daughter, Constance, recalled growing
up in that house, where she lived until she was almost twenty. It was a two-

1898 wedding portrait. This formal portrait was taken on the occasion of the wedding of
Joshua Houston, Jr., and Georgia Carolina Orviss in October of 1898. Joshua Houston, Sr.,
is seated proudly in the middle of members of both the Houston and the Wilson families,
although his sister Virginia Wilson is not in the picture. L–R: back row, *Lawrence Wilson,*
John Wilson, Isreal Wilson, Wesley (C. W.) Wilson; second row, *Clarence Wilson, Joshua*
Houston, Jr., Georgia Carolina Orviss, George Wilson, unidentified woman, Samuel W.
Houston; third row (seated), *Cornelia Orviss, Cadolie Wilson, Reverend Brooks, Joshua*
Houston, Sr., Ellen Houston, Ida Wilson; front row, *Viola Wilson, Minnie Houston.*
Courtesy Constance Houston Thompson and the Sam Houston Memorial Museum—
Huntsville, Texas.

bedroom Victorian styled home. She especially remembered the piano in the
parlor. Although pianos were not the novelty at this point in time that they
had been when the first one arrived in Texas for the home of Margaret and
Sam Houston, they were nevertheless prized possessions that only a few families in Huntsville—particularly in the black community—could afford.[72]

On a statewide level, this group of upper-class blacks would have included
mostly those who were lucky enough to have received an education some-
where along the way—the businessmen, medical doctors, teachers, and (now

Joshua Houston. By the time this photograph was taken in 1898, Joshua had come a long way from his roots as a slave in Alabama. It is believed that the cane he holds in this picture was given to him by Sam Houston.
Courtesy Constance Houston Thompson and the Sam Houston Memorial Museum—Huntsville, Texas.

fewer in number than during Reconstruction) the politicians. These blacks were in the forefront, making progress for themselves, their families, and their race in spite of active opposition to their attempts to move forward.

As Joshua entered the twentieth century, he could look back with pride at the progress his people had made. Just thirty-five years before, in 1865, they had come out of slavery with few skills, no education, no money, little clothing, no roofs over their heads, and no organized social structure for support and nurturing. In this short period of time, they had established churches, schools, farms, businesses and fraternal organizations, bought land, built houses, and survived in an often hostile environment. By 1900, according to John Hope Franklin, "there were 28,560 Negro teachers and more than 1,500,000 Negro students" in the United States. There were thirty-four institutions providing college training for blacks and some 2000 black college graduates.[73]

Joshua was proud not only of his own progress but his children's. Joshua, Jr., had attended Prairie View and his wife Georgia was a teacher at Grant's Colony; Samuel W. was at school in the East; and Minnie was well on her way to becoming a teacher. In addition, his Crockett family was prospering, and many were entering the field of education. He and his wife Sylvester had established in Huntsville a comfortable and stable environment for their family. Together they contributed to the community by helping build churches, schools, and even a college.

Joshua never entirely lost touch with his roots in slavery. There is a record of his continued contact with former Houston slaves Prince and Albert,[74] and it is likely he maintained contact with others as well. Fellow ex-Houston-slave Jeff Hamilton had remained in Independence, eventually finding work as a janitor at Baylor University.[75] Eliza had stayed there also, as a cook for the Houston family long after her mistress, Margaret Lea Houston, died.[76] One of the General's first and most colorful servants, Tom Blue, lived to be at least ninety-three years old, at which time he was probably living in Harris County, where he signed an affidavit attesting that he had been with Houston during the battle of San Jacinto.[77]

As he neared the end of his life, Joshua Houston must have felt a deep sense of accomplishment. He died on 8 January 1902, at the age of eighty.[78] He was buried beside his wife Sylvester, just a few yards from the grave site of his beloved ex-master, General Sam Houston, without whose help he might not have achieved all he accomplished. His life had spanned some of the most tur-

Jeff Hamilton and Samuel Walker Houston. Jeff (left) *is the ex-slave of Sam Houston whose memoirs are recorded in* My Master. *He is shown here with Samuel W. Houston, son of the man he used to call "Uncle Joshua." This photo was probably taken at the Texas Centennial in Dallas in 1936.*
Courtesy Sam Houston Regional Library and Research Center—Liberty, Texas.

Eliza and the Williams Family. Eliza and Joshua both came to Texas in 1840 with the General and Margaret. Both slaves proved loyal to the Houston family long after slavery ended. Clockwise from Eliza, *Sam Houston Hearne, Madge W. Hearne, Franklin Williams, Marian Williams, Royston Williams, Maggie Houston Williams, and Houston Williams.*

Courtesy Madge Thornall Roberts.

bulent times ever experienced by Texans. The first half of it he experienced as a slave and the second half as a free man.

Joshua had witnessed so many historic events in Texas that in his later years he became a resource for at least one historian writing on early Texas history. A. W. Jackson, in his book *A Sure Foundation,* about pioneer African American Texans, wrote that "much of the data in the old Pennybacker history was first-hand information furnished by Joshua Houston."[79] An observer of Huntsville history and former president of the Sam Houston Normal Institute, Harry Estill, verified this when he recalled that Joshua, when he was "over seventy-five years of age" loved to "tell of his first impressions of the stalwart Texas statesman [General Sam Houston] when he came courting his young mistress, Miss [Margaret] Lea of Alabama, in 1839. There are few distinguished Texans of the period 1840 to 1860 whom Josh does not distinctly remember."[80]

Joshua had not gotten his knowledge of Texas from books; he was an eye-witness to the events he recounted. He began the eight decades of his life as a slave on the Lea plantation in Alabama. His educational foundation began with the teachings of his owner Margaret Lea. When she married Sam Houston and moved to Texas, Joshua began to witness firsthand the growing pains of Texas. He watched the General hold an infant Republic together and then manipulate the political situation there in order to acquire statehood. When the General was elected United States Senator, Joshua helped keep his household together during the thirteen years when the General was mostly absent because of traveling back and forth from and living in Washington, D. C. When the General was home, Joshua traveled the roads between major Texas cities with him, heard his rousing speeches, and slept under the stars with him. Joshua lived in many Texas communities with the Houston family, including Cedar Point, Houston, Raven Hill, Huntsville, Washington-on-the-Brazos, Independence and Austin. He met many of Texas's most powerful leaders, most of whom were friends of the General. Toward the end of Sam Houston's life, Joshua shared his sorrows and disappointments, and he remained loyal to the family even after the General told him he was free.

After the General died, Joshua began a life of his own as a free man. He was more prepared for the transition from slavery than most freedmen in Texas. He could read and write and had acquired experience in business matters while handling the General's affairs when he was away. With this background, Joshua was able to begin his journey toward statesman immediately after slavery ended in Texas on 19 June 1865. Joshua's commitment to education became one of his greatest assets. This was buoyed by the $2000 he had managed to save. He put this money to good use, supporting his family and providing a formal education for those who wanted the opportunity. This money, along with his own informal education and his contacts with Texas leaders, made him invaluable to other blacks during Reconstruction, a time when they really needed help. He was able to help them purchase land for the establishment of churches and schools, vital institutions for the survival of Texas freedmen. In Walker County, as elsewhere in Texas, the building of churches became the single most important goal of freedmen besides providing for their personal needs. "The church became the hidden passage to education and sociocultural development," according to Huntsville native and author Naomi Lede.[81]

Joshua Houston and his family were at the forefront of this passageway. Once the churches were built, schools became an integral part of their services. Joshua and others who could read and write helped those less fortunate than they were. So important was education that classes were held not just during the week, but on Sundays too. They were filled with both young and old who wanted to learn. Booker T. Washington also experienced this fervor firsthand, and described it in his autobiography, *Up From Slavery:*

> In every part of the South during the Reconstruction period, schools, both day and night, were filled to overflowing with people of all ages and conditions. . . . The idea was . . . that as soon as one secured a little education, in some unexplainable way he would be free from most hardships of the world, and, at any rate, could live without manual labor. There was a further feeling that a knowledge, however little, of the Greek and Latin languages, would make one a very superior human being, something bordering almost on the supernatural.[82]

Whatever progress was achieved by the ex-slaves had to be made, unfortunately, within an atmosphere of violence. Many of the atrocities committed freely during slavery were perpetuated during and after Reconstruction to keep blacks from voting, especially in areas of East Texas such as Walker County, where black voters either outnumbered or nearly reached the number of white voters. During the 1860s, right after the Civil War, this violence was rampant due to the lawlessness at the time. Author Merline Pitre has noted that "there was nothing subtle or hidden about the imposition of coercion as it relates to keeping blacks from voting. Violence appeared when the first black was elected and lasted until the final one left office in 1898."[83]

Joshua's journey from slave to statesman illustrates how one seemingly ordinary man can, when he decides to make his life extraordinary, make a vital difference in his world. He beat all the odds that were against his success in a society that generally regarded people of African descent as inferior. He rose from slave to freedman; then to property owner, city alderman, college trustee, and county commissioner. Joshua was in the forefront of every progressive movement for his race.

Piecing together the life of a slave, even one who attained such heights, is a slow and tedious process. But all the clues gathered about Joshua Houston, both the written and the oral, indicate that he was much more than just a trusted body servant to General Sam Houston, as most of the history books say. A detailed examination of Joshua's life in the context of his times reveals a rags to riches story not ordinarily seen in African American history of that time. In a sense, he is proof of the theory of one black writer, Dennis Kimbro, that:

Scenes from black life in Huntsville/Walker County

Unidentified Huntsville minister. Early clergymen, sometimes called exhorters, played a key role as leaders of the freedmen and their families.
Courtesy Samuel Walker Houston Cultural Center—Huntsville, Texas.

Ben Bradley. A resident of Walker County, Ben Bradley supplemented his income by selling peanuts. He is an example of what many freedmen were forced to do if they had not been taught a trade (like Joshua's blacksmithing) or been given an opportunity for an education.
Courtesy Samuel Walker Houston Cultural Center—Huntsville, Texas.

Unidentified Walker County WW I soldier. Following World War I, black soldiers returned to the United States disillusioned and angry that they could not enjoy the rights they had fought for. Interracial Commissions such as the one on which Samuel W. Houston served were formed across the South to address the problem. Courtesy Samuel Walker Houston Cultural Center—Huntsville, Texas.

Unidentified Walker County class. The early county schools taught both academic and vocational skills to the surrounding community and were the centers for both educational and social activities.
Courtesy Samuel Walker Houston Cultural Center—Huntsville, Texas.

Interior of school/church in Walker County. This rare photograph of an unidentified schoolroom/churchroom in Walker County reveals the variety of uses to which the room was put. Most churches conducted both Sunday school and regular school for young people and adults.
Courtesy Samuel Walker Houston Cultural Center—Huntsville, Texas.

Wilma Pace's class at Wesley Grove School. Wilma Pace is one of the many teachers who graduated from the Houston Institute and carried throughout Texas the educational legacy begun by Joshua. She is shown here with one of her classes from the Wesley Grove School in Walker County.
Courtesy Samuel Walker Houston Cultural Center—Huntsville, Texas.

Community Band. Music has always been an important part of the Negro heritage. Dave Williams, pictured near the center in the dark suit, was the first certified teacher and an early music instructor in the black community.
Courtesy Samuel Walker Houston Cultural Center—Huntsville, Texas.

Buggy and unidentified riders. A major social event from the early days of First Baptist Church, of which Joshua and Sylvester were members, was the annual picnic at Nelson Creek. Gentlemen rented their buggies for the event months in advance.
Courtesy Samuel Walker Houston Cultural Center—Huntsville, Texas.

Every black American can trace his or her genealogy to Africa . . . [Each] can take pride in [his] genetic roots. Why? Because [he] is the offspring of survivors. The weakest slaves, unfortunately, did not clear the middle passage. Some died aboard ship. Some threw themselves overboard and were drowned. Others died [as] soon as they reached these foreign shores. But those Africans who survived the tumultuous ordeal . . . had the courage, fortitude, and state of mind that would not let them die. They were emotionally superior—they would not give up hope in spite of the obstacles! Every black American is a genetic descendant of the toughest and best bloodlines.[84]

Joshua's life is a prime example of what Kimbro describes. He not only survived, but survived *well,* proving to himself and others that a black man could achieve anything he set his mind to. Although a devoted husband and father, he did not limit his vision or his efforts to his own family, but worked at the local, state, and national levels for the betterment of the whole black race. His descendants retain the image of him as a dignified man, of few words but of powerful influence. He utilized a calm, intellectual approach to dealing with the challenges of his time. Joshua, respected by both blacks and whites, was often able to bridge the deep chasms between the two races.

Joshua's life was woven like a fine piece of Kente, the colorful silk cloth dating back several centuries to the intricate patterns woven for royal tribe members in Ghana, West Africa. Each piece of Kente cloth became a work of art that was handed down for generations. Now his story is told with the hope that generations of Texans will savor his memory for years to come and add another hero to their repertoire.

NOTES

1. Naomi Lede, *Samuel W. Houston and His Contemporaries,* p. 15; also Mae Wynne McFarland Collection, Peabody Library, Sam Houston State University (hereinafter simply McFarland).

Much of the information for this chapter was taken from the McFarland Collection, and a special explanation about them is in order. McFarland was a historian with a degree from the University of Texas (1912) who served as State Regent of the Texas Society of the DAR and President of the Harris County Historical Society. She interviewed hundreds of people during the 1930s and copied this information into her unpaginated, hardcover notebooks, along with excerpts from newspapers, journals, and any other written sources she could find. Although she did not always record where her information came from, her notes contain, in many cases, the *only* information about people and events which have long since disappeared. The notebook of most value to us is marked "Negroes" on the front. We realize that much of the information in it is unsubstantiated, but because so little about black history in Texas has been put on paper at all, we are grateful that McFarland took the time to record so much.

Most of the information on Bishop Ward Normal and Collegiate Institute is from the "Negroes" notebook. She lists as her sources Memphis Allen, Sam Houston [son of Joshua], Noah Crawford, C. W. Wilson [Joshua's nephew], Will Williams, Dave Williams, and Hurrioms Herndon.

2. McFarland.

3. Lede, *Samuel W. Houston,* p. 15.

4. McFarland.

5. Crews, p. 42.

6. McFarland.

7. Ibid.

8. Ibid.

9. Ibid.

10. Lede, *Samuel W. Houston,* p. 15.

11. Cecil Williams, interview with Jane Monday, 1992, Huntsville, Texas.

12. Walker County Deed, 18 December 1880, Book W/63, Walker County Courthouse, Huntsville, Texas.

13. Vernon McDaniel, *History of Teachers State Association of Texas* (Washington, D.C.: National Education Association, 1977.)

14. McFarland.

15. Rice, p. 233.

16. Walker County Commissioners Court Minutes, May Term 1884, Minute Book, p. 295.

17. Walker County Election Reports, 4 November 1884.

18. In 1888 he went to the Republican National Convention as a delegate.

19. McFarland; also Lede, *Samuel W. Houston,* p. 16.

20. J. A. Chatman, *Lone Star State Medical, Dental, Pharmaceutical History,* (self-published, circa 1959), p. 335.

21. Chatman, p. 335.

22. Hazel Price, interview with Jane Monday, 1992.

23. Heintze, p. 33.

24. Lede, *Precious Memories,* p. 35.

25. Lede, *Precious Memories,* p. 36.

26. William Oliver Bundy, *The Life of William Madison McDonald, PhD* (Fort Worth: Bunker Printing, 1925), p. 83.

27. Bundy, p. 83.

28. Ibid.

29. Franklin, p. 335.

30. Rice, p. 181–2.

31. Rice, p. 120.

32. Pitre, p. 212.

33. Pitre, p. 194.

34. Pitre, p. 106; Budd, p. 93.

35. Walker County Election Returns, V. 1, 1873–1896, Walker County Courthouse, Huntsville, Texas.

36. Lede, *Samuel W. Houston,* p. 24; also Scott Johnson, interview with Jane Monday, 1992, Huntsville.

37. McFarland.

38. Ibid.

39. Constance Houston Thompson, interviews with Jane Monday and Patricia Smith Prather, 1991–1992, Houston, Texas.

40. Pitre, p. 213.

41. Rice, p. 180–82.

42. Rice, p. 181.

43. Rice, p. 183.

44. Franklin, p. 397.

45. Franklin, p. 393.

46. Wilson, p. 26.

47. Jesse Baker Wilson and Kijana Wiseman (descendants), interviews with Jane Monday and Pat Prather, 1992–93.

48. Wilson, p. 27.

49. Lede, *Samuel W. Houston,* p. 39.

50. Pitre, p. 212.

51. Emmett J. Scott, *The Red Book of Houston: A Compendium of Social, Professional, Educational and Industrial Interests of Houston's Colored Population* (Houston: Sotex Publishing, [1915]), p. 11.

52. Heintze, p. 34.

53. Roberta Willie Gardner, *Pearls (A Book of Poems)* (Jackson, Tennessee: C.M.E. Publishing House, n.d.). Book in possession of Harold Fobbs, a descendant of Lucy living in Houston, who says that Roberta was descended from Joshua.

54. Wilson, p. 17.

55. Thomas, p. 40.

56. Wilson, p. 34–40.

57. Melvin M. Sanee, Jr., *The Afro-American Texans,* (San Antonio. Institute of Texan Cultures, 1987), p. 17; also, Thomas, p. 53.

58. Thomas, p. 48–53.

59. Thomas, p. 27.

60. Thomas, p. 58.

61. Lede, *Samuel W. Houston*, p. 25.

62. Lede, *Samuel W. Houston*, p. 32–34.

63. Franklin, p. 390–93.

64. Lede, *Samuel W. Houston*, p. 33; Franklin, p. 393.

65. Crews, p. 88.

66. Lede, *Precious Memories*, p. 41.

67. The house is no longer owned by the Houston family.

68. Lede, *Precious Memories*, p. 41.

69. History Book Committee of Houston County Historical Commission, *Houston County History*, (Tulsa: Heritage Publishing, 1979), p. 416. The cane may have been given to him by the General.

70. Lovie Wilson, letter to Constance Houston, 30 August 1991, copy in possession of Patricia Smith Prather. The letter lists who is who in the photograph.

71. She is buried in Oakwood Cemetery not far from the grave site of General Houston. We have taken her death date from the headstone itself.

72. Constance Houston Thompson, interviews with Jane Monday and Patricia Smith Prather, 1991 and 1992, Houston, Texas.

73. Franklin, p. 389.

74. McFarland.

75. Hamilton/Hunt, p. 130.

76. Madge Roberts, interview with Jane Monday, 1992.

77. Court records, Harris County, Texas.

The affidavit states: "My name is Thomas Blue, my age is 93 years. I was a slave to General Sam Houston and attended him as his body servant during the war of Texas Independence, and in that capacity was with him at the battle of San Jacinto and during the campaign up to that time. A short time before the battle of San Jacinto was fought, General Houston encamped with his army on the place of Mr. Matthew Burnet on Cypress Creek about 25 miles Northwest from the present city of Houston. Being out of provisions the army seized and slaughtered for food one hundred head of hogs, then worth 9.00 per head and thirty-five head of cattle, then worth 5.00 per head. They also used for food about 1000 bushels of corn worth at that time 1.50 per bushel and consumed for fuel about 4000 rails worth at that time one dollar per hundred—all belonging to Mr. Matthew Burnet. As far as I ever heard, these articles were never paid for." It is signed with an "X".

78. Death date from tombstone in Oakwood Cemetery, Huntsville, Texas.

79. A. W. Jackson, *A Sure Foundation*, (Houston: Self-published, [1936]), p. 134. The Pennybacker history was one of the early textbooks used by school children in Texas.

80. Crews, p. 19.

81. Lede, *Samuel W. Houston,* p. 35.

82. Booker T. Washington, *Up From Slavery,* (New York: A. L. Burt Company, 1900), p. 65.

83. Pitre, p. 203.

84. Dennis Kimbro, *Think and Grow Rich: A Black Choice,* (New York: Fawcett Crest, 1991), p. 180.

CHAPTER EIGHT

The Family Legacy
1903–present

"Lift Every Voice and Sing"

Joshua's four sons and four daughters continued his educational legacy, each in his or her own way, but Samuel chose perhaps the most traditional road.

Samuel W. Houston—following the lead of his father and of his namesake, General Sam Houston—seemed destined to become an educational leader. He possessed the drive to establish a school which would become known as the "Tuskegee of Texas" and which would train yet another generation of scholars to build on the educational legacy that began long before he was born.

But Samuel's parents no doubt saw this potential early and began to prepare him as soon as he was able to decipher letters and numbers. His 1864 birth date predated Emancipation by one year.[1] His childhood was almost the exact opposite of what his father's had been, although as ex-slaves, his family faced some difficult times. Samuel would never be anyone's property. Instead, he was raised by loving parents who could afford to give him advantages the previous generation of blacks could only dream of. As a boy, he watched his father build a home of his own, one of the first of his race to do so in their Rogersville community.[2] He watched him leave home in the mornings to work across the street in his own blacksmith shop. Young Samuel could walk with his parents to a beautiful church building just a block from their home. He could learn to read and write from the direct teachings of and the examples set by both his parents. Samuel's older sister Ellen was also a teacher,[3] and he was probably the recipient of her teachings as well.

Samuel also saw his father change from his blacksmith clothes to the clothes he would wear as city alderman or county commissioner when he went to the courthouse to make decisions which would affect the lives of both blacks and whites in the community. Throughout Samuel's formative years, he was surrounded by outstanding black leaders who were friends and acquaintances of his father, men like Memphis Allen, Richard Williams, Joe Mettawer, Billy Kittrell, Joe Watkins, Tip Hightower, John Clark, Reverend Rhinehardt, C. W. Luckie, Dave Williams, Joe Spivey, Madison McKinney, Strother Green, Joe Kimball Watkins, William Baines and Alex Wynne.

He also came face-to-face with strong and achieving women like Aunt Jane Ward and Joshua's half sister, Virginia Wilson. Virginia was married to George Wilson, a farmer with considerable land holdings. She had obviously learned many of the same lessons that Joshua had, as she was just as determined that her children would become educated. So Samuel and his cousins would have heard from all sides the message that education was the key to freedom and success.

Samuel was probably entered in one of the church or community schools to supplement his home learning. Sometime during his early training, he had the opportunity to study music with Professor O. A. C. Todd, who taught at several schools and churches in Huntsville.[4] It may have been from Todd that Samuel developed the love for and skill in music that sustained him throughout his life. By the time his father and other leaders established Bishop Ward College in 1883, Samuel was nearly twenty years old. He attended that school for only a short time (it closed just one and a half years after opening)[5] before Professor C. W. Luckie persuaded him to further his studies outside of Texas,[6] which he was able to do because of his father's hard work and thrift. It was no doubt an emotional experience for both Samuel and his parents when he left Huntsville heading for greener educational pastures in eastern schools of higher learning.

While at Atlanta University he was called the "other Sam Houston"—identifying him with his father's ex-master—and also "little Sam Houston," probably due to his small stature. While there, he did not limit himself to academic pursuits, but extended his activities to include sports. One of his teammates on the baseball team was James Weldon Johnson, who would became one of America's best known black songwriters. Johnson and his brother composed the song "Lift Every Voice and Sing," which became known as the Negro National Anthem.[7] Samuel later told his family that when the Johnsons were composing this song they would get so emotional that they paced the floor and cried.[8] Among the words to the song are these: "Facing the rising sun of a new day begun, let us march on, til victory is won." This phrase became the battle cry of generations of descendants of ex-slaves.

Samuel's first job following school was in the nation's capital. Ironically, he worked as a government clerk in the Old Ford Theater building where the "great emancipator" President Abraham Lincoln had been assassinated. During his five-year tenure in Washington, D.C., he worked for the War, State and Navy Departments.[9] Given the regard with which his family held General Sam Houston's memory, Samuel is likely to have thought about his father's mentor as he lived and worked in the same city where Houston had fought legislative battles that prepared the way for the freedoms Samuel and his family now enjoyed.

When Samuel returned to Huntsville around 1900,[10] one of the first things he did was to establish a newspaper for the city's black citizens, the *Huntsville Times*. Like the white-owned papers, this one informed its readers about local, state and national events of interest to all,[11] such as the Galveston storm which killed thousands of Texas residents.[12] It would also have covered information of interest to blacks which some white newspapers would not be interested in printing, such as Booker T. Washington's establishment of the National Business League, a network for the growing numbers of black businessmen in America.

Thirty-six years old in 1900, with a fine education and high-level work experience to his credit, Samuel now turned his attention to his personal life. Specifically, he started making wedding plans. He and Cornelia Orviss had known each other for most of their lives. She was one of seven daughters of Reverend George Orviss and his wife Mary. She had been in the wedding party along with Samuel two years earlier when Joshua, Jr., had married her sister Georgia Carolina. Samuel and Cornelia became man and wife on 4 June 1901, and Reverend Walter "Watty" Watkins performed the ceremony.[13] About a year after the marriage they were blessed with a son, Harold.[14] Not long afterwards, Cornelia became pregnant again. Unfortunately, the results of this pregnancy were not so happy. She and her baby girl died in childbirth.[15] After waiting so long to start his own family, Samuel must have been devastated at the loss. He sent his young son Harold to live with his Orviss grandparents,[16] and Samuel buried himself in his work.

Samuel became a teacher in nearby Grimes County in the Red Hill community school. Subjects he taught included basic skills, vocational work and classical training, mainly in music. Samuel had an outstanding bass voice and

Cornelia and Georgia Carolina Orviss, sisters. Photo taken around 1898. These two daughters of George and Mary Orviss married the two sons of Joshua Houston. Cornelia (left) *became Samuel W. Houston's wife and Georgia Carolina* (right) *became Joshua Houston, Jr.'s, wife.*
Courtesy Constance Houston Thompson and Sam Houston Memorial Museum— Huntsville, Texas.

also played the drums. He organized a community quartet for which he arranged and wrote music.[17]

About 1906, Samuel began teaching school in the small community of Galilee, located about five miles west of Huntsville. The building at Galilee which had previously been used as a house and converted to a school was a twelve-by-fourteen foot wooden box with one door and two windows. It was so dilapidated that Samuel refused to teach there. Instead he used $4 of his own $35 a month salary to rent the Galilee Methodist Church. He taught grades four through six, and hired an assistant, Miss Mamie Arnold, to teach grades one through three.[18]

Samuel had learned a great deal from his father, particularly the ability to organize. In 1907, he decided to organize a Board of Trustees to help him establish a proper school for Galilee, in much the same way that his

Samuel W. Houston. Son of Joshua Houston, Samuel Walker Houston became an outstanding educator, helping to carry on his father's educational legacy. Courtesy Samuel Walker Houston Cultural Center—Huntsville, Texas.

father and other leaders had set up the Bishop Ward College. John Henry Randall, Milton Jones, Eastern Dickie, Bud Mills, Noble Naylor, Sterling Jones, Adam Walker, Bill Williams, Nathan O'Neals, Henderson Naylor and W. H. Appling consented to be trustees. Mrs. Melinda Williams (widow of Sanford Williams) and her heirs, conveyed one acre of land for the sum of $6.50, and thus the Sam Houston Industrial and Training School was launched.[19]

The citizens listed on a warranty deed—filed 1 December 1906 selling land to the trustees rather than the school itself—were J. M. Mettawer, Memphis Allen, J. R. Mills, E. W. Dirden, M. J. Mills, G. W. Cotton, A. S. Barnes, P. R. Cotton, Milton Jones, Eph Dickie, J. H. Randall, Sam O. Bryant and Samuel W. Houston.[20] Many of these men had been contemporaries of Joshua, and in signing this document showed they stood by his son's commitment to carrying on the educational legacy.

Money was raised for the school by a series of programs, concerts, bake sales and baseball games. In this way the trustees were able to build a four-room school, with a separate vocational shop, in the first year. By the second year of operation, the trustees voted to increase Houston's salary from $35 to $45 per month. He refused the raise, however, and requested the extra money be used to hire another teacher, as the student population had grown to eighty. New teachers were added. J. Paul Chretien was hired to teach manual training, Jack Beauchamp taught woodwork and Hope G. Harville, a graduate of Tuskegee, was hired to teach homemaking. An additional 4.5 acres was purchased to add dormitories and other facilities.[21]

Houston modeled his school on the philosophy established by General Samuel Chapman Armstrong, founder of Hampton Institute. He believed in training students to become not only educated, but also self sufficient.[22] The most famous of Armstrong's students was Booker T. Washington, who followed Armstrong's philosophy when he started Tuskegee Institute in 1881, thus helping spread this philosophy throughout many other Negro institutions of higher learning. At the time Tuskegee opened there was a major disagreement among those interested in black education. While Booker T. Washington agreed with those who thought vocational training was the way to help blacks on the road to self-sufficiency, Harvard graduate W. E. B. DuBois (convener of the Niagara movement, forerunner of the NAACP) felt that classical learning should also be included in their education.[23]

Both forms of teaching were used in the school at Galilee. The program included both theoretical and practical training. The homemaking and domestic

Houston Industrial and Training School. Joshua's son, Samuel W. Houston, founded the
Houston Industrial and Training School in 1906. It provided a strong Industrial
Department and excellent agricultural courses for both male and female students, as well as
excellent classical studies. Affiliated with Prairie View, Wiley, Tuskegee, and Hampton,
Houston Industrial and Training School was one of the few accredited black schools whose
graduates could go directly into college.
Courtesy Dr. Naomi Lede.

science program for girls, for instance, included sewing, cooking, and basic
science. The boys were taught woodwork, manual training, carpentry, basic
subjects, mathematics and the principles of problem-solving. Classical subjects
were also available, including music, humanities and nature.[24]

Houston's emphasis on the humanities meant that students in the higher
grades were required to study Kipling, Tennyson, Shakespeare and Keats.
The lower grades studied the works of Henry Ward Beecher, Hans Christian Andersen and William B. Rands.[25] Teachers at Sam Houston Industrial
and Training School would have had to work hard to overcome some of the
negative images of blacks which this literature perpetuated.

Houston received some criticism concerning his hiring practices when he
chose several teachers who had graduated from schools outside of Texas. Ap-

Hope G. Harville Houston. The second wife of Samuel W. Houston, Hope was a graduate of Tuskegee and an early teacher at the Houston Industrial and Training School. Courtesy Mrs. Hazel Houston Price and family and Samuel W. Houston, Jr., and family.

parently his reason for this was that the majority of teachers trained at Texas colleges received certificates after attending only one year of college. Houston sought teachers with full degrees and with wide experiences in order that the students' educations be as broadly-based as possible. To help achieve this goal, he and fellow teacher Hope Harville taught classes during the summers to help teachers continue their certification programs.[26]

The professional relationship between Houston and Harville soon blossomed into a personal one and on 28 April 1915, they married.[27] They moved into a house across the street from the school, where they both continued to work.[28] The Houstons contributed vegetables from their garden to supplement the students' diet, and students would help with upkeep of the house and garden.[29] One of these students in the school's later years was Mary Oliphant. Mary grew up in the Cotton Creek community where she had picked cotton with her family. Recognizing Mary's intelligence, several people encouraged her mother to send her to Galilee. Some of Mary's memories of going to school at Galilee show that even though times were better for blacks by this time, the threat of violence was always close by. For instance, she recalls that a man named Mr. Cole was accused of rape. Without benefit of a trial, he was presumed guilty and tarred, feathered, and dragged around the square in downtown Huntsville. She also remembers the Ku Klux Klan coming to her house one night and searching it.[30]

By the time Mary Oliphant arrived in Galilee, Samuel and Hope had three young children: Samuel W. Houston, Jr., born on 9 May 1916; Helen Hope, born on 25 August 1917; and Hazel Sylvester, born on 30 September 1919.[31] In her later years the youngest child, Hazel Houston Price, remembered her father as a kind, caring and intelligent man who was always studying. He especially loved drama and Shakespeare. She described him as a quiet man who spoke with "a voice of authority that came from within," with a "personality [that] made him seem larger than he was." Her earliest memories always include music as a part of their home atmosphere, and she remembers that her father's record collection included a mixture of classical and jazz recordings. He also had a "children's classics" record set that the children listened to. Hazel Price remembers using ideas and songs from this set many times during her long teaching career. Samuel read several black newspapers such as the *Houston Informer, Houston Defender* and *Pittsburgh Courier,* along with the *Houston Chronicle, Houston Post* and *New York Times.* Hazel recalls him sitting down to read in the evenings surrounded by his papers, a bag of "Fig Newtons" at his side. By morning, newspapers would be scattered everywhere. Samuel also read "cowboy books," like those of Luke Short and Max Brand. His wife Hope kept up with current events through reading such magazines as *Time, Harper's Bazaar, Good Housekeeping, McCalls* and *Ladies Home Journal,* which she would then share with the school homemaking classes. According to Hazel Price, her mother Hope also taught "social graces" to her students, including ballroom dancing—an unusual course in black schools of the time.[32]

A particularly revealing insight into Samuel's personality comes from a piece of advice that Hazel Price remembers her father repeating time and time again. He was adamant that his children always behave in a way that was opposite to what was expected of them as stereotypical Negroes. He would say: "If people thought they [Negroes] would be loud, then be quiet. If they expected them to be dirty, then be spotless with perfectly polished shoes. If they think they will try to draw attention to themselves, then do just the opposite."[33]

Herma Owens (later Johnson), who had been a playmate to the Houston children when she was young, recalls that Hope Houston was very particular about who her daughters, Hazel and Helen, could associate with. Hope approved of the Johnson family because she knew the parents and children, and "there were no boys at home then."[34]

Samuel Houston, like his father Joshua, always stayed on course and pursued his goals even when surrounded by hostility. As the school continued to expand, he launched a capital plan to raise money. In 1909, he applied for and received $300 from the Quaker Fund in Philadelphia. He also managed to get money from such private sources as the Rosenwald Fund, the Slater Fund, W. S. Gibbs, H. C. Meachum and Will Hogg of Houston. When he managed to get money from the General Education Fund of the state of Texas, the trustees turned over their assets to Walker County, and the Sam Houston Industrial and Training School changed its name to the Sam Houston Institute, and became part of the state of Texas education system.[35]

Community support for the school continued to be strong even after it became part of the state system. The men in Galilee and surrounding areas cut timber, hauled it in their wagons and sold it to help build three dormitories and two academic buildings. The school purchased additional land to expand to thirty-five acres. Houston hired a mechanic and the community responded by loading the school grounds with plows, wagons, buggies, stoves, watches, clocks and "everything imaginable for the boys to fix" according to historian Naomi Lede.[36] Constance Houston Thompson adds that "white citizens also donated equipment and money estimated at $600. Other contributions included a chair and scenery from the Henry Opera House in Huntsville."[37]

Samuel Houston had a special relationship with the opera house. He had always insisted that his family and his students see and experience as many musical programs and performances as they could. Florence Thompson, the music teacher at the school, took her students to the Henry Opera House often.[38]

Houston's niece, Constance Houston Thompson, was a student at her uncle's school during the 1910's, and remembers that "when black patrons arrived at the concerts, they had to wait and enter the Henry Opera House only on the side [entrance], and after whites entered, even if they had been assigned restricted seating." Thompson said she "deplored the scenes of whites racing up the steps from carriages driven by black men" and the fact that the blacks were relegated to seats in the "peanut gallery."[39]

The opera house had been an important part of the social circle of Huntsville dating back to the days of Joshua and his contemporaries. Those who attended the concerts were exposed to composers like Bach, Beethoven, Brahms, Schubert and Chopin. Because Huntsville was an important stopover on the road between Houston and Dallas, many famous performers would stop there and give a show.[40] Among the local performers was an outstanding black pianist known as "Blind Tom" who was able to play most of the major pieces by ear even though he had had no formal training.[41]

By 1922, enrollment at Sam Houston Industrial and Training School had grown to 400 students. Described by P. R. Thomas as "the leading school of East Texas, [which] had advanced under the leadership of the sage, Professor Houston . . . from a low[ly] hut to a low estimate of $15,000," the school was rated as the best rural black school in Texas. Unlike some of the others, this school was accredited so its graduates could enter college.[42]

Since many of the families who wanted their children educated could not afford tuition, alternate ways of payment were often arranged. Frequently, the students worked off their bills in the Houston house or garden, or at one of the dormitories or in the school kitchen. Tuition could also be paid in the form of produce from a family's farms or by donating a calf, hog, horse or chickens.[43]

A glimpse into how students were treated while at school is provided by one of its former students, Herma Owens (Johnson). She remembers an incident which particularly illustrates Houston's quiet but effective disciplinary tactics. One day he caught a couple of older boys smoking at school. As he approached them, they attempted to hide the cigarettes by putting them behind their backs. Houston pretended he had not seen them, and began an extended conversation with the boys while the cigarettes smoldered between their fingers. No words were apparently necessary for him to make his point and teach the boys a lesson.[44]

Herma also recalled that a "Challenge" assembly was held each day at the school. These always started with a Biblical or literary quote, with teachers taking turns being in charge of the programs. The assemblies also included at least two songs. Often it would be noisy before things got started, but as soon as Houston entered, a hush would fall over the room. Though he had a quiet voice and he never raised it, he "commanded complete respect from faculty and students." Occasionally he would be forced to "clap his hands together if he heard talking," or "raise his eyebrows" or point a finger at someone not being respectful.[45]

Another of Houston's students who later provided a glimpse into "The Professor's" way of doing things was Champ Anderson. He recalled running errands for Houston, sometimes going to town for him as often as ten times a week. If it was a special errand, Houston would insist that Champ wear his own clothes, (except for the derby that Houston always wore). On one of Champ's trips to town in the professor's buggy and horse, he collided with another buggy and bent a wheel. He took the wheel to Joshua Houston, Jr.'s, blacksmith shop for repair, and Champ's secret was protected. Champ remembers serving as Professor Houston's "right arm" at school, often settling fights or other disagreements in the dormitory. In addition, he also guarded the girl's dormitory at times, as no one could visit a young lady without permission.[46]

Others who remembered Professor Houston were four of the ten children of Jesse and Fanny Baker: Jesse, Nannie Lee, James, and Wendell. The senior Jesse was a large landowner who arranged for homemaking students from the Galilee school to help can beef and vegetables on his farm as part of their curriculum. Baker also employed a large number of tenant farmers and operated a large cotton and timber business. When it was cotton picking time, thirty-five to forty people, some of them students, would come to the farm and either sleep in the cotton house or in the open fields. All the Baker children would help, the girls with cooking and the boys with the picking. Breakfast would be a slice of fried salt pork, biscuits, syrup, butter, fried or scrambled eggs and rice. Lunch would be served in the fields and included peas, corn, corn bread, pork in beans, potatoes and meat. Sometimes they would have coffee,

Wagons on the Jesse Baker farm. Andrew Smithers (left) *and Kintz Curtis* (right) *are shown working on the Jesse Baker farm in Walker County. Farmers like Baker (and Joshua) used wagons to haul their produce and do other work on the farm.*
Courtesy Samuel Walker Houston Cultural Center—Huntsville, Texas.

milk, grape juice or wine made from wild grapes that grew on the farm. Night meals would include greens, peas, corn bread and meat.[47]

Baker's sons Wendell and James ("Pap") were both honor students. They remembered Samuel Houston had eyes "like a whip." One of his favorite sayings was: "Great minds discuss ideas; Average minds discuss events; Small minds discuss people." They also recalled that one of Houston's idols was Frederick Douglass, who had lived during the same time as Joshua Houston. The Professor would quote Douglass' saying that "You cannot enslave any man unless you enslave his mind." And James Baker recalled when W. E. B. DuBois visited Professor Houston in Huntsville in the late 30's and spoke to the students and community about education.[48] Booker T. Washington was another famous educator documented to have visited Samuel Houston, in 1914.[49]

In 1928, Houston appealed to the Huntsville Independent School District for consolidation. Funds were becoming difficult to obtain and the cost of the physical plant at Galilee was growing. Within two years, the Samuel W. Houston Industrial Training School became incorporated into the Huntsville Independent School District. Samuel Houston became the County Superintendent of Schools and then principal of the new high school that was later named in his honor.[50]

Thus Samuel Houston's dream, begun in the small community of Galilee in 1906, had for twenty-four years been able to provide a quality education for blacks from all over the state of Texas. It is estimated that more than 250 of his students went on to complete college degrees and later become black leaders both within and outside of the state of Texas.[51] The Samuel W. Houston High School became a visual reminder and legacy of the professor's accomplishments.

But Houston had not confined his efforts just to education during this time. True to the foundation laid by his father Joshua, he also took part in efforts to improve race relations in his native state. In 1920, he became a founding member of the Texas Commission on Interracial Cooperation. The history behind this organization begins following World War I, when two hundred thousand Negro youth returned home from fighting. Thousands of others had participated in indirect efforts to win the war. When peace was declared, these black Americans looked forward to enjoying the freedom and equality promised to all. Instead, overt racism, which had been largely overshadowed by devotion to the common cause of fighting the war, began to reassert itself. Mob violence burst out anew among whites and Negroes.[52] Ironically, this scenario was similar to the one Joshua, Sr., had faced during Reconstruction. But just as his father had done, Samuel was determined to serve as a bridge between the two races as they moved toward reconciliation.

In 1919, a small group of leaders representing businesses, churches, the YMCA and the War Work Council, met in Atlanta to address the nation's race problems. Calling themselves the Commission on Interracial Cooperation, they set up headquarters in Atlanta and began to promote the establishment of interracial committees in every state in the South. The Commission's major task, which they called "an adventure in goodwill," was long range improvement of race relations.[53]

The call for a Texas branch was made on 27 March 1920, by the President of the University of Texas, R. E. Vinson, along with L. A. Coulter, YMCA Secretary for the state of Texas, who assembled twenty white and Negro men. That summer Samuel W. Houston and Matthew W. Dogan, along with two white men, J. L. Clark and H. L. Grey, traveled around the state organizing local interracial committees. This gave Houston ongoing contact with outstanding leaders in education throughout Texas, including Vinson, Dogan (President of Wiley College), J. C. Hardy (President of Baylor), and J. L. Clark (Head of the History Department of Sam Houston State University). Financial support from the group came from such diverse places as the Houston Community Chest, the Alphin Club of Houston, Pythian Temple of Dallas, Pricilla Art Club of Dallas, Alphin Club of Ft. Worth and many churches, both black and white.[54]

The Texas Commission on Interracial Cooperation operated more than thirty years and achieved many successes during its existence. Although it dealt with other aspects of life, its major focus was education. For example, in 1935, when no Texas schools offered graduate courses to Negroes, the Commission made out-of-state aid available to pay tuition and travel for those accepted at schools outside the state. The Commission also encouraged the introduction of race relations courses in Texas colleges.[55]

The Commission's health initiatives included providing for black tuberculosis patients who had been denied medical services. In 1929, the death rate among blacks having the disease was triple that for whites, but the only place which would accept them as patients was the state penitentiary. In 1935, thanks to the Commission's work, the legislature made an appropriation of $200,000 for a tubercular hospital for Negroes. The Commission also promoted care for the blind and training for black doctors.[56]

One of the Commission's greatest challenges was in the area of criminal justice. Whenever there had been a lynching or there seemed to be the danger of one, a member of the Commission was sent to the area and responsible citizens were called upon to investigate and/or take preventative action.[57] Hazel Price, daughter of Samuel W. Houston, vividly recalls the times her father investigated lynchings. The Commission would call ahead to alert the community that someone was coming. Houston sometimes went to an area by himself, but other times Dr. J. L. Clark of Sam Houston State University accompanied him. They were an effective team because each could work separately with the black and white communities before coming together to move toward resolving the problem in a peaceful way. Hazel recalls her father telling her how he would enter a community quietly and try to reason with the parties concerned to see if he could gather facts and make his report.[58]

Another problem tackled by the Commission was that of sporadic arrests of innocent Negroes who happened to be traveling through Texas in cars. The Commission also concerned itself with equal treatment of blacks in the courts as well as in the penitentiaries.[59]

When plans were being made to celebrate Texas's one hundredth birthday in Dallas in 1936, the Commission worked for the inclusion of blacks in the celebration. J. L. Clark led this effort by having twenty key members of the Commission send telegrams to Senator George Purl, Chairman of the Senate Subcommittee considering the bill to fund the Centennial Celebration. The telegrams asked that the committee, while considering whether to include blacks in their program, hear testimony from leading Negroes such as Dr. C. T. Pinkston, Dallas; W. R. Banks, Prairie View; M. W. Dogan, Marshall; John W. Rice, Houston; and Samuel W. Houston, Huntsville. Over one hundred telegrams, sent 21 October 1934, were received by the Senator. As a result, $50,000 was appropriated for a Hall of Negro Life, and another $50,000 was appropriated for exhibits and administrative costs. So great was interest in this exhibit that Dr. George Washington Carver from Tuskegee personally set up the school's agriculture exhibit.[60] And on 19 October 1936, known officially as "Negro Education Day" at the Centennial, over 66,000 blacks visited the Hall of Negro Life building.[61]

Samuel W. Houston, as Director of Public Relations in the effort for Negro participation, traveled throughout the state prior to the Centennial, meeting with municipal authorities, editors and business leaders of both races in an effort to improve harmony and understanding between them. Houston was also a major speaker during the Centennial.[62] It was fitting that he, namesake of General Sam Houston, should be chosen to represent the accomplishments of his people and their contributions to the state of Texas during the seventy-one years since slavery had ended.

In the process of organizing their involvement in the Centennial, Samuel and other members of the Interracial Commission had also involved churches, chambers of commerce, teachers associations, labor unions, college presidents, professors, doctors, attorneys and other prominent men and women of Texas to support their cause.[63] These groups also became involved in other community efforts aimed at providing services for blacks in the community, such as building libraries, parks, and public school facilities and even encouraging the press to use a capital "N" when printing the word Negro.[64]

Even with all his hard work for the Interracial Commission, Samuel's major goal in life always lay in the area of education. Beginning in 1931, he divided his time between his duties as principal of Samuel W. Houston High School and those he had as a member of the commission. Like his father before him, he encouraged everyone around him to obtain an education.

One of his outstanding students, Scott Johnson, recalled that Professor Houston would share some of his own books with him to encourage him to read. He would also visit Scott's parents to discuss with them the importance of their son's education.[65] Houston's niece, Constance Houston Thompson, recalled that he would deny his own needs to help pay for the education of some of his outstanding students.[66]

The special relationship between Houston and Dr. Clark of Sam Houston State University in Huntsville meant that Samuel W. Houston High School received benefits unavailable to many other black high schools. For example, Houston's students were allowed use of the university's football field for their games. Students also received used uniforms from the university which they then dyed maroon to match their high school colors.[67]

Houston's daughter, Hazel Price, recalled that Huntsville was different from many Texas communities because of the university. She stated that "most of the people had respect for education," so that they admired her father because of his college degree. The references to her father as a "smart nigger" because of his college training were good-natured. Price summed up her father's work by saying, "He set a standard and the community followed."[68]

That standard had been set by Joshua Houston, and thus by those who influenced him, including General Sam Houston and his wife Margaret. Samuel had participated in many of the same activities as his father had, including serving as delegate to the Republican National Convention and involvement in state politics. However, Samuel also extended his efforts to areas unavailable to Joshua during his lifetime. He served, for example, as a member of the State Executive Committee of the Y.M.C.A.; a member of the State Advisory Committee of the Older Boy's Conference; a member of the Southern Sociological Congress; a member of the State Centennial Committee; and Chairman of the State Good Will Committee appointed by Governor Allred. While serving as the latter, he was described by a contemporary as having the "confidence of both races" and being "closer in touch and ha[ving] the ear of more distinguished white citizens of Texas than any other member of our group in the state."[69]

Among the hundreds of other students he taught were Samuel W. Houston's own four children. Only Harold, his oldest, who had been raised in California by Orviss relatives, chose not to go to college. He worked as a porter with a railroad company. His half brothers and sisters would sometimes go to Houston to see him when his trains stopped there. Houston's namesake, Samuel W. Houston, Jr., attended Houston Junior College and Wiley College, and later worked for the Oklahoma City Postal Department. His daughter Helen went to Wiley College and Talladega College, graduated

Harold Houston. Harold was born to Samuel W. Houston and his first wife Cornelia Orviss about 1902. His mother died from complications of childbirth, so Harold was raised by the Orviss family.
Courtesy Mrs. Hazel Houston Price and family and Samuel W. Houston, Jr., and family.

Samuel W. Houston, Jr., Family. Son of Samuel W. Houston and Hope Harville,
Samuel, Jr., was born in 1916. He is pictured above with his family. L–R, back row,
Samuel Houston III, Hyder Hope Houston, Willie Houston; front row, *Samuel W.*
Houston, Jr., Heavenly Houston (child), Hyder Houston.
Courtesy Mrs. Hazel Houston Price and family and Samuel W. Houston, Jr., and family.

Constance Houston Thompson and Helen Hope Houston. These two granddaughters of Joshua Houston are pictured in the garden of Constance's home in Houston, Texas. Constance (left), was the daughter of Joshua Houston, Jr., and Hope (right), was the daughter of Samuel W. Houston.
Courtesy Constance Houston Thompson and the Samuel Walker Houston Cultural Center, Huntsville, Texas.

Hazel Houston Price Family, 1970's. Hazel, granddaughter of Joshua Houston,
is an example of the many descendants who went on to become school teachers
and carry on the educational legacy. L–R, back row, Hazel Houston Price,
William Price (holding granddaughter Marina Harris); front row, grandchildren
James Harris and Angel Stephens.
Courtesy Mrs. Hazel Houston Price and family and Samuel W. Houston, Jr., and family.

from Virginia State, and then worked for the IRS and taught as a substitute teacher in New York. She was employed by IBM as a supervisor in the Data Processing Department for thirty-three years. After moving to California, she worked at the Naval Supply Center until her death. His daughter Hazel attended Prairie View and graduated from Tillotson. She taught in the Oakland (California) Unified School District and retired in Oakland after twenty-three years of service in the district's Child Development Program.[70]

Professor Houston delivered his last public speech at the commencement of the 1944 graduating class of Sam Houston High School in Huntsville. He told the graduates:

> It matters not how gifted one may be, or what genius may be manifested in his life—he can be a true leader only as he becomes the follower of Him, who said, "I am the way, the truth and the light." Regardless of the encouragement he may find in others and regardless of the opposition that may come to him, he will press forward and carry to a successful conclusion the great purpose to which he has given his life.[71]

He ended the speech with the following words:

> True humility is a necessary quality for one who would be successful in the accomplishment of a great task. Another quality that is required for one who would be a leader is courage. He is not a real leader unless his courage remains steadfast and he can move forward with his convictions whether there is a visible majority with him or not.[72]

Samuel W. Houston died on 19 November 1945, and was buried beside his father, not far from General Sam Houston's grave.[73] He had carried with distinction the baton of leadership that Joshua Houston had passed on to him. These two men, father and son, influenced educational advancement for African Americans in Texas for eighty years, beginning with their Emancipation in 1865 and ending with Samuel's death in 1945.

Unlike his half-brother Samuel, Joshua Houston, Jr., made his mark in society by following in his father's business footsteps. Born just before slavery ended, he probably lived with his mother, Mary Green, before she died when he was still quite young.[74] At that point, it is likely that he went to live with Joshua and his new wife Sylvester, where he apprenticed in the blacksmith shop. He was probably in the same school and class as Samuel, since they were about the same age.

As a young apprentice, Joshua, Jr., would have worked in the blacksmith shop located diagonally across the street from his father's house on 10th street. Young Joshua probably assisted with such things as keeping the shop filled with wood, caring for the horses, carriages and wagons, and making household tools such as pots, pans, utensils and fireplace hardware. When he was in his late teens, Prairie View College added courses in blacksmithing and young Joshua may have taken advantage of the opportunity for more formal learning in his chosen field.[75]

Joshua also followed in his father's footsteps in matters of property and marriage. The senior Joshua reportedly advised his sons not to marry until they were sure they could provide for a family. By 1898, Joshua, Jr., was ready. The bride he chose was Georgia Carolina Orviss, a school teacher and musician whom he had known since childhood. She was educated at Mary Allen Seminary in Crockett, her parents having sold produce from their 600-acre farm to pay tuition.[76] The wedding photograph supports the view that Joshua and the rest of the Houstons were able to partake of a standard of living that old Joshua, seventy-six years old in the picture, could only have dreamed of when he was his son's age.

Within one year of marriage, Joshua, Jr., and his wife welcomed their first child. The senior Joshua was present, along with several members of the Orviss family, when Constance Eloise Houston was born on 7 August 1899. The baby was described as a "beautiful redhead child with large, hazel eyes and wavy hair."[77]

A second daughter was welcomed into the Houston household in 1902, just after the death of Joshua, Sr. But this baby lived only about six months. She is buried near Joshua, Sr., and Sylvester in Oakwood Cemetery.[78] The next year another daughter, Hortense Cornelia, was born on 22 February 1903.[79]

Constance remembered a great deal about growing up in the Huntsville house with her parents and younger sister Hortense. At one time, her father located his blacksmith shop in the large yard behind the house. She recalled that people would bring their horses and wagons into the yard, tie them up and leave them until Joshua could find time for repairs. Joshua also continued to work at a blacksmith shop downtown. Constance was always good with horses and at a early age remembers that when her father finished his work, she would deliver the horses back to their owners.[80]

The two sisters' childhood days were generally filled with activities quite dissimilar from those of their parents and grandparents. There was still plenty of discrimination against their race at the turn of the century, but the Houston

*Joshua Houston, Jr. The child of Joshua Houston and Mary Green, Joshua, Jr., was born in
1860 or 1861. His mother died soon afterward, leaving him and his sister Ellen (born in
1856) behind. He became a blacksmith like his father.
Courtesy Constance Houston Thompson and Sam Houston Memorial Museum—
Huntsville, Texas.*

family had support in both the black and the white communities, so Constance and Hortense were afforded privileges others were not privy to. Their father made special efforts to provide them with comforts by getting up early in the morning to heat up the house, bringing them hot drinks in the morning while they were still in bed, and polishing their shoes during the night and placing them under their beds. Their mother, being a school teacher, began

Constance Houston. Joshua Houston, Sr., was present at the birth of Joshua, Jr.'s, first child Constance, born in 1899. This photograph was probably taken shortly after he died in 1902. Courtesy Constance Houston Thompson and Sam Houston Memorial Museum— Huntsville, Texas.

Teacher training class. This picture shows the 1924 teacher training class at Prairie View
Normal School. Georgia Carolina Houston (third from the left on the front row) attended
the Trades and Industries training class during the summer of 1924.
Courtesy Constance Houston Thompson and Sam Houston Memorial Museum—
Huntsville, Texas.

schooling them at home when they reached the age of two. When Georgia Houston returned to formal teaching while her children were still small, she would put them in her buggy every morning as she drove the three miles to the large, two-story school at Grants Colony. Thus the girls were exposed to education both in their own home and in a school atmosphere at a early age. During the summers, the Houston girls would wave goodbye to their mother as she left to attend certification classes at Prairie View.[81]

Constance remembers that her mother's educational teachings included lessons in survival as well. Georgia Houston taught her two daughters to design and sew their own clothing, as well as giving them piano lessons. She had a habit of writing down verses and sayings for her daughters. To Constance she quoted the words of A. Mackenzie: "If we look down, then our shoulders stoop. . . . It is only when our thoughts go up that our lives become upright." For Hortense she wrote, "Success comes only to those who set for themselves a goal and, by continued work, study and perseverance in that direction, reach it."[82]

Constance enrolled in her Uncle Samuel's school in Galilee when it opened in 1906. Her sister Hortense continued to go to the Grants Colony school with her mother. Rather than going back and forth each day, Constance would often stay out at the school with her uncle Samuel and her aunt Mary Orviss, who was school matron. When Constance got older, her father would often "mail her a horse" on Friday afternoons. Joshua would tie a horse to the back of the mailman's buggy, and it would be delivered with the mail for the school. She would then ride the horse back to town to spend the weekend with her parents and sister. When her sister got old enough to join her at Galilee, Constance recalled, they would take their buggy to school. Whenever they would stay late for evening programs, she and her sister would get in the buggy heading toward Huntsville. Often they would fall asleep on the way home and the horse would take them right up to their house, paw the ground, and their father would come lift them out of the buggy and carry them to bed.[83]

The children of Joshua Houston, Jr., continued the family tradition of participating in both social and cultural activities centered around First Baptist Church, which Joshua, Sr., and his wife Sylvester had begun. They were encouraged to take part in such youth activities as the "Starlight Leaders" (composed of young people who had achieved in the literary profession), Sunday School activities, and the Baptist Young People's Union (BYPU).[84]

They were taught many lessons at church which influenced the way they lived their lives. Constance, for instance, remembered when a highly respected founding member, Mrs. Sarah "Mother" Rolling, suffered a leg injury. Her father suggested that Constance help take care of her. So she stayed with her, cleaned her house and ran errands. She would take food from her house that their cook had prepared for the family and share with Mother Rolling. If her father was too busy to take her, Constance would walk to Mother Rolling's house and encourage her to eat, change the bed linens, help her bathe and get her to bed. In appreciation for her efforts, Mother Rolling willed her house to Constance. Since she was still a minor, Joshua, Jr., was given legal right to the house.[85]

The girls' own home became a place of refuge, where they could surround themselves with beauty in a world not ready to give it to members of the Negro race. Constance recalled that her mother taught her "a taste and way of life" that included the best of music and books. Because most public facilities were unavailable to them as they got older, more and more of the girls' social events took place in private homes. Constance recalled having parties in their home for which they would spend days designing invitations and making plans.[86]

She also remembered box suppers, picnics and revivals at church and elsewhere where both boys and girls would participate.[87] But once out of the safety of their homes and churches, young blacks in Huntsville, including Constance and Hortense, still had to be careful. Constance remembered that the young men attending Sam Houston State Teachers College would sometimes "tease" her: "I would be riding my horse and they would catch the bridle and hold it." But these boys would be told by other whites to leave the horse alone because "That's Joshua's girl." The Houston girls were always welcome, however, in the Huntsville stores, where they had charge accounts because of their father's position.[88]

But Constance's most vivid memories always included the importance her family placed on education. During an interview with Naomi Lede, she stated:

As children we were taught to model ourselves after our parents and other members of the family or successful people such as Booker T. Washington, R. R. Moton and my Uncle, Professor Samuel W. Houston, who was considered to be one of the national Black leaders. Because of his national status, we met a lot of important people because of their association with Uncle Sam. I remember to this day how excited I was to meet and talk with Emmett J. Scott, Dr. R. H. Boyd, and Professor C. W. Luckie. Within our home, there was the constant flow of educational materials and living personalities. This exposure opened our eyes to a larger world that demanded skills and creative talent. We were introduced to achievers like Marian Anderson, the great opera singer, and James Weldon and Rosamond Johnson, great composers and songwriters. There were Dr. R. Nathaniel Dett, who directed the choir at Hampton Institute and Carter G. Woodson, the great historian. . . . We were given books as gifts for birthdays and holidays. Like most children, we were socialized to play specific roles . . . I appreciated the works of the great masters of music (Bach, Beethoven, Puccini, Rachmaninoff, Nathaniel Dett and William Dawson). All of us were fond of music. Before radio and television, we had to make our own music and other forms of entertainment. All of us were musically inclined. Even Uncle Sam played an instrument and was a member of the Hampton Institute, Virginia choir.[89]

Constance and Hortense were not completely sheltered from the reality of their world, however. They, like their parents and grandparents, were constantly exposed to the effects of prejudice and racism. This did not diminish much as they got older. After Constance married, whenever she and her husband would drive from Houston to Huntsville, they would have to go through Conroe, which was known for its extreme racial prejudice. He would put on a chauffeur's hat and drive, and she would take her place in the back of the car.[90]

As children, Constance and Hortense were warned "to stay close to home, because the Ku Klux Klan members were hanging people."[91] In 1918, that possibility became a reality: a black man in Huntsville was lynched.[92] Ironically, Constance Houston was visiting the prison when a prisoner was taken out and hanged.[93]

In 1918, out of fear for the safety of his family, Joshua, Jr., began making plans to move to Houston. Constance remembered: "We loaded all our household belongings including the family cow in a railroad boxcar and boarded the train for Houston." Joshua continued his blacksmithing when he moved, first working with a white man in Bellaire to get himself established.[94] He had been approached to become an instructor in the blacksmith shop at Prairie View, but turned down the offer.[95] He arrived ahead of his wife and daughters, who stayed for a while in Huntsville with their Uncle Sam in the house that their grandfather Joshua had built in Rogersville right after Emancipation.[96]

Joshua, Jr., purchased a home on Bayou Street in Houston just north of Buffalo Bayou in a community known as "Fifth Ward." He soon established a blacksmith shop with another black man on Lyons Avenue, the main thoroughfare of Fifth Ward, not far from his new home. Later he would locate the shop right behind his house.[97]

The Houston home at 1303 Bayou Street became the setting for many social gatherings, beginning about the time Constance and Hortense were in their teens. Constance recalled that at parties they would often gather around the piano and sing together. The piano was one of the wedding gifts Joshua, Jr., had presented his young wife Georgia when they married in 1898.

Joshua and Georgia remained hard workers, he as a businessman and she as a teacher at nearby Crawford Elementary School and later at Atherton Elementary. They continued to encourage their daughters to become educated,

*The Houston Place. Located on 1303 Bayou in Houston, Texas, this is the home that Joshua
Houston, Jr.'s family lived in beginning about 1918. It became the setting for many social
gatherings for blacks in Houston. Guest books noting all its visitors form a "who's who" of
famous black entertainers, educators, doctors, clergy, and businessmen.*
Courtesy Brenda Smith Long.

and provided for both of them to attend college in the 1920s when most
women were not even finishing high school. Constance attended Hampton,
Prairie View and Columbia University, while Hortense was educated at Fisk
University.[98]

Hortense was the first to marry. Her husband was Dr. C. Milton Young, a
surgeon. They made their home in Louisville, Kentucky. Hortense became a
well-known civic leader, businesswoman and columnist, writing "Tense Topics" for the *Louisville Defender* newspaper. Their son, C. Milton Young III,
following his father's footsteps, is a surgeon. Their daughter Yvonne Young
Clark teaches in the Engineering Department at Tennessee State University.[99]

Constance married Tracy Thompson in an elegant wedding in Houston's
historic Antioch Church in 1928. Their wedding, like Constance's parents'
wedding thirty years before, was among the most fashionable in the community. The bridesmaids' dresses were made of lavender chiffon ordered from
New York and each of their hats was made by Constance's friend who owned

*Constance Houston's Wedding Photo. Joshua's granddaughter Constance was a stylish young
woman who taught in the Houston public schools for many years. Her wedding in 1928 was
an elegant affair. On the left of the bride is her husband, Tracy Thompson, and on the right
is her uncle, Samuel W. Houston, who gave her away due to the death of her father,
Joshua, Jr., shortly before. Photo taken at the Houston Place.
Courtesy Houston Metropolitan Research Center, Houston Public Library.*

Ann's Hat Shoppe, a black-owned business in downtown Houston. The wedding of Constance, a teacher, and Tracy, a maître d' at Houston's number one
private club, set the stage for over 400 weddings and receptions that they
would host at their elegant home over many years. And, in fact, the home on
Bayou Street soon became known as the "Houston Place" because of all the
weddings, elegant parties, luncheons and other social activities hosted there
during the years of segregation when blacks could not sponsor events at hotels
and other public places.[100]

Joshua, Jr., was not to witness Constance's wedding because he died just
months before the event, so her uncle Samuel gave her away. Joshua's wife
Georgia continued both her teaching and her involvement in civic affairs. She
also continued to open her elegant home to travelers. Visitors included clergy,

Georgia Carolina (Orviss) Houston. The wife of Joshua Houston, Jr., and mother of Constance and Hortense, Georgia Houston opened her home on Bayou Street for weddings, parties, luncheons, and other social activities during the years when blacks were not allowed in most public places.

Courtesy Constance Houston Thompson and Sam Houston Memorial Museum— Huntsville, Texas.

educators, sports teams and others. Although they were charged a fee, they were made to feel at home and meals were served them.[101] Such arrangements are now known as "Bed and Breakfast Inns," but during the days of segregation, private homes were often the only places available to Negro travelers.

Constance and her mother kept guest books noting all the visitors to the "Houston Place." These books form a "Who's Who" of locally and nationally known Negro high society of the time. Among the notables are Matthew W. Dogan, who was President of Wiley College in Marshall, Texas, for nearly 50 years; entertainers such as Ethel Waters, Lionel Hampton and the Mills Brothers; and principals of high schools, medical doctors, business owners and clergy.[102]

Although Samuel W. Houston and Joshua Houston, Jr., seem to have been the two children to follow most closely their father's educational legacy, Joshua, Sr.'s, other children also led successful lives. Because they lived a lower-profile existence, however, less has been written about them and their lives are more difficult to document.

Joshua, Sr.'s, first born son, Joe Houston, lived to be over a hundred years old. His mother was Anneliza,[103] who is believed to have come from Alabama as a slave.[104] She and Joshua became Joe's parents at an early age, but as slaves, they were not permitted to marry. According to laws of the time, children belonged to the families that owned the slave mothers. So it is likely that Joe grew up with his mother, probably on a plantation. Given the care Joshua showed for his other children, he probably traveled to see Joe and Anneliza whenever he could.

Joe Houston was a grown man by the time slavery ended, and had not had the benefits of an education. Soon after Emancipation he began acquiring property in a community near Crockett known as Hall's Bluff, probably with his father's help.[105] He eventually acquired over 200 acres of land.[106] On the 1880 census, he is listed as a farmer and a widower. His children are listed as a daughter (Paralee), age eight, and two sons—Andrew, age seven, and Joe, age four.[107] The elder Joe's first wife's name was Caroline Todd, and he later married her sister Mariah Todd, with whom he did not have children.[108]

Joe was considered well-to-do among blacks in Crockett because of the amount of land he owned. According to several of his descendants, he was frugal with his money and did not believe in lending or borrowing.[109] He has been described as a very dark man.[110]

The home in which he was living when he died in 1938 still stands, although

Joe Houston's House. Joshua's oldest son built this home in the Hall's Bluff community near Crockett, Texas, in the late 1800's. After he died, it was used for several years as a community center. It is still standing today.
Courtesy Chester Hines.

it is empty. It is not known exactly when the house was built, but it is said to be over 100 years old. One of Joe's granddaughters, Minnie Houston Woodall, recalled that this "Big House," as it was called by the family, was used for a while as a Community Center after Joe Houston died.[111]

During his farming days, Joe had both a syrup mill and grist mill operation. He and his second wife Mariah were active in the Union Chapel Methodist church located not far from their home in the Hall's Bluff community.[112] Mariah preceded Joe in death and she, along with her sister and many other members of her family, are buried in Campbell's Cemetery in Hall's Bluff. Also buried there is Joe's mother, Anneliza Halyard, and her husband Wharton.[113]

One of Joe's sons, Andrew, learned and practiced the trade of concrete and cement finisher and utilized his trade as a means to support his family. At the time, highway and bridge construction were big business, and Andrew was involved in this. It is believed that Joe, Jr., went to New York when he left Crockett.[114] Joe's oldest child, Paralee, married a Mr. Warfield.[115]

In addition to their son Joe, Joshua and Anneliza had two daughters who also were born during slavery and therefore remained with their mother. Julie Houston married Coleman Wagner in 1865, the year of Emancipation in Texas. The marriage took place in St. Daniel Baptist Church in Crockett, where the young people had both been members. Before her marriage, Julie had lived with her mother on land which, according to her descendants, belonged to Joshua, Sr. Her husband either purchased that land or they inherited it after Joshua's death, and the couple lived in the same house her mother had lived in. The house was described by one of her descendants as a "neat, clean house with a beautiful yard filled with flowers. Crepe myrtles still grace the premises and are attributed to Julie herself." [116]

The couple reared nine children: Walter, Herbert, Joe, Tom, John, Sarah, Alice, Mariah and Lucy. Their daughter Sarah entered the teaching profession and their son John married a teacher who had attended nearby Mary Allen College located in Crockett. Julie Houston Wagner died in 1918 and is buried in the same cemetery as her brother Joe and her mother Anneliza. [117]

Joshua and Anneliza's other daughter, Lucy, was born in 1840. [118] She is remembered by her descendants (who refer to her as "Aunt Lucy") as a strong-willed woman, and her photograph seems to bear this out. Lucy married Willis Gardner, a carpenter, and they lived near Crockett and had ten children: Bettye, Henry, William, Anna Lisa, Rachel, Dora, Jesse, Aaron, Andrew and Julia. Two of their daughters, Rachel and Julia, became school teachers. Their son William became a gospel preacher, and another son Henry owned eighty acres of land in Hall's Bluff. [119] Lucy's descendants (one of whom is Tony Sherman, Houston artist), report that after Willis's death she married a man whose last name was Brooks and they moved to Lovelady, Texas. Lucy died around 1916. [120]

Joshua also had a daughter by Mary Green, the mother of Joshua, Jr. Ellen Houston was born a slave around 1856. [121] What education Ellen received as a child was at home, since there were no schools—not even church schools—available to her before Emancipation. When First Baptist Church was founded in 1869, Ellen became one of the first members along with her father. She also became one of the first church Sunday School teachers. [122]

It is not known if Ellen ever lived with Joshua. Most of what is known about her came from the memory of her niece, Constance Houston Thompson, who recalled that in the 1920s, her aunt lived in "Fourth Ward," a community of

Julie Houston. In a letter dated May 24, 1848, Margaret Houston wrote from Huntsville: "Joshua and Anne have a baby girl." The authors believe that baby girl was Julie, who is pictured above, and who later lived in Crockett.
Courtesy Ruby Sims, descendant of Joshua through Julie Houston.

Lucy Houston. This is an artist's copy (made in 1983) of the original picture, which was unavailable for reproduction. Lucy was Joshua's oldest daughter, born to Anneliza around 1840. Lucy and her brother Joe lived with their mother, who eventually settled in Crockett, Texas.
Courtesy Tony Sherman, Houston artist and descendant of Joshua through Lucy Houston.

African Americans located just west of downtown Houston. Thompson recalled that when she was about nine years old she came to Houston from Huntsville to visit her Aunt Ellen while her parents traveled. "Aunt Ellen owned a croquet garden in the Fourth Ward and she charged a fee. The garden was beautiful and had landscaped arches of greenery. The garden was located near the home of Thelma Patten Law, who was Houston's first Negro woman pediatrician and a native of Huntsville." [123]

Ellen Houston married twice, first to Sam Dillard and then to Ed Spears. She had three children—one daughter and two sons. One son, called "Monkey Tom," lived in Houston at 1900 Grove Street and was older than Constance, who especially remembered that he once gave her a $20 gold piece.[124] Land records reveal that one of Ellen's sons was named Joshua Dillard and the other was Sam Dillard.[125] Constance Thompson believed that the daughter's name was Minnie, and that she raised horses in Houston when she got older.[126]

Ellen acquired property in both Huntsville and Houston.[127] One of her prized possessions, according to an old, undated newspaper article, was a chest owned by General Sam Houston made of white cedar. The article noted that Joshua, Sr., had told Ellen that General Houston used the chest during his trips to Washington from Texas during the years he served as United States Senator.[128]

Ellen may also have lived in both Chicago and New York in her later years. Her niece Hazel Price recalled that she visited her Aunt Ellen in Chicago after Hazel's mother Hope died.[129] The last Constance Thompson heard of her Aunt Ellen, she was living in New York.[130]

The child of Joshua Houston who perhaps enjoyed the most freedom was Minnie Houston, whose mother was Sylvester. She was born on 5 December 1875, ten years after slavery ended.[131] Joshua was well established in the Rogersville community by then. Both Minnie's parents and her brother Samuel, who lived at home when she was small, were education-oriented, so there is little doubt that her own education started at home while she was very young. It would have been augmented by Sunday School lessons at First Baptist Church, taught by her older half sister, Ellen.[132]

Minnie would have started school around age six. St. James Methodist Church school was open at that time, and is likely where she went.[133] By that time, the Freedmen's Bureau schools had ceased to exist and the only options for ex-slaves were church schools, which had to charge tuition to cover costs. When Bishop Ward Normal and Collegiate Institute opened in 1883 with Joshua as one of the trustees, Minnie was probably enrolled in the school's elementary classes. After that, she entered Prairie View Normal Institute to make preparations for a teaching career.[134] At the time Minnie enrolled, Prairie View was training nearly all of the Negro teachers in the state, and its graduates were much sought after by the growing number of Negro schools throughout Texas.[135] Minnie had several choices of travel to Prairie View. L. C. Anderson, founder and first president of the Colored Teachers State

Association of Texas, was principal of Prairie View at this time.[136] According to her niece Constance Thompson, Minnie returned to Huntsville to teach under principal Dave Williams, where Constance's mother also taught.[137]

As a teacher, Minnie would have been able to share with her students some of her dad's stories about General Sam Houston. By the time she began teaching, her father was over seventy years old and her mother around sixty. They would probably not have had to remind her about her good fortune in being born after the end of slavery. By comparing her own life with that of her students and other black children in Huntsville, Minnie would have known that her own life was the exception rather than the rule for children of ex-slaves.

Minnie left Huntsville in the early 1900s. At some point, she married Ben Dillard, who worked for the railroad, and they lived on Oats Street in Fifth Ward in Houston, within walking distance of Southern Pacific Railroad operations. For some reason, Minnie apparently never taught school in Houston. Constance Thompson recalled that she worked at the Rosonian Hotel and as a nanny, tutoring white children. Minnie never had children of her own. She died in the early 1940s and is buried in Huntsville.[138]

Joshua and Sylvester were parents of one more child, a son named Thomas, who died in his twenties. Nothing else is known about him. He is buried next to them, and his partially destroyed marker reads:

Thomas, s/o J and S Houston, aged 22 years, 20 Jan 1888.[139]

The educational legacy established by Joshua Houston for his children helped each of them to attain greater heights than most children of ex-slaves. His promise to Margaret that he would educate his children was indeed fulfilled. Many of his family went on to become school teachers and educators, and through them generations of black children were educated. They made a difference in African American history not only in Texas, but across the United States. The $2000 in gold was indeed a "golden" legacy which reaped rich rewards.

NOTES

1. Samuel W. Houston gravestone, Oakwood Cemetery, Huntsville, Texas.
2. Lede, *Samuel W. Houston,* p. 22.
3. Lede, *Samuel W. Houston,* p. 11.

4. P. R. Thomas, p. 35.

5. McFarland.

6. Lede, *Precious Memories,* p. 36.

7. Lede, *Samuel W. Houston,* p. 26.

8. Constance Houston Thompson interview, 1992.

9. Lede, *Samuel W. Houston,* p. 25.

10. Estimation of when he returned is based on the fact that he got married in Texas in 1901.

11. Lede, *Samuel W. Houston,* p. 25; also McFarland.

12. At the time of the storm, Aunt Jane Ward's granddaughter was in Galveston with her father, who was in medical school there. She described the flood as she saw it from the third story of a building. She watched large bundles of money floating down the street from the bank, and she saw dead horses and people floating by. R. H. Williams interview, 1992.

13. Marriage license, Walker County, Texas.

14. Affidavit by Samuel W. Houston; Birth Certificate, Walker County, Texas; Hazel Houston Price interview, 1992.

15. Hazel Price interview; Lede, *Precious Memories,* p. 42.

16. Hazel Price interview, 1992.

17. Lede, *Samuel W. Houston,* p. 26; Hazel Price interview, 1992.

18. Lede, *Samuel W. Houston,* 27–28.

19. Lede, *Samuel W. Houston,* p. 28.

20. Ibid.

21. Lede, *Samuel W. Houston,* p. 29–35.

22. Lede, *Samuel W. Houston,* p. 31.

23. Franklin, p. 390–93; Lede, *Samuel W. Houston,* p. 32–34.

24. Lede, *Samuel W. Houston,* p. 32–34.

25. Lede, *Samuel W. Houston,* p. 38.

26. Lede, *Samuel W. Houston,* p. 31–39; Constance Houston Thompson interview, 1992.

27. Lede, *Samuel W. Houston,* p. 36.

28. Herma Johnson interview, 1992.

29. Scott Johnson interview, 1992.

30. Mary Oliphant interview, 1992.

31. Lede, *Samuel W. Houston,* p. 36–37.

32. Hazel Price interviews, 1992, 1993.

33. Ibid.

34. Herma Johnson interview, 1992.

35. Lede, *Samuel W. Houston,* p. 35–39.

36. Lede, *Samuel W. Houston,* p. 36.

37. Constance Houston Thompson interview, 1992.

38. Lede, *Samuel W. Houston,* p. 36.

39. Lede, *Precious Memories,* p. 82.

40. Ibid.

41. Lede, *Samuel W. Houston,* p. 36.

42. As quoted in Lede, *Samuel W. Houston,* p. 42.

43. Herma Johnson, Scott Johnson, and Mary Oliphant interviews, 1992.

44. Herma Johnson interview, 1992.

45. Ibid.

46. Champ Anderson interview, 1992.

47. Jesse Baker Wilson, Nannie Lee Eckford, James Baker, and Wendell Baker interviews, 1992.

48. James Baker interview, 1992.

49. Lede, *Samuel W. Houston,* p. 79.

50. Lede, *Samuel W. Houston,* p. 45–47.

51. Lede, *Samuel W. Houston,* p. 76.

52. Donnal M. Timmons, "The Texas Commission on Interracial Cooperation," Master's thesis, Sam Houston State University, 1971, p. 2–9.

53. Timmons, p. 3.

54. Timmons, p. 4–11.

55. Timmons, p. 23, 38.

56. Timmons, p. 49–59.

57. Timmons, p. 59.

58. Hazel Price interview, 1992.

59. Timmons, p. 63–64.

60. Timmons, p. 72–74.

61. Jesse O. Thomas, *Negro Participation in the Texas Centennial Exposition,* (Boston: The Christopher Publishing House, 1938), p. 56, 92–93.

62. Hazel Price interview, 1992.

63. Timmons, p. 2.

64. Constance Houston Thompson interview, 1992; Timmons, p. 2.

65. Scott Johnson interview, 1992.

66. Constance Houston Thompson interview, 1992.

67. Percy Howard interview, 1992.

68. Hazel Price interview, 1992.

69. A. W. Jackson, *A Sure Foundation,* (Houston: self-published, [1936]), p. 134–35.

70. Hazel Price interview, 1992.

71. Lede, *Samuel W. Houston,* p. 127–28.

72. Ibid.

73. Harris County, Texas, death certificate; Constance Houston Thompson interview, 1992.

74. Samuel W. Houston affidavit in Walker County.

75. Hazel Price interview, 1992.

76. Lede, *Precious Memories,* p. 41–42; Constance Houston Thompson interview, 1992.

77. Lede, *Precious Memories,* p. 48–49. One of Mary Orviss's sisters also had red hair.

78. Lede, *Precious Memories,* p. 52.

79. Constance Houston Thompson interview, 1992.

80. Ibid.

81. Constance Houston Thompson interview, 1992; Lede, *Precious Memories,* p. 49.

82. Lede, *Precious Memories,* p. 53.

83. Constance Houston Thompson interview, 1992.

84. P. R. Thomas, p. 28.

85. Constance Houston Thompson interview, 1992.

86. Lede, *Precious Memories,* p. 63, 69.

87. Constance Houston Thompson interview, 1992.

88. Lede, *Precious Memories,* p. 73.

89. Lede, *Precious Memories,* p. 63.

90. Constance Houston Thompson interview, 1992.

91. Ibid.

92. Lede, *Precious Memories,* p. 71.

93. Constance Houston Thompson interview, 1992.

94. Lede, *Precious Memories,* p. 71; Constance Houston Thompson interview, 1992.

95. Hazel Houston Price interview, 1992.

96. Constance Houston Thompson interview, 1992.

97. Ibid.

98. Ibid; also Lede, *Precious Memories,* p. 107.

99. Lede, *Precious Memories,* p. 109–110.

100. Constance Houston Thompson interview, 1992.

101. Ibid.

102. Ibid.

103. Death certificate of Joe Houston, #33206, dated 1 August 1938, Houston County, Texas.

104. McFarland.

105. Desdamona Fobbs interview, 1991.

106. Port Arthur Todd interview, 1991.

107. 1880 census, Houston County, Texas.

108. Houston County Historical Commission, *History of Houston County, Texas, 1687–1979* (Tulsa: Heritage Publishing, 1979), p. 415–16, 460.

109. Port Arthur Todd and Desdamona Fobbs interviews, 1991.

110. Georgia Jolley interview, 1991.

111. Houston County Historical Commission, p. 608.

112. Ibid.

113. Houston County Historical Commission, *Houston County Cemeteries (Texas)*, (Marceline, Missouri: Walsworth Publishing, 1977), p. 341.

114. Constance Houston Thompson interview, 1991.

115. WCGS & WCHC, p. 460.

116. Desdamona Fobbs interview, 1991; also Houston County Historical Commission, p. 460, 608.

117. Ibid.

118. 1900 Census; also, Ruby Sims interview, 1992.

119. Houston County Historical Commission, p. 360.

120. Desdamona Fobbs interview.

121. Affidavit no. 88 by Samuel W. Houston to the Public, Walker County, Texas, 5 September 1940.

122. P. R. Thomas, 9–12.

123. Constance Houston Thompson interview, 1991.

124. Ibid.

125. Walker County Deeds, Vol. 8, p. 56; Vol. 23, p. 110; Vol. 35, p. 326. Walker County Court House.

126. Constance Houston Thompson interview, 1991.

127. Ibid.

128. Undated and unidentified newspaper article, in possession of Patricia Smith Prather.

129. Hazen Houston Price interview, 1992.

130. Constance Houston Thompson interview, 1991.

131. Birth certificate, Walker County, Texas.

132. P. R. Thomas, p. 9–12.

133. There are no school records for St. James, but it was open at the time she was of age to enter school and it was not far from where she lived.

134. Constance Houston Thompson interview, 1991.

135. Woolfolk, p. 68.

136. Woolfolk, p. 94.

137. Constance Houston Thompson interview, 1991.

138. Ibid.

139. Cemetery marker, Oakwood Cemetery, Huntsville, Texas.

Appendix

Documents relating to Joshua Houston

1858

Genl Sam Houston

1858　　　　　In a/c with T & S Gibbs

August To Balance as per a/c Rendered $384.84

" 4 " 1 Memorandum Book per Son 25

" 5 " 1 Double bit Jacob Plane by Albert 1

" " " 1¾ lbs Cate Fish 2/ 31

" 7 " 1 Bell No 3 per J. Kern 1 75

" " " Juniper Buckets 135-65 . . . . 2 00

" 9 " Rent Grass Rope per Self 30

" " " 1½ lbs Grass Rope " " 22/ . . 33

" " " ¼ lb wrought Nails 07 40

" " " ¼ 16 Candles per Book . . 1 00

" " " 1 Paper Composition . . . . .13 . . 1 13

" 10 " 1 Brier Scythe per Book . . 1 25

" " " 1 pr Mij Cot Adr Pants . . . 1 37

" " " 1 pr Do . . . . 75 . . 3 37

" " " 1 pr Tin Cups per Self 10

" 12 " 1 pr Pants Cot Ado " Jacob . . 1 25

" 13 " 13 yds Pink Check Calico Son Sam 13¾ . . 50

" 17 " 6 Hand Saw files by Albert . . 75

" " " 1 2 ft Rule . . . . . 45 . . 1 20

" " " 16 Candles per Book . . 1 00

" 28 " 16 Candles 1 00

" " " 1 Ham 16 lbs per Louis 18¾ . . 3 00

" 30 " ¼ m Bro Flat Thread per request . . 31

Sept 3 " 1 Doz Spools Thread Taylors coats per book . . 1 00

" 11 " 2 Balls dress cord per Book . . .10

" " " 1 Pad Lock . . . . . 45 . . 55

" " " 1 lb Col Rope per don Sam . . 25

" 7 " 27 lbs Round Iron per Albert . . 8/ . . 2 16

" " " 1 Fancy Shirt Collar per Son Sam . . 20

" 8 " 1 Brooch in Gold 130 00

" " " 2 pr Candle Sticks per Self . . 80 . . 1 60

" " " 2 yds Checkea Calico " Son Sam 16¾ . . 33

" 9 " 3 Hanks Harper Flax . Book . . 25

" " " 1 Ass Candles " Girl . . 10

Sam Houston account at T&S Gibbs. These three pages from the 1858 store ledger of T&S Gibbs have several entries involving two of Sam Houston's slaves. Albert is listed under

Am'l br't over $660.74

Sept 25 To Cash to Renfro 49.00
" " " 13 lb Clarified Sugar per Book 2.00
Oct 1 " Cash to Randolph & Son 200.00
" 4 " 2 Collars for Mules per M Leigh 2.20
" 5 " 2 pr Boa Drill Drawers per Sam 1.30
" 6 " 3 lb Salt Petre " Book 54
" 9 " 2 yds Gauze Flannel per don Sam 90¢ 1.80
" 11 " 1½ lb Grass Rope for Carriage per self 22¢ 33
" " " Cash in Silver per self 10.00
" " " 1 Counter Brush 50 10.50
" 12 " 1 Bunch Linen Cord per self 22
" " " 1 Can Lard 53½ @ 11¢ 119 lb 16¼ (817) 617
" " " 1 Bot Laudanum 15
" 16 " 2 lb 12 d Nails per Book 18
" " " 1 pr Calf Shoes per Joshua 2.00
" " " 4 Boxes Matches " Book 10
" 19 " 4 yds Calico in 2 pc " Mrs M 15¢ 61
" 20 " 6 lb Dried Apples " Book 1.00
" 25 " 1 pr Russels No 8 1.50
" " " 1 Bot Spts Turpentine 35 1.85
" 26 " 7½ lb Bro Sugar per Book 1.00
" 28 " 1 pr Grey Blankets " Albert 2.75
Nov 1 " Cash paid Walker & Caruol 104.13
" 4 " 4 pr Grey Blankets per self 2½ 10.30
" 5 " Paid S Kern for Flour 81½ lb 5¢ (448) 4.08
" " " 1 pr Kip Brog Shoes 2.00
" 8 " 1 Blk Knapsd over Coat per son Sam 10.50
" 9 " 1 Hat (13 m) per don Sam 1.35
1858 Cr $1077.09
Aug 3 By Dft on N. York $500.00
5 1 Paper bin ".10
27 By Ceiling 1354 ft @ 2½ 33.85
Sept 25 Dft on Washington 50000 $1033.95
1858 $0043.14

August 17, September 7, October 28, and (December?) 7. Joshua is listed under October 17, for one pair "Calf Shoes" costing $2.

"	"	" 1 for Col Rope per son Sam		25
"	7	" 27 lbs Round Iron per Albert	8 f	2 16
"	"	" 1 Fancy Shirt Collar per son Sam		20
"	8	" 1 Bush in Gold		130 00
"	"	" 2 pr Candle Sticks per Self	80 f	1 60
"	"	" 2 yd Checked Calico " Son Sam	16¾ f	33
"	9	" 3 Hanks Dressed Flax " Book		25
"	11	" 1 Paper No 12 Needles " Girl		10
"	15	" 1 Hickory Shirt " Order		65
"	17	" 2 Balls Tape " Book		15
"	21	" 6½ lbs Clarified Brn Sugar "		1 00
"	"	" 1 Plug Tobacco	25	1 25
"	24	" 1 Doz Cakes Soap per Self		40
"	"	" 2 pr Trace Chains		2 25
"	"	" 1 lb Shot per son Sam	14	
"	"	" ½ lb Powder	25	
"	"	" 1 Box Head Caps	5 n	89
"	25	" Cash to Shirts		115 00
				$660 74

Affidavit concerning Ellen Houston. Evidently written by the former owner of Ellen Houston, this affidavit documents her age and the fact that Joshua Houston was her father. It states: "I hereby certify that one Ellen *now called Ellen Houston, the daughter of Joshua Houston was originally—before Emancipation proclamation—my slave—that she was born January 15, 1856—as appears from the Family (Bible) in my possession and is therefore over eighteen years of age. This July 9, 1874."*

[Handwritten manuscript page — Walker County Commissioners Court Minutes]

Minutes Commissioners Court Walker
County — Call Session — Dec. 16. 1882

It appearing to the satisfaction of the Court that E.S. Augur late Tax Collector, in the settlement of his accounts as such, had paid an excess of $8.42 into the County Treasury on account of general Revenue or Class No. 3 : it is therefore ordered by the Court that the County Clerk draw his warrant on the County Treasurer in favor of said Augur for said amount — payable out of any moneys on hand belonging to the 3rd Class, without reference to time of registration

Ordered that the Commissioners in attendance on this day be allowed their per diem — as follows —

Co. Judge J. M. Smither	1 day	$	3.00
" Com. J. Houston	1 "	$	3.00
" Com. W. M. Mann	1 "	$	3.00
" Com. D. McAngle	1 "	$	3.00

And that the Clerk issue drafts to them payable from 6th Class fund
Whereupon Court adjourned until the 2nd monday in January A.D. 1883

Attest   J. M. Smither
M. P. Rome   Co. Judge Walker Co.
Clk C. C. W. C.

Minutes Called Session — Commissioners Court — Walker County — Dec. 23. 1882
On this 23 day of Dec. 1882 the Commissioners Court of Walker County convened

Commissioners Court Minutes. This page from Book B of the Walker County Commissioners Court minutes shows that on December 16, 1882, "Co. Com. J. Houston" was paid $3 per diem for one day's work.

In the Name of God; Amen:
Realizing the Uncertainty of life, I Joshua
Houston of Huntsville, Walker County, Texas,
though in feeble health, yet, in the Possession
of Sound Mind and Memory do Make and
Ordain this my last Will and Testament,
hereby revoking all former Wills by me made
I bequeath to my beloved daughter Mineola
Houston, the house in which I now reside
With the Ground on which it is Situated
extending North to the branch and West to the
dividing fence between me and Kirdin Brown,
Also all furniture and bedding in my
residence owned by me; also eight acres of
land Purchased by me from Mrs R A Smith,
Also My Jersey Cow and her heifer Calf.
I bequeath to my beloved Son Sam W Houston
the lot on which my blacksmith Shop is Sit-
uated Conveyed to me by A. G. Creath and his
Wife Elizabeth Creath —
I bequeath to my beloved Son Joshua Houston
Jn all my blacksmith tools of every description
and Kind.
I bequeath to the Children of my beloved daughter
Mrs Spear, to Sam W Houston and Joshua Houston
Jn my farm of thirty three acres More or less,
Purchased by me from Mrs Ella Smither, also
My horse and Wagon to go with the farm; the
land I bequeath in the following manner;
Seven acres to Joshua Houston Jr, and the Residue
to be equally divided between the Children

Joshua Houston's Last Will and Testament.

Minutes of County Court of Walker County, In Probate Matters   Regular Session May Term as 1904

of my beloved daughter Mrs Ellen Spears,
And Sam W Houston; and it is my wish
that the unpaid Venders lien note, on above
thirty three aens more or less, Shall be paid
by the legatees of Same pro rata —
It is my will that Mrs Ellen Spears have
the use of above land bequeathed to her
Children, as long as She Shall live —
I appoint my friend E L Anguin executor of
this, my last will and Testament, and
it is my will that he be not required to give
bond for Security for the performance of his
duties as executor; and that no action Shall
be had by the Court Concerning this will, except the probate of Same; and recine or
Inventory of the estate —
In testimony Whereof I hereto Sign my name
this Feby 15 as 1900

           J Houston

Signed and declared by Joshua Houston as
his last will and testament, in the presence
of us, who hereto Subscribe our Names, at
his request as Witnesses thereto in the presence of the Said testator and of each
other   Dr J C Clarke
                Geo Moen

Filed June 9 1904.   Recorded June 11 1904
                J E Ballee cen exactx

Bibliography

BOOKS, ARTICLES AND THESES

Barr, Alwyn. *Black Texans: A History of Negroes in Texas, 1528–1971*. Austin: Jenkins Press, 1973.
———. *Reconstruction to Reform, Texas Politics 1876–1906*. Austin: University of Texas Press, 1971.
Blassingame, John W. *The Slave Community*. New York: Oxford University Press, 1972.
Braider, Donald. *Solitary Star*. New York: Putnam, 1974.
Brewer, J. Mason. *Negro Legislators of Texas*. Dallas: Mathis Publishing, 1935.
Budd, Harrell T. "The Negro in Politics, 1867–1898." Master's thesis, University of Texas at Austin, 1925.
Bundy, William Oliver. *The Life of William Madison McDonald, PhD*. Fort Worth: Bunker Printing and Book Company, 1925.
Campbell, Randolph B. *An Empire for Slavery: The Peculiar Institution in Texas, 1821–1865*. Baton Rouge: Louisiana State University Press, 1989.
Cartwright, Gary. *Galveston*. New York: Atheneum/Macmillan, 1991.
Chatman, J. A. *Lone Star State Medical, Dental, Pharmaceutical History*. n.p.: self-published, [1959].
Crews, D'Anne McAdams, ed. *Huntsville and Walker County, Texas: A Bicentennial History*. Huntsville: Sam Houston State University, 1976.
Daughters of the Republic of Texas. *Fifty Years of Achievement*. Dallas: Banks Upshaw and Company, 1942.
De Bruhl, Marshall. *Sword of San Jacinto: A Life of Sam Houston*. New York: Random House, 1993.
Dickenson, Johnnie Jo, compiler. *Walker County, Texas, 1850–60 Census*. Huntsville: Dickenson Research, 1985.
Dresel, Gustav. *Gustav Dresel's Houston Journal*. Max Freund, translator. Austin: University of Texas Press, 1954.
Dudar, Helen. "'Griot New York' Sets the City's Rhythm Dance." *Smithsonian Magazine* (September 1922): 102–09.
Elliot, Claude. "The Freedmen's Bureau in Texas." *Southwestern Historical Quarterly* 56 (1952): 1–24.

Ellis, Joseph Henry Harrison. *Sam Houston and the Related Spiritual Forces*. Houston: Concord Press, 1945.

Ericson, J. E. "Delegates to the Texas Constitutional Convention of 1875, A Reappraisal." *Southwestern Historical Quarterly* 67 (1963): 22–27.

Escott, Paul. *Slavery Remembered*. Chapel Hill: University of North Carolina Press, 1979.

Farrell, Mary D. and Elizabeth Silverthorne. *First Ladies of Texas*. Belton, Texas: Stillhouse Publishers, 1976.

Fehrenbach, T. R. *Lone Star: A History of Texas and Texans*. New York: Collier Books, 1985.

Flanagan, Sue. *Sam Houston's Texas*. Austin: University of Texas Press, 1964.

Franklin, John Hope. *From Slavery to Freedom*. New York: Knopf, 1967.

Friend, Llerena. *Sam Houston: The Great Designer*. Austin: University of Texas Press, 1954.

Fuermann, George. *Houston: The Feast Years*. Houston: Premiere Printing Company, 1962.

Gage, Larry Jay. "The City of Austin on the Eve of the Civil War." *Southwestern Historical Quarterly* 63 (1959): 428–38.

Gammel, H. N. P., compiler. *The Laws of Texas 1822–1889*. 10 vols. Austin: Gammel Publishing, 1898.

Goree, Thomas Jewett. *The Thomas Jewett Goree Letters*. Compiled and edited by Langston James Goree V. Bryan, Texas: Family History Foundation, 1981.

Hamilton, Jeff, as told to Lenoir Hunt. *My Master: The Inside Story of Sam Houston and His Times*. Dallas: Manfred, Van Nort, and Company, 1940.

Hayman, Bettie. *A Short History of the Negro of Walker County, 1860–1942*. Master's thesis, Sam Houston State College, 1942.

Heintze, Michael R. *Private Black Colleges in Texas, 1865–1954*. College Station: Texas A&M University Press, 1985.

History Book Committee of Houston County Historical Commission, compilers and editors. *Houston County History*. Tulsa: Heritage Publishing, 1979.

Holland, J. K. "Freedmen in the Legislature." *Southwestern Historical Quarterly* 1 (1897): 125–126.

Hopewell, Clifford. *Sam Houston: Man of Destiny*. Austin: Eakin Press, 1987.

Houston County Historical Commission. *Houston County Cemeteries (Texas)*. Marceline, Missouri: Walsworth Publishing, 1977.

———. *Houston County History, 1687–1979*. Tulsa: Heritage Publishing, 1979.

Houston, Sam. *The Writings of Sam Houston*. Amelia Williams and Eugene Barker, eds. 8 vols. Austin: University of Texas Press, 1938–1943.

Jackson, A. W. *A Sure Foundation & Sketch of Negro Life in Texas*. Houston: self-published, [1936].

James, Marquis. *The Raven*. Indianapolis: Bobbs-Merrill Company, 1929.

Kimbro, Dennis. *Think and Grow Rich: A Black Choice*. New York: Fawcett Crest, 1991.

Lede, Naomi. *Precious Memories of a Black Socialite*. Houston: D. Armstrong Company, 1991.

———. *Samuel W. Houston and His Contemporaries*. Houston: Pha Green Printing, 1981.

Looscan, Adele B., "Reminiscences of Reconstruction in Texas." *Southwestern Historical Quarterly* 11 (1907): 56–65.

McAshan, Marie Phelps. *On the Corner of Main and Texas: A Houston Legacy*. Houston: Hutchins House, 1985.

McComb, David G. *Houston, the Bayou City*. Austin: University of Texas Press, 1969.

McDaniel, Vernon. *History of Teachers State Association of Texas*. Washington, D.C.: National Education Association, 1977.

McDonald, Archie, ed. *Adolphus Sterne, Hurrah for Texas*. Waco: Texian Press, 1969.

———, compiler. *Nacogdoches, Past and Present: A Legacy of Texas Pride*. Odessa: B&C Publishing, 1986.

Madison, Meredith Morrow. "Margaret Lea Houston." Master's thesis, University of Texas at El Paso, 1960.

Mellon, James, E. *Bullwhip Days: The Slaves Remember*. New York: Weidenfeld and Nicolson, 1988.

Oats, Stephen B. "Texas Under the Secessionists." *Southwestern Historical Quarterly* 67 (1963): 167–212.

Orr, Lyndon. *The Wives of General Houston*. Vol 3 in *Famous Affinities of History, The Romance of Devotion*. New York: Harper & Brothers, 1909.

Owens, Leslie Howard. *This Species of Property*. New York: Oxford University Press, 1976.

Pitre, Merline. *Through Many Dangers, Toils and Snares: Black Leadership in Texas, 1868–1900*. Austin: Eakin Press, 1985.

Prather, Patricia Smith. "A Celebration of Freedom." *Texas Highways* (June 1988): 2–8.

"Proceedings of Eighty-First Annual Communication of the Free and Accepted Masons of the Most Worshipful Prince Hall Grand Lodge," Fort Worth, 1956. (Collection of Patricia Smith Prather.)

Ramsdell, Charles W., "Texas from the Fall of the Confederacy to the Beginning of Reconstruction." *Southwestern Historical Quarterly* 11 (1907): 199–219.

Rice, Lawrence D. *The Negro in Texas 1874–1900*. Baton Rouge: Louisiana State University Press, 1971.

Richter, William L. *The Army in Texas During Reconstruction, 1865–1870*. College Station: Texas A&M University Press, 1987.

———. *Overreached on All Sides: The Freedmen's Bureau Administrators in Texas, 1865–1868*. College Station: Texas A&M Press, 1971.

Roberts, Madge Thornall. *Star of Destiny: The Private Life of Sam and Margaret Houston*. Denton: University of North Texas Press, 1992.

Sance, Melvin M., Jr. *The Afro-American Texans*. San Antonio: Institute of Texan Cultures, 1987.

Scott, Emmett J. *The Red Book of Houston: A Compendium of Social, Professional, Religious, Educational and Industrial Interests of Houston's Colored Population*. Houston: Sotex Publishing, [1915].

Seale, William. *Sam Houston's Wife*. Norman: University of Oklahoma Press, 1970.

Sellers, James Benson. *Slavery in Alabama*. Birmingham: University of Alabama Press, 1950.

Shuffler, Henderson. *The Houstons of Independence*. Waco: Texian Press, 1966.

Silverthorne, Elizabeth. *Plantation Life in Texas*. College Station: Texas A&M Press, 1986.

Singletary, Otis A. *Negro Militia and Reconstruction*. Austin: University of Texas Press, 1957.

———. "The Texas Militia During Reconstruction." *Southwestern Historical Quarterly* 60 (1956): 23–35.

Smallwood, James M. *Time of Hope, Time of Despair*. Port Washington, New York: Kennikat Press, 1981.

Study Club of Huntsville. *Taste and Traditions*. Kearney: Morris Press, 1992.

Texas Almanac. Dallas: A. H. Belo Corporation, 1956.

Thomas, Jesse O. *Negro Participation in the Texas Centennial Exposition*. Boston: The Christopher Publishing House, 1938.

Thomas, P. R. *Outline History of the First Baptist Church, Huntsville, Texas*. Huntsville: published privately, 1922.

Timmons, Donnal M. "The Texas Commission on Interracial Cooperation." Master's thesis, Sam Houston State University, Huntsville, Texas, 1971.

Turner, Kathryn. *Stagecoach Inns of Texas*. Waco: Texian Press, 1972.

Vonder Mehden, Fred R. *Ethnic Groups of Houston*. Houston: Rice University Press, 1984.

Walker County Genealogical Society and Walker County Historical Commission. *Walker County, Texas: A History*. Dallas: Curtis Media Corporation, 1986.

Washington, Booker T. *Up From Slavery*. New York: N. L. Burt, 1900.

Webber, Thomas L. *Deep Like the Rivers*. New York: W. W. Norton, 1978.

White, W. W. "The Texas Slave Insurrection in 1860." *Southwestern Historical Quarterly* 55 (1948): 259–85.

Williams, Amelia. *Following General Sam Houston, 1793–1863*. Austin: The Steck Company, 1935.

Wilson, C. W. "The Negro in Walker County." Huntsville: Sam Houston State University, 1934.

Wintz, Cary D. *Blacks in Houston*. Houston: Center for Humanities, 1982.

Wood, W. D. "The Ku Klux Klan." *Southwestern Historical Quarterly* 9 (1905): 262–68.

Woolfolk, George Ruble. *History of Prairie View: A Study in Public Conscience 1878–1946.* New York: Pagent, 1962.

Young, S. O. *Thumb Nail History of the City of Houston, Texas.* Houston: Rein and Sons, 1912.

INTERVIEWS

(JCM = Jane Clements Monday; PSP = Patricia Smith Prather)

Anderson, Champ. Interview with JCM, Fall 1992, at his home in Hopewell Community, Walker County, Texas.

Baker, James. Interview with JCM, Summer 1992, at the Samuel W. Houston Alumni Reunion, Huntsville, Texas.

Baker, Wendell. Interviews with JCM, Summer and Fall 1992, at his home and at the Samuel W. Houston Alumni Reunion, Huntsville, Texas.

Demby, Helen. Interview with PSP, Winter 1992, at her home in Houston, Texas.

Douglas, Stanford, Director of Samuel W. Houston Cultural Center. Interviews with JCM on numerous occasions throughout 1992, Huntsville, Texas.

Eckford, Nannie Lee. Interview with JCM, Summer 1992, at the Samuel W. Houston Alumni Reunion, Huntsville, Texas.

Everitt, Peggy. Phone interview with JCM, Spring 1992, and personal interview with JCM, Summer 1992, Sam Houston State University, Huntsville, Texas.

Fobbs, Chelisa. Interview with JCM, Spring 1992, in Monday's home, Huntsville, Texas.

Fobbs, Desdamona. Interview with JCM and PSP, 1992, in her home in Crockett, Texas.

Fobbs, Harold. Phone interview with JCM throughout 1992 and 1993.

Hines, Chester. Interview with JCM and PSP, 1992, at his law office in Crockett, Texas.

Houston, Otho Morrow. Interview with JCM and PSP, 1992, at Chester Hines law office in Crockett, Texas.

Howard, Alice. Interview with JCM, 1992, at Monday's home in Huntsville, Texas.

Howard, Percy. Interview with JCM, 1992, at Monday's home in Huntsville, Texas.

Hudley, Elnora. Phone interview with JCM, December 1992.

Johnson, Herma. Interview with JCM, 1992, at the Samuel W. Houston Cultural Center, Huntsville, Texas.

Johnson, Scott E. Interviews with JCM, throughout 1992, at his home in Huntsville, Texas.

Jolley, Georgia Mac Wagner. Interview with JCM and PSP, 1992, at her home in Crockett, Texas.

Jones, Felder. Interview with JCM, January 1993, at the Samuel W. Houston Cultural Center, Huntsville, Texas.

Oliphant, Mary. Interview with JCM, 1992, at the Samuel W. Houston Cultural Center, Huntsville, Texas.

Patton, James. Interviews with JCM, 1993, at the courthouse and the Samuel W. Houston Cultural Center in Huntsville, Texas.

Price, Hazel Houston. Interviews with JCM, throughout 1992 and 1993, at the Samuel W. Houston Cultural Center and in her home, Huntsville, Texas.

Roberts, Madge Thornall. Interview with JCM in Huntsville, Texas, 1992.

Ross, Joseph. Interview with JCM, Summer 1992, at the Samuel W. Houston Cultural Center, Huntsville, Texas.

Sherman, Tony. Interviews with PSP, throughout 1992, at his home in Houston, Texas.

Sims, Ruby. Interview with PSP, winter of 1992, at her home in Houston, Texas.

Spangler, Meredith. Interviews with JCM, 1992, at Sam Houston State University, Huntsville, Texas.

Teasdale, Mary Louise (Mrs. A. R.). Interviews with JCM, 1992, at Sam Houston State University, Huntsville, Texas.

Thompson, Constance Houston. Interviews with PSP, from 1986 to 1992, at the Houston Place, Houston, Texas. Interviews with JCM, 1992, at the Samuel W. Houston Cultural Center, Huntsville, Texas, and at the Houston Place, Houston, Texas. Interview with JCM and PSP, 1992, at the Samuel W. Houston Cultural Center, Huntsville, Texas.

Todd, Port Arthur. Interview with JCM and PSP, 1991, in his home in Crockett, Texas.

Watkins, Lovie. Interview with JCM, 1992, in Monday's home in Huntsville, Texas, and phone interview, 1992.

Watkins, Richard. Interview with JCM, 1992, in Monday's home in Huntsville, Texas, and phone interview, 1992.

Williams, Cecil. Interview with JCM, 1992, in Monday's home in Huntsville, Texas, and phone interviews, 1992.

Williams, R. H. Interview with JCM, 1992, at his business, Huntsville, Texas.

Wilson, Jesse Baker. Interview with JCM, Summer 1992, at the Samuel W. Houston Alumni Reunion, Huntsville, Texas.

Wiseman, Kijana. Phone interview with JCM, 1992, Huntsville, Texas, and interview with PSP, 1992, Houston, Texas.

COUNTY RECORDS

Harris County (Texas). Death Records. Birth Records.
Houston County (Texas). Death Records. Deed Records.

Marion, Perry County (Alabama). Probate Records.

Walker County (Texas). Court Records. Deed Records. Election Records. Marriage Records. Registration Records. Tax Records.

STATE RECORDS

Adjutant General's Reconstruction Records. Court Martial Reports. Texas State Archives, Austin, Texas.

County Legislative Acts. Walker County. Barker History Library, University of Texas, Box 409, VI.

Fifth Military District/District of Texas Records, 1865–1870. Boxes 401–1000, Texas State Archives, Austin, Texas.

Freedmen's Bureau Records, Estelle Owens Collection, Series M821, Reels 3386, 3393, 3397, Texas State Archives, Austin, Texas.

Register of Elected/Appointed Local Officials 1870–1873. Elected/Appointed Officials, 1870–75. Reel 3502. Texas State Archives, Austin, Texas.

MANUSCRIPT COLLECTIONS

Hill, Laura E. Papers. Mae Wynne McFarland Collection. Peabody Library, Sam Houston State University, Box 34.

Houston, Margaret Bell. Papers. Sam Houston Memorial Museum, Huntsville, Texas.

McFarland, Mae Wynne. Papers. Peabody Library, Sam Houston State University, Huntsville, Texas.

Morrow, Temple Houston. Collection. Sam Houston Memorial Museum, Huntsville, Texas.

Newcomb, J. P. State Papers. James Pearson Collection. Barker History Library, University of Texas, Austin.

Williams, Franklin. Collection of Houston Letters 1839–1861. Sam Houston Memorial Museum, Huntsville, Texas.

WPA Interviews. "Slave Stories." Transcripts, 1937. Dist 8, A-12, Archives Box 4H360, Barker History Center, Austin, Texas. (Interviewees: Lizzie Atkins, Harriet Barrett, Andy McAdams, John McAdams, Mary Gaffeny, Rosa L. Pollard, Harre Quarls.)

MISCELLANEOUS RECORDS

Davis, Ruth. "Stage Routes of Huntsville." Map. Thomason Room, Sam Houston State University, Huntsville, Texas.

Goree, Thomas J. Diary. Thomason Room, Sam Houston State University Library, Huntsville, Texas.

Hightower, Goree. Interview with Gerald Holder, 1976, Huntsville, Texas. Tape in possession of James Patton, Huntsville, Texas.

Leigh, Mrs. W. A. "Map of Houston home and gardens." Sam Houston Memorial Museum, Huntsville, Texas.

Minutes of the First Baptist Church, in the minutebook at the church in Huntsville, Texas.

Sugg, Paul. "The Freedmen's Bureau in Walker County, 1866–68." Typescript, 21 January 1990. Courtesy of James Patton, Walker County Historical Association, Huntsville, Texas.

Teasdale, A. R., compiler. "General Sam Houston 1793–1863: Descendants." Computer printout, Dallas, March 3, 1991.

Index